Neo4j in Action

ALEKSA VUKOTIC
NICKI WATT
with
TAREQ ABEDRABBO
DOMINIC FOX
JONAS PARTNER

MANNING
SHELTER ISLAND

For online information and ordering of this and other Manning books, please visit
www.manning.com. The publisher offers discounts on this book when ordered in quantity.
For more information, please contact

> Special Sales Department
> Manning Publications Co.
> 20 Baldwin Road
> PO Box 761
> Shelter Island, NY 11964
> Email: orders@manning.com

Manning Publications Co.
20 Baldwin Road
PO Box 761
Shelter Island, NY 11964

Development editor:	Karen Miller
Technical development editor	Gordon Dickens
Copyeditor:	Andy Carroll
Proofreader:	Elizabeth Martin
Technical proofreader:	Craig Taverner
Typesetter:	Dennis Dalinnik
Cover designer:	Marija Tudor

ISBN: 9781617290763
Printed in the United States of America
1 2 3 4 5 6 7 8 9 10 – EBM – 19 18 17 16 15 14

brief contents

contents

v

foreword

The database world is experiencing an enormous upheaval, with the hegemony of relational databases being challenged by a plethora of new technologies under the NoSQL banner. Among these approaches, graphs are gaining substantial credibility as a means of analyzing data across a broad range of domains.

Most NoSQL databases address the perceived performance limitations of relational databases, which flounder when confronted with the exponential growth in data volumes that we've witnessed over the last few years. But data growth is only one of the challenges we face. Not only is data growing, it's also becoming more interconnected and more variably structured. In short, it's becoming far more networked.

In addressing performance and scalability, NoSQL has generally given up on the capabilities of the relational model with regard to interconnected data. Graph databases, in contrast, revitalize the world of connected data, outperforming relational databases by several orders of magnitude. Many of the most interesting questions we want to ask of our data require us to understand not only that things are connected, but also the differences between those connections. Graph databases offer the most powerful and best-performing means for generating this kind of insight.

Connected data poses difficulties for most NoSQL databases, which manage documents, columns, or key/value pairs as disconnected aggregates. To create any semblance of connectedness using these technologies, we must find a way to both denormalize data and fudge connections onto an inherently disconnected model. This is not a trivial undertaking, as we have discovered in building Neo4j itself!

Neo4j has come to fruition over the same timeframe as the other frontrunners in the NoSQL world. (In fact, Neo4j predates many other NoSQL technologies by several years.) Neo4j provides traditional database-like support (including transactional safety) for highly connected data, while also providing orders of magnitude ("minutes to milliseconds") better performance than relational databases. For domains as varied as social computing, recommendation engines, telecoms, authorization and access control, routing and logistics, product catalogs, datacenter management, career management, fraud detection, policing, and geospatial, Neo4j has demonstrated it's an ideal choice for tackling complex data.

Because Neo4j is by far the most popular graph database, it's the one that most developers will encounter. We know that this "first contact" with a new technology like Neo4j can be bewildering. The tyranny of choice regarding different APIs, bindings, query languages, and frameworks can be daunting, and it's easy to be put off.

Neo4j in Action addresses these concerns by getting developers up and running quickly with Neo4j. It takes a pragmatic programmatic tour through Neo4j's APIs and its query language, and provides examples based on the authors' extensive real-world use of the database. Complementing this development advice, the authors also discuss deployment options and solution architectures. The result is a rounded, holistic view of Neo4j as seen in the context of the full systems development lifecycle.

As Neo4j contributors and authors ourselves, we value *Neo4j in Action* for its no-nonsense, hands-on approach, and its willingness to back its assertions using reproducible tests. The authors are some of the most experienced Neo4j users around, and we're very pleased to see their authority and knowledge made available to all developers through this book.

JIM WEBBER
CHIEF SCIENTIST, NEO TECHNOLOGY

IAN ROBINSON
ENGINEER, NEO TECHNOLOGY

preface

Graph issues are some of the most common problems in computer programming, and have been since the early days. Back then, hierarchy trees, access control lists, and mapping tables were built, typically, in code. When it came time to store the graphs, programmers transformed them into tables and used the relational database as underlying storage. We had to do a lot of plumbing to save the most basic graph data, but there was no other option—until graph databases, with Neo4j leading the parade, entered the scene.

Neo4j started its journey more than a decade ago, with the first official version, the 1.0 release, coming out in 2010, and the more recent 2.0 release coming out in December 2013. Most of us have been involved with actively using Neo4j and watching it evolve over this period on various projects for clients. The hype and excitement around graph databases, and Neo4j in particular, have been gaining more and more traction, with many people and companies realizing that Neo4j is uniquely placed in the graph database space to provide a robust and solid solution capable of solving complex and challenging, interconnected business problems.

It is with great pleasure that we tried to distill much of this real-world experience and knowledge into this hands-on book in a way that lays solid foundations and then builds on those to help you get up and running with Neo4j as soon as possible.

acknowledgments

This book has been some time in the making, so first and foremost a big thank you goes out to all of our families and friends who tirelessly stood by us, put up with us, and made those late evening coffees to keep us going through the many additional late hours of work required to write this book. Thank you!

First, we'd like to thank Open Credo, the company for whom we currently work (or worked) while writing this book, for the opportunity afforded us to be able to share and contribute our experiences to this book—mostly after hours, but for those precious paid hours as well. This was most appreciated!

A big thanks to the Neo4j guys, Jim Webber and Ian Robinson in the UK, Michael Hunger in Germany, and the whole clan, for their continued work on Neo4j, but most importantly, for their useful comments and feedback in helping us fine-tune this book appropriately. It was great having the UK guys just down the hall from our Open Credo office so we could call on them for help with some of those "interesting" challenges.

Thanks to Karen Miller, our development editor at Manning, for her endless patience and understanding over this period, plus the entire Manning team for the fantastic effort they put out to finally get us to this point. It was hard work, and we ended up doing a fair few rounds, but we are grateful for their support and guidance and for the solid product that has emerged as a result.

Many thanks to our MEAP readers, who posted corrections and comments in the Author Online forum, and to the following reviewers, who read the manuscript during development and provided invaluable feedback: Adam Frankl, Bill LaPrise,

Brian Gyss, Christoph Jasinski, Frank Uzzolino, Fred Patton, Janeen Johnson, John D. Lewis, Joshua White, Mark Watson, Philippe Lamote, Pouria Amirian, Rikke Willer, Robert Gimbel, Rod Hilton, and Stephen Kitt.

Thanks also to Jim Webber and Ian Robinson for contributing the foreword to our book, and to Craig Taverner for his technical expertise as he reviewed the manuscript and code examples one more time, just before production.

There are many others who contributed in various ways as well. We cannot mention everyone by name as this would mean that the acknowledgments would roll on and on, but we'd like to send a big thank you to everyone else who had a hand in helping make this book possible!

about this book

Neo4j as a graph database has evolved quite a bit over the last decade or so. Starting as a database operating purely within the Java-based world, it has since evolved to cater to many languages and frameworks.

When we first embarked on writing this book, it was targeting the then-latest 1.9 release. The Neo4j 2.0 release was a real game changer, introducing new features, including the much-desired (built-in) concept of node labels. Though there is still some 1.x related material, you will be pleased to know that the content of this book has indeed been updated to cover 2.0 features, with all the associated sample code and examples having been specifically validated against the 2.0.1 release. No doubt there will be later releases by the time this book hits the printing press; however, the deliberate step-by-step approach taken by *Neo4j in Action* should provide you with the core foundational knowledge and skills necessary to learn about, and get up and running with, any Neo4j 2.0+ release—subject to any unforeseen breaking changes introduced, of course.

With Java being the language used to give birth to Neo4j, we decided to use Java as the primary language for demonstrating the various techniques and approaches in this inaugural Neo4j book. Besides the fact that this was previously one of the only options available, the language choice has also afforded us the ability to include chapters and sections detailing how you can explicitly take advantage of some of the native core Neo4j APIs for performing certain tasks. This certainly has major benefits for Java-based clients. However, if we were starting from scratch again, more time and attention would probably have been given to Cypher. Using Cypher where possible to interact with the graph promotes easier integration regardless of the client—Java, shell, or something else. In any case, we leave this for a potential second edition as we still believe there are many core fundamental concepts and approaches in this book that need to be conveyed first. The book assumes the latest version of JDK 7 is being used. Additionally, the sample code that accompanies this book makes use of Maven as our build dependency tool of choice. For those unfamiliar with Maven, we provide a quick getting started section in appendix B to help get you up and running.

It should be noted that this is not meant to be a reference book; it would be a lot longer if that were the case. It does aim to arm you with enough knowledge and understanding in each area to be relatively proficient before moving on. Links are provided to appropriate content where you can get more information should you want to explore any specific area further.

Roadmap

This book is divided into three parts. Part 1 is an introduction and covers data modeling, starting development with Neo4j, and the power of transversals. Part 2 takes on application development and covers Cypher and Spring. Part 3 covers Neo4j in production.

Chapter 1 introduces graph database concepts in general, including looking at some of Neo4j's key aspects and the typical use cases which it is well suited to address. The chapter goes on to address some of the questions about where Neo4j fits within the so-called NoSQL space, including comparing it with more traditional relational databases.

Chapter 2 examines how and why we model data in Neo4j, including common approaches to data modeling scenarios in a graph database. Examples from a variety of domains are also presented, giving you a sense for just how flexible data modeling in Neo4j can be.

Chapter 3 is where we really start getting our hands dirty. This chapter introduces you to the Neo4j Core Java API, where you are taken through the steps of creating a graph representing a social network of users and the movies they like. This chapter covers creating and connecting nodes and capturing additional information against these nodes. It also looks at strategies for differentiating between types of nodes, including the use of labels.

Chapter 4 builds on this social network domain, exploring the core API in more depth and focusing specifically on traversals—in this case the Neo4j Traversal API—as a powerful way of querying graph data.

Chapter 5 introduces the indexing strategies available in Neo4j. Creating and traversing graph data is great, but you will need a strategy for finding the starting point, or points, in your graph from which to begin. This chapter covers these options. You will begin by looking at the manual (legacy) indexing options, before moving on to the built-in indexing options available from Neo4j 2.0 onward.

Chapter 6 introduces Cypher, Neo4j's human-readable query language. The nature of Cypher is explained, its basic syntax for graph operations is demonstrated, and advanced features that can be useful in day-to-day development and maintenance of Neo4j databases are also covered.

Chapter 7 focuses on one of the unique selling points of Neo4j in the NoSQL space—the fact that it fully supports ACID-based transactions, providing examples of different uses as well as taking a more in-depth look at certain aspects.

While chapter 4 provides your initial foray into the world of traversals, writing efficient traversals is the key to successfully querying graph data. In chapter 8 we dig deeper into the inner workings of the Traversal API so you can learn how to solve the most complex graph problems in an efficient manner with the native API.

Chapter 9 looks at Spring Data Neo4j library (SDN), the object graph-mapping library. Though not an official Neo4j offering, this chapter focuses on demonstrating how the Neo4j-specific open source framework can be used as a library to provide a robust and seamless mapping experience between a rich object graph model and data backed by Neo4j. Once again our trusty social network of users and their favorite movies is used to demonstrate these points.

Chapter 10 explores the two main usage modes in Neo4j, namely embedded and server. Much of the book has focused on demonstrating core concepts using the embedded mode. This chapter additionally introduces the server mode, which can be used by just about any client, and explores each mode in a bit more depth, weighing the pros and cons of each, including how to get the most out of your server if you choose to use this option.

Chapter 11 finishes off with an overview of the high-level Neo4j architecture. Framed with this knowledge, the chapter explores what should be considered when you want to take Neo4j to production, including scaling and other requirements for making Neo4j highly available, finishing off with instructions for how to back up and restore your database should it be required.

The four appendixes guide you through installing, setting up, and running Neo4j, Maven, and SDN, and offer guidance for seeking more help.

Code conventions and downloads

All source code in the book is in a `fixed-width font like this`, which sets it off from the surrounding text. In many listings, the code is annotated to point out the key concepts, and numbered bullets are sometimes used in the text to provide additional information about the code.

Most of the code shown in the book can be found in various forms in the sample source code that accompanies it. The sample code can be downloaded free of charge from the Manning website at www.manning.com/Neo4jinAction, as well as at https://github.com/opencredo/neo4j-in-action.

The sample code is structured as a set of JUnit style tests that aim to highlight and/or demonstrate the particular code under discussion. Instructions for how you can run the sample code are provided in appendix B.

Author Online forum

Purchase of *Neo4j in Action* includes free access to a private web forum run by Manning Publications where you can make comments about the book, ask technical questions, and receive help from the authors and from other users. To access the forum and subscribe to it, point your web browser to www.manning.com/Neo4jinAction. This page provides information on how to get on the forum once you're registered, what kind of help is available, and the rules of conduct on the forum.

Manning's commitment to our readers is to provide a venue where a meaningful dialog between individual readers and between readers and the authors can take place. It's not a commitment to any specific amount of participation on the part of the authors, whose contributions to the AO remain voluntary (and unpaid). We suggest you ask the authors challenging questions lest their interest stray!

The Author Online forum and the archives of previous discussions will be accessible from the publisher's website as long as the book is in print.

about the authors

ALEKSA VUKOTIC started out as a data management practice lead at Open Credo, and now works as the Head of Platform Development at Noble Group. Aleksa is a software architect and developer, agile advocate, author, and trainer, and has been a developer on a number of Neo4j projects that leverage the graph-data model to solve complex access control list and recommendation engine problems.

NICKI WATT is a lead consultant at Open Credo. Pragmatic, hands on, and a techie at heart, she's a problem solver who enjoys using "the right tool for the job." Nicki has been involved on various projects using Neo4j and other open source tools and frameworks, including insight and recommendation engine-based problems. She's also a contributor on the Spring Data Neo4j project.

TAREQ ABEDRABBO is the CTO of Open Credo. Tareq has a strong interest in programming languages, ranging from Scala and Python to Google Go. He has expert knowledge in a number of NoSQL technologies, including Neo4j, MongoDB, and Redis. Tareq has been actively involved with the Spring project since the early days, and has been a committer on Spring Web Services.

DOMINIC FOX is a consultant at Open Credo, with a particular interest in translating the insights of programming language theory into practice. His varied career as a developer has included work in the domains of document management, telecommunications, and finance, and also involves training people in Neo4j. Constant throughout his career has been a desire to build tools and libraries that make the everyday tasks of programming more intuitive and reliable.

JONAS PARTNER is CEO of Open Credo, a service partner of Neo Technology, and an expert in solving complex data-centric problems. He's also the coauthor of *Spring Integration in Action* (Manning, 2012).

about the cover illustration

The figure on the cover of *Neo4j in Action* is captioned a "Man from Šibenik, Dalmatia, Croatia." The illustration is taken from a reproduction of an album of Croatian traditional costumes from the mid-nineteenth century by Nikola Arsenovic, published by the Ethnographic Museum in Split, Croatia, in 2003. The illustrations were obtained from a helpful librarian at the Ethnographic Museum in Split, itself situated in the Roman core of the medieval center of the town: the ruins of Emperor Diocletian's retirement palace from around AD 304. The book includes finely colored illustrations of figures from different regions of Croatia, accompanied by descriptions of the costumes and of everyday life.

Šibenik, unlike other cities along the Adriatic coast which were established by Greeks, Illyrians, and Romans, was founded by Croats. It is the oldest native Croatian town on the eastern shores of the Adriatic. The figure on the cover is wearing red woolen pants and a red woolen jacket over a black vest, all richly embroidered in the blue and green colors typical for this region.

Dress codes and lifestyles have changed over the last 200 years, and the diversity by region, so rich at the time, has faded away. It is now hard to tell apart the inhabitants of different continents, let alone of different hamlets or towns separated by only a few miles. Perhaps we have traded cultural diversity for a more varied personal life—certainly for a more varied and fast-paced technological life.

Manning celebrates the inventiveness and initiative of the computer business with book covers based on the rich diversity of regional life of two centuries ago, brought back to life by illustrations from old books and collections like this one.

Introduction to Neo4j

What is Neo4j? What is it good for? Is it the right database for your problem domain and what kind of things can it do? In part 1 of *Neo4j In Action*, we'll answer these questions and more.

Chapter 1 introduces general graph database concepts, and begins to explore some of Neo4j's key aspects. Chapter 2 continues looking at general graph-related problems and domains, with a focus on graph data modeling techniques and approaches for various circumstances. Chapters 3 to 5 are where we really start getting our hands dirty. Using an example social network of users and the movies they like, we begin exploring Neo4j starting with how to use the core API to perform the basic functionality of creating and connecting nodes, and techniques for identifying different types of nodes. Traversing graph data is also a key feature of Neo4j and chapter 4 addresses this by investigating the Neo4j Traversal API.

Chapter 5 introduces the various "indexing" strategies and options available in Neo4j, beginning by looking at the manual (legacy) option, before moving on to the built-in indexing option available from Neo4j 2.0 onward.

A case for
a Neo4j database

This chapter covers

- Use cases for Neo4j graph databases
- How Neo4j compares with more traditional relational databases
- Neo4j's place in the larger NoSQL world
- Key characteristics of Neo4j

Computer science is closely related to mathematics, with a lot of its concepts originally coming from mathematical philosophy. Algorithms, cryptography, computation, automation, and even basic theories of mathematical logic and Boolean algebra are all mathematical concepts that closely couple these two disciplines. Another mathematical topic can often be found in computer science books and articles: *graph theory*. In computer science, graphs are used to represent specific data structures, such as organizational hierarchies, social networks, and processing flows. Typically, during the software design phase, the structures, flows, and algorithms are described with graph diagrams on a whiteboard. The object-oriented structure of the computer system is modeled as a graph as well, with inheritance, composition, and object members.

But although graphs are used extensively during the software development process, developers tend to forget about graphs when it comes to data persistence. We try to fit the data into relational tables and columns, and to normalize and renormalize its structure until it looks completely different from what it's trying to represent.

An access control list is one example. This is a problem solved over and over again in many enterprise applications. You'd typically have tables for users, roles, and resources. Then you'd have many-to-many tables to map users to roles, and roles to resources. In the end, you'd have at least five relational tables to represent a rather simple data structure, which is actually a graph. Then you'd use an object-relational mapping (ORM) tool to map this data to your object model, which is also a graph.

Wouldn't it be nice if you could represent the data in its natural form, making mappings more intuitive, and skipping the repeated process of "translating" the data to and from a storage engine? Thanks to graph databases, you can. Graph databases use the graph model to store data as a graph, with a structure consisting of *vertices* and *edges*, the two entities used to model any graph.

In addition, you can use all the algorithms from the long history of graph theory to solve graph problems more efficiently and in less time than using relational database queries.

Once you've read this book, you'll be familiar with Neo4j, one of the most prominent graph databases available. You'll learn how a Neo4j graph database helps you model and solve graph problems in a better-performing and more elegant way, even when working with large data sets.

1.1 Why Neo4j?

Why would you use a graph database, or more specifically Neo4j, as your database of choice? As mentioned earlier, it's often quite natural for people to logically try to model, or describe, their particular problem domain using graph-like structures and concepts, even though they may not use a graph database as their ultimate data store. Choosing the right data store (or data stores—plural, in today's polyglot persistence world) to house your data can make your application soar like an eagle; it can come crashing to the ground just as easily if the wrong choice is made.

A good way to answer this question, then, is to take a problem that naturally fits very well into the graph-based world and compare how a solution using Neo4j fares against one using a different data store. For comparison purposes, we'll use a traditional relational database, as this is generally the lowest common denominator for most people when it comes to understanding data storage options. More importantly, it's what most people have turned to—and sometimes still turn to—to model such problems.

The example we're going to explore is a social network—a set of users who can be friends with each other. Figure 1.1 illustrates the social network, where users connected with arrows are friends.

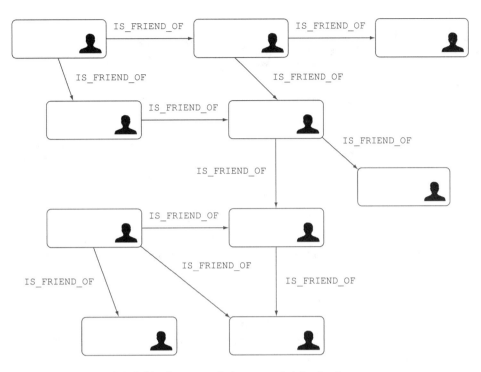

Figure 1.1   Users and their friends represented as a graph data structure

NOTE   To be semantically correct, the friendship relationship should be bidirectional. In Neo4j, bidirectionality is modeled using two relationships, with one direction each. (In Neo4j, each relationship must have a well-defined direction, but more on that later.) So you should see two separate friendship relationships for each pair of friends, one in each direction. For simplicity we have modeled friendships as single, direct relationships. In chapters 2 and 3 you'll learn why this data model is actually more efficient in Neo4j.

Let's look at the relational model that would store data about users and their friends.

1.2   Graph data in a relational database

In a relational database, you'd typically have two relational tables for storing social network data: one for user information, and another for the relationships between users (see figure 1.2).

The following listing shows the SQL script for creating tables using a MySQL database.

Listing 1.1   SQL script defining tables for social network data

```
create table t_user (
  id bigint not null,
  name varchar(255) not null,
  primary key (id)
);
```

⟵⌐ **Table definition for storing user information**

```
create table t_user_friend (                    Table definition for storing
    id bigint not null,                         friendship relations
    user_1 bigint  not null,
    user_2 bigint  not null,
    primary key (id)
);
alter table t_user_friend
    add index FK416055ABC6132571 (user_1),
    add constraint FK416055ABC6132571
    foreign key (user_1) references t_user (id);    Foreign key
alter table t_user_friend                           constraints
    add index FK416055ABC6132572 (user_2),
    add constraint FK416055ABC6132572
    foreign key (user_2) references t_user (id);
```

Table t_user contains columns with user information, while table t_user_friend simply has two columns referencing table t_user using a foreign key relation. The primary key and foreign key columns have indexes for quicker lookup operations, a strategy typically employed when modeling relational databases.

1.2.1   Querying graph data using MySQL

How would you go about querying relational data? Getting the count for direct friends of a particular user is quite straightforward. A basic `select` query such as the following would do the trick:

```
select count(distinct uf.*) from t_user_friend uf where uf.user_1 = ?
```

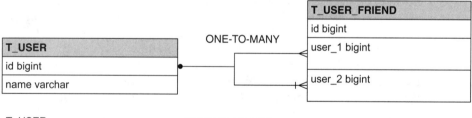

T_USER

id	name
1	John S
2	Kate H
3	Aleksa V
4	Jack T
5	Jonas P
5	Anne P

T_USER_FRIEND

id	user_1	user_2
1000	1	2
1001	3	5
1002	4	1
1003	6	2
1004	4	5
1005	1	4

Figure 1.2   SQL diagram of tables representing user and friend data

NOTE We're counting the friends in all examples, so we don't overload the CPU or memory by loading the actual data.

How about finding all friends of a user's friends? This time you'd typically join the t_user_friend table with itself before querying:

```
select count(distinct uf2.*) from t_user_friend uf1
   inner join t_user_friend uf2 on uf1.user_1 = uf2.user_2
   where uf1.user_1 = ?
```

Popular social networks usually have a feature where they suggest people from your friendship network as potential friends or contacts, up to a certain degree of separation, or depth. If you wanted to do something similar to find friends of friends of friends of a user, you'd need another join operation:

```
select count(distinct uf3.*) from t_user_friend uf1
   inner join t_user_friend uf2 on uf1.user_1 = uf2.user_2
   inner join t_user_friend uf3 on uf2.user_1 = uf3.user_2
   where uf1.user_1 = ?
```

Similarly, to iterate through a fourth level of friendship, you'd need four joins. To get all connections for the famous six degrees of separation problem, six joins would be required.

There's nothing unusual about this approach, but there's one potential problem: although you're only interested in friends of friends of a single user, you have to perform a join of all data in the t_user_friend table, and then discard all rows that you're not interested in. On a small data set, this wouldn't be a big concern, but if your social network grows large, you could start running into serious performance problems. As you'll see, this can put a huge strain on your relational database engine.

To illustrate the performance of such queries, we ran the friends-of-friends query a few times against a small data set of 1,000 users, but increased the depth of the search with each invocation and recorded the results each time. On a small data set of 1,000 users, where each user has on average 50 friends, table t_user contains 1,000 records, whereas table t_user_friend contains $1,000 \times 50 = 50,000$ records.

At each depth, we ran the query 10 times—this was simply to warm up any caches that could help with performance. The fastest execution time for each depth was recorded. No additional database performance tuning was performed, apart from column indexes defined in the SQL script from listing 1.1. Table 1.1 shows the results of the experiment.

Table 1.1 Execution times for multiple join queries using a MySQL database engine on a data set of 1,000 users

Depth	Execution time (seconds) for 1,000 users	Count result
2	0.028	~900
3	0.213	~999
4	10.273	~999
5	92.613	~999

NOTE   All experiments were executed on an Intel i7–powered commodity laptop with 8 GB of RAM, the same computer that was used to write this book.

NOTE   With depths 3, 4, and 5, a count of 999 is returned. Due to the small data set, any user in the database is connected to all others.

As you can see, MySQL handles queries to depths 2 and 3 quite well. That's not unexpected—join operations are common in the relational world, so most database engines are designed and tuned with this in mind. The use of database indexes on the relevant columns also helped the relational database to maximize its performance of these join queries.

At depths 4 and 5, however, you see a significant degradation of performance: a query involving 4 joins takes over 10 seconds to execute, while at depth 5, execution takes way too long—over a minute and a half, although the count result doesn't change. This illustrates the limitation of MySQL when modeling graph data: deep graphs require multiple joins, which relational databases typically don't handle too well.

Inefficiency of SQL joins

To find all a user's friends at depth 5, a relational database engine needs to generate the Cartesian product of the t_user_friend table five times. With 50,000 records in the table, the resulting set will have $50,000^5$ rows (102.4×10^{21}), which takes quite a lot of time and computing power to calculate. Then you discard more than 99% to return the just under 1,000 records that you're interested in!

As you can see, relational databases are not so great for modeling many-to-many relationships, especially in large data sets. Neo4j, on the other hand, excels at many-to-many relationships, so let's take a look at how it performs with the same data set. Instead of tables, columns, and foreign keys, you're going to model users as nodes, and friendships as relationships between nodes.

1.3   *Graph data in Neo4j*

Neo4j stores data as vertices and edges, or, in Neo4j terminology, *nodes* and *relationships*. Users will be represented as nodes, and friendships will be represented as relationships between user nodes. If you take another look at the social network in figure 1.1, you'll see that it represents nothing more than a graph, with users as nodes and friendship arrows as relationships.

There's one key difference between relational and Neo4j databases, which you'll come across right away: data querying. There are no tables and columns in Neo4j, nor are there any SQL-based select and join commands. So how do you query a graph database?

The answer is not "write a distributed MapReduce function." Neo4j, like all graph databases, takes a powerful mathematical concept from graph theory and uses it as a powerful and efficient engine for querying data. This concept is *graph traversal*, and it's one of the main tools that makes Neo4j so powerful for dealing with large-scale graph data.

1.3.1 Traversing the graph

The *traversal* is the operation of visiting a set of nodes in the graph by moving between nodes connected with relationships. It's a fundamental operation for data retrieval in a graph, and as such, it's unique to the graph model. The key concept of traversals is that they're localized—querying the data using a traversal only takes into account the data that's required, without needing to perform expensive grouping operations on the entire data set, like you do with `join` operations on relational data.

Neo4j provides a rich Traversal API, which you can employ to navigate through the graph. In addition, you can use the REST API or Neo4j query languages to traverse your data. We'll dedicate much of this book to teaching you the principles of and best practices for traversing data with Neo4j.

To get all the friends of a user's friends, run the code in the following listing.

Listing 1.2   Neo4j Traversal API code for finding all friends at depth 2

```
TraversalDescription traversalDescription =
   Traversal.description()
   .relationships("IS_FRIEND_OF", Direction.OUTGOING)
   .evaluator(Evaluators.atDepth(2))
   .uniqueness(Uniqueness.NODE_GLOBAL);
Iterable<Node> nodes = traversalDescription.traverse(nodeById).nodes();
```

Don't worry if you don't understand the syntax of the code snippet in listing 1.2—everything will be explained slowly and thoroughly in the next few chapters. Figure 1.3 illustrates the traversal of the social network graph, based on the preceding traversal description.

Before the traversal starts, you select the node from which the traversal will start (node *X* in figure 1.3). Then you follow all the friendship relationships (arrows) and collect the visited nodes as results. The traversal continues its journey from one node to another via the relationships that connect them. The direction of relationships does not affect the traversal—you can go up and down the arrows with the same efficiency. When the rules stop applying, the traversal stops. For example, the rule can be to visit only nodes that are at depth 1 from the starting node, in which case once all nodes at depth 1 are visited, the traversal stops. (The darker arrows in figure 1.3 show the relationships that are followed for this example.)

Table 1.2 shows the performance metrics for running a traversal against a graph containing the same data that was in the previous MySQL database (where the traversal is functionally the same as the queries executed previously on the database, finding friends of friends up the defined depth). Again, this is for a data set of 1,000 users with an average of 50 friends per user.

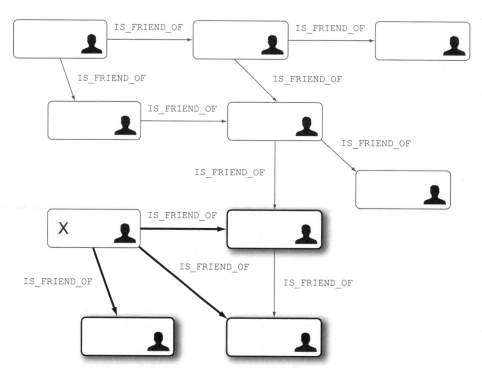

Figure 1.3   Traversing the social network graph data

Table 1.2   The execution times for graph traversal using Neo4j on a data set of 1,000 users

Depth	Execution time (seconds) for 1,000 users	Count result
2	0.04	~900
3	0.06	~999
4	0.07	~999
5	0.07	~999

NOTE   Similar to the MySQL setup, no additional performance tuning was done on the Neo4j instance. Neo4j was running in embedded mode, with the default configuration and 2,048 MB of JVM heap memory.

The first thing to notice is that the Neo4j performance is significantly better for all queries, except the simplest one. Only when looking for friends of friends (at depth 2) is the MySQL performance comparable to the performance of a Neo4j traversal. The traversal of friends at depth 3 is four times faster than the MySQL counterpart. When performing a traversal at depth 4, the results are five orders of magnitude better. The depth 5 results are 10 million times faster for the Neo4j traversal compared to the MySQL query!

Another conclusion that can be made from the results in table 1.2 is that the performance of the query degrades only slightly with the depth of the traversal when the count of nodes returned remains the same. The MySQL query performance degrades with the depth of the query because of the Cartesian product operations that are executed before most of the results are discarded. Neo4j keeps track of the nodes visited, so it can skip nodes it's visited before and therefore significantly improve performance.

To find all friends at depth 5, MySQL will perform a Cartesian product on the t_user_friend table five times, resulting in $50,000^5$ records, out of which all but 1,000 are discarded. Neo4j will simply visit nodes in the database, and when there are no more nodes to visit, it will stop the traversal. That is why Neo4j can maintain constant performance as long as the number of nodes returned remains the same, whereas there's a significant degradation in performance when using MySQL queries.

> **NOTE** Graph traversals perform significantly better than the equivalent MySQL queries (thousands of times better with traversal depths of 4 and 5). At the same time, the traversal performance does not decrease dramatically with the depth—the traversal at depth 5 is only 0.03 seconds slower than the traversal at depth 2. The performance of the most complex MySQL queries is more than 10,000 times slower than the simple ones.

But how does this graphing approach scale? To get the answer, let's repeat the experiment with a data set of 1 million users.

1.4   *SQL joins versus graph traversal on a large scale*

For this experiment, we used exactly the same data structures as before; the only difference was the amount of data.

In MySQL we had 1,000,000 records in the t_user table, and approximately 1,000,000 × 50 = 50,000,000 records in the t_user_friend table. We ran the same four queries against this data set (friends at depths 2, 3, 4, and 5). Table 1.3 shows the collected results for the performance of SQL queries in this case.

Table 1.3   The execution times for multiple join queries using a MySQL database engine on a data set of 1 million users

Depth	Execution time (seconds) for 1 million users	Count result
2	0.016	~2,500
3	30.267	~125,000
4	1,543.505	~600,000
5	Not finished	—

Comparing these results to the MySQL results for a data set of 1,000 users, you can see that the performance of the depth 2 query has stayed the same, which can be explained by the design of the MySQL engine handling table joins efficiently using indexes. Queries at depths 3 and 4 (which use 3 and 4 `join` operations, respectively) demonstrate much worse results, by at least two orders of magnitude. The SQL query for all friends at depth 5 did not finish in the hour we ran the script.

> **NOTE**   To store the large amount of data required for these examples, a significant amount of disk space is required. To generate the sample data and run examples against it, you'll need in excess of 10 GB of disk space available.

These results clearly show that the MySQL relational database is optimized for single `join` queries, even on large data sets. The performance of multiple `join` queries on large data sets degrades significantly, to the point that some queries are not even executable (for example, friends at depth 5 for a data set of 1 million users).

Why are relational database queries so slow?

The results in table 1.3 are somewhat expected, given the way `join` operations work. As we discussed earlier, each `join` creates a Cartesian product of all potential combinations of rows, then filters out those that don't match the `where` clause. With 1 million users, the Cartesian product of 5 joins (equivalent to a query at depth 5) contains a huge number of rows—billions. Way too many zeros to be readable. Filtering out all the records that don't match the query is too expensive, such that the SQL query at depth 5 never finishes in a reasonable time.

We repeated the same experiment with Neo4j traversals. We had 1 million nodes representing users, and approximately 50 million relationships stored in Neo4j. We ran the same four traversals as in the previous example, and we got the performance results in table 1.4.

Table 1.4   The execution times for graph traversal using Neo4j on a data set of 1 million users

Depth	Execution time (seconds) for 1 million users	Count result
2	0.01	~2,500
3	0.168	~110,000
4	1.359	~600,000
5	2.132	~800,000

As you can see, the increase in data by a thousand times didn't significantly affect Neo4j's performance. The traversal does get slower as you increase the depth, but the main reason for that is the increased number of results that are returned. The performance slows linearly with the increase of the result size, and it's predictable even with a larger data set and depth level. In addition, this is at least a hundred times better than the corresponding MySQL performance.

The main reason for Neo4j's predictability is the localized nature of the graph traversal; irrespective of how many nodes and relationships are in the graph, the traversal will only visit ones that are connected to the starting node, according to the traversal rules. Remember, relational `join` operations compute the Cartesian product before discarding irrelevant results, affecting performance exponentially with the growth of the data set. Neo4j, however, only visits nodes that are relevant to the traversal, so it's able to maintain predictable performance regardless of the total data set size. The more nodes the traversal has to visit, the slower the traversal, as you've seen while increasing the traversal depth. But this increase is linear and is still independent of the total graph size.

What is the secret of Neo4j's speed?

No, Neo4j developers haven't invented a superfast algorithm for the military. Nor is Neo4j's speed a product of the fantastic speed of the technologies it relies on (it's implemented in Java after all!).

The secret is in the data structure—the localized nature of graphs makes it very fast for this type of traversal. Imagine yourself cheering on your team at a small local football stadium. If someone asks you how many people are sitting 15 feet around you, you'll get up and count them—you'll count people around you as fast as you can count. Now imagine you're attending the game at the national stadium, with a lot more spectators, and you want to answer the same question—how many people are there within 15 feet of you. Given that the density of people in both stadiums is the same, you'll have approximately the same number of people to count, taking a very similar time. We can say that regardless of how many people can fit into the stadium, you'll be able to count the people around you at a predictable speed; you're only interested in the people sitting 15 feet around you, so you won't be worried about packed seats on the other end of the stadium, for example.

This is exactly how the Neo4j engine works in the example—it visits nodes connected to the starting node, at a predictable speed. Even when the number of nodes in the whole graph increases (given similar node density), the performance can remain predictably fast.

If you apply the same football analogy to the relational database queries, you'd count all the people in the stadium and then remove those not around you, which is not the most efficient strategy given the interconnectivity of the data.

These experiments demonstrate that the Neo4j graph database is significantly faster in querying graph data than using a relational database. In addition, a single Neo4j instance can handle data sets of three orders of magnitude without performance penalties. The independence of traversal performance on graph size is one of the key aspects that make Neo4j an ideal candidate for solving graph problems, even when data sets are very large.

In the next section we'll try to answer the question of what graph data actually is, and how Neo4j can help you model your data models as natural graph structures.

1.5   *Graphs around you*

Graphs are considered the most ubiquitous natural structures. The first scientific paper on graph theory is considered to be a solution of the historical seven bridges of Königsberg problem, written by Swiss mathematician Leohnard Euler in 1774. The seven bridges problem started what is now known as graph theory, and its model and algorithms are now applied across wide scientific and engineering disciplines.

There are a lot of examples of graph usage in modern science. For example, graphs are used to describe the relative positions of the atoms and molecules in chemical compounds. The laws of atomic connections in physics are also described using graphs. In biology, the evolution tree is actually a special form of graph. In linguistics, graphs are used to model semantic rules and syntax trees. Network analysis is based on graph theory as well, with applications in traffic modeling, telecommunications, and topology.

In computer science, a lot of problems are modeled as graphs: social networks, access control lists, network topologies, taxonomy hierarchies, recommendation engines, and so on. Traditionally, all of these problems would use graph object models (implemented by the development team), and store the data in normalized form in a set of tables with foreign key associations.

In the previous section you saw how a social network can be stored in the relational model using two tables and a foreign key constraint. Using a Neo4j graph database, you can preserve the natural graph structure of the data, without compromising performance or storage space, therefore improving the query performance significantly.

When using a Neo4j graph database to solve graph problems, the amount of work for the developer is reduced, as the graph structures are already available via the database APIs. The data is stored in its natural format—as graph nodes and relationships—so the effects of an object-relational mismatch are minimized. And the graph query operations are executed in an efficient and performant way by using the Neo4j Traversal API. Throughout this book we'll demonstrate the power of Neo4j by solving problems such as access control lists and social networks with recommendation engines.

If you're not familiar with graph theory, don't worry; we'll introduce some of the graph theory concepts and algorithms, as well as their applicability to graph storage engines such as Neo4j, when they become relevant in later chapters.

In the next section we'll discuss the reasons why graph databases (and other NoSQL technologies) started to gain popularity in the computer industry. We'll also discuss categories of NoSQL systems with a focus on their differences and applicability.

1.6   *Neo4j in NoSQL space*

Since the beginning of computer software, the data that applications have had to deal with has grown enormously in complexity. The complexity of the data includes not only its size, but also its interconnectedness, its ever-changing structure, and concurrent access to the data.

With all these aspects of changing data, it has been recognized that relational databases, which have for a long time been the de facto standard for data storage, are not the best fit for all problems that increasingly complex data requires. As a result, a number of new storage technologies has been created, with a common goal of solving the problems relational databases are not good at. All these new storage technologies fall under the umbrella term *NoSQL*.

> **NOTE** Although the NoSQL name stuck, it doesn't accurately reflect the nature of the movement, giving the (wrong) impression that it's against SQL as a concept. A better name would probably be *nonrelational databases*, as the relational/nonrelational paradigm was the subject of discussion, whereas SQL is just a language used with relational technologies.

The NoSQL movement was born as an acknowledgment that new technologies were required to cope with the data changes. Neo4j, and graph databases in general, are part of the NoSQL movement, together with a lot of other, more or less related storage technologies.

With the rapid developments in the NoSQL space, its growing popularity, and a lot of different solutions and technologies to choose from, anyone new coming into the NoSQL world faces many choices when selecting the right technology. That's why in this section we'll try to clarify the categorization of NoSQL technologies and focus on the applicability of each category. In addition, we'll explain the place of graph databases and Neo4j within NoSQL.

1.6.1 *Key-value stores*

Key-value stores represent the simplest, yet very powerful, approach to handling high-volume concurrent access to data. Caching is a typical key-value technology. Key-value stores allow data to be stored using very simple structures, often in memory, for very fast access even in highly concurrent environments.

The data is stored in a huge hash table and is accessible by its key. The data takes the form of key-value pairs, and the operations are mostly limited to simple put (write) and get (read) operations. The values support only simple data structures like text or binary content, although some more recent key-value stores support a limited set of complex data types (for example, Redis supports lists and maps as values).

Key-value stores are the simplest NoSQL technologies. All other NoSQL categories build on the simplicity, performance, and scalability of key-value stores to better fit some specific use cases.

1.6.2 *Column-family stores*

The distributed key-value model scaled very well but there was a need to use some sort of data structure within that model. This is how the column-family store category came on the NoSQL scene.

The idea was to group similar values (or columns) together by keeping them in the same column family (for example, user data or information about books). Using this approach, what was a single value in a key-value store evolved to a set of related values.

(You can observe data in a column-family store as a map of maps, or a key-value store where each value is another map.) The column families are stored in a single file, enabling better read and write performance on related data. The main goal of this approach was high performance and high availability when working with big data, so it's no surprise that the leading technologies in this space are Google's BigTable and Cassandra, originally developed by Facebook.

1.6.3   *Document-oriented databases*

A lot of real problems (such as content management systems, user registration data, and CRM data) require a data structure that looks like a document. Document-oriented databases provide just such a place to store simple, yet efficient and schemaless, document data. The data structure used in this document model enables you to add self-contained documents and associative relationships to the document data.

You can think of document-oriented databases as key-value stores where the value is a document. This makes it easier to model the data for common software problems, but it comes at the expense of slightly lower performance and scalability compared to key-value and column-family stores. The convenience of the object model built into the storage system is usually a good trade-off for all but massively concurrent use cases (most of us are not trying to build another Google or Facebook, after all).

1.6.4   *Graph databases*

Graph databases were designed with the view that developers often build graph-like structures in their applications but still store the data in an unnatural way, either in tables and columns of relational databases, or even in other NoSQL storage systems. As we mentioned before, problems like ACL lists, social networks, or indeed any kind of networks are natural graph problems. The graph data model is at the core of graph databases—you're finally able to store an object model that represents graph data as a persisted graph!

This data model can naturally represent a lot of complex software requirements and the efficiency and performance of graph traversal querying are the main strengths of graph databases.

1.6.5   *NoSQL categories compared*

Table 1.5 illustrates the use cases and representative technologies for each of the NoSQL categories.

Table 1.5   An overview of NoSQL categories

NoSQL category	Typical use cases	Best-known technologies
Key-value stores	▪ Caches ▪ Simple domain with fast read access ▪ Massively concurrent systems	▪ Redis ▪ Memcached ▪ Tokyo Cabinet

Table 1.5 An overview of NoSQL categories

NoSQL category	Typical use cases	Best-known technologies
Column-family stores	■ Write on a big scale ■ Colocated data access (for reading and writing)	■ Cassandra ■ Google BigTable ■ Apache HBase
Document-oriented databases	■ When domain model is a document by nature ■ To simplify development using natural document data structures ■ Highly scalable systems (although on a lower level than the key-value and column-family stores)	■ MongoDB ■ CouchDB
Graph databases	■ With interconnected data ■ Domain can be represented with nodes and relationships naturally ■ Social networks ■ Recommendation engines ■ Access control lists	■ Neo4j ■ AllegroGraph ■ OrientDB

So far in this chapter, you've seen examples of the efficient use of Neo4j to solve graph-related problems, seen how common real-world problems can be naturally modeled as graphs, and learned where graph databases and Neo4j in particular sit within the wider NoSQL space. But there's one key aspect of Neo4j that none of the other NoSQL stores have—one that's very important when it comes to the adoption of new storage technologies in the enterprise world: transactional behavior.

1.7 *Neo4j: the ACID-compliant database*

Transaction management has been a prominent talking point in discussions of NoSQL technologies since they started to gain popularity. Trading off transactional attributes for increased performance and scalability has been a common approach in nonrelational technologies that targeted big data. Some (such as BigTable, Cassandra, and CouchDB) opted to trade off consistency, allowing clients to read stale data in some cases in a distributed system (eventual consistency). In key-value stores that concentrated on read performance (such as Memcached), durability of the data wasn't of too much interest. Similarly, atomicity on a single-operation level, without the possibility to wrap multiple database operations within a single transaction, is typical for document-oriented databases.

While each of the approaches mentioned here are valid in specific use cases (such as caching, high data-read volumes, high load, and concurrency), the lack of ACID-based transaction handling is usually the first hurdle when it comes to introducing nonrelational databases to any enterprise or corporate environment. Although they were devised a long time ago for relational databases, transaction attributes still play an important and fundamental part in many practical use cases. Neo4j has therefore taken a different approach.

Neo4j's goal is to be a graph database, with the emphasis on *database*. This means that you'll get full ACID support from the Neo4j database:

- *Atomicity (A)*—You can wrap multiple database operations within a single transaction and make sure they're all executed atomically; if one of the operations fails, the entire transaction will be rolled back.
- *Consistency (C)*—When you write data to the Neo4j database, you can be sure that every client accessing the database afterward will read the latest updated data.
- *Isolation (I)*—You can be sure that operations within a single transaction will be isolated one from another, so that writes in one transaction won't affect reads in another transaction.
- *Durability (D)*—You can be certain that the data you write to Neo4j will be written to disk and available after database restart or a server crash.

NOTE   It's very important to note that Neo4j is a transactional database. Everything you know about transactions from the relational world applies to Neo4j as well. Transaction support is one the key differentiators between Neo4j and the other NoSQL databases we mentioned earlier, which don't support all ACID properties.

The ACID transactional support provides a seamless transition to Neo4j for anyone used to the guarantees provided by relational databases, and it offers safety and convenience in working with graph data. Transactional support is one of the strong points of Neo4j, which differentiates it from the majority of NoSQL solutions and makes it a good option not only for NoSQL enthusiasts, but in enterprise environments as well.

1.8   Summary

In this chapter you learned how much more efficient and performant Neo4j can be compared to relational databases for solving specific problems, such as the social network in the example. We illustrated the performance and scalability benefits of graph databases, as represented by Neo4j, showing the clear advantage Neo4j has over a relational database when dealing with graph-related problems.

You also learned about some of the key characteristics of Neo4j, as well as its place within the larger NoSQL movement of related data-storage technologies.

Using graph databases to store the data affects the way you should think about data. This is where data modeling becomes very important. There are no tables and columns any more, like in relational databases, or keys and values, like in other NoSQL technologies. You have to switch your mind to think of graph representations of your data. In the next chapter we'll give you some guidance and explain the best practices for modeling your graph data.

Data modeling in Neo4j

In this chapter, we're going to talk about how and why we model data in Neo4j, and discuss approaches to data modeling in a graph database. We'll look at alternative ways to model a given domain, making use of nodes, relationships, properties and labels in different ways. We'll also present examples from different domains to give a sense of how flexible data modeling in Neo4j can be.

We'll look at queries written in the Cypher query language. These are shown purely for illustration, to give an idea of how simple it is to query the models shown here: you don't need to know anything about Cypher to start modeling data, and the language will be introduced in more detail later on.

2.1 What is a data model for Neo4j?

Unlike a traditional RDBMS (relational database management system), Neo4j is a *schemaless* database. You don't need to define tables and relationships before you can start adding data. A node can have any properties you like, and any node can be related to any other node. The data model for a Neo4j database is implicit in the data it contains, rather than explicitly defined as part of the database itself. It's a description of what you want to put in your database, rather than a set of prescriptions enforced by the database that constrain what it will accept.

Because Neo4j data modeling is descriptive rather than prescriptive, it's easy to make changes when your application's view of the world expands or alters. But it's also useful to have a consistent description of the data the database will contain, so that you can frame queries in the expectation that similar entities will be represented in similar ways. The Neo4j query language, Cypher, works by matching patterns in the data, so one way to see your data model is as an inventory of basic patterns. For example,

- A person *lives at* an address.
- An underground station *is connected to* another underground station *on* an underground line.
- A smartphone bundle *includes* a smartphone and a call allowance.

These patterns fit collections of facts:

- Peter *lives at* The Gables. Mary *lives at* 13 Acacia Avenue.
- Bank Station *is connected to* Moorgate Station. Bank Station and Moorgate Station are both *on* the Northern Line.
- The light usage bundle *includes* a FictoPhone smartphone, and 150 minutes per month of mobile-to-mobile calls.

Once you have a consistent description of the data that will be stored in the database, you can use this description to reason about the queries you'll put to that database in the future.

A common way of expressing such a description is through diagrams. By drawing fragments of graphs that represent common patterns in your data, you can visualize your model in an intuitive way. In the early stages of Neo4j data modeling, a pen and a whiteboard, a sheet of paper, or a napkin is often all you need to start discussing what your data will look like.

2.1.1   *Modeling with diagrams: a simple example*

Suppose that instead of friendships between individuals, you were interested in modeling associations between groups of people. A group might contain several people, and a person might belong to several groups. In a traditional RDBMS, you'd typically model this scenario using three tables: a table for people, a table for groups, and a join table that would be used to link people to groups in a many-to-many relationship (figure 2.1).

Figure 2.1   Users and groups in an RDBMS with a join table

In Neo4j, you could model the same scenario by representing users and groups as *nodes*, and group membership as a *relationship* between nodes (figure 2.2).

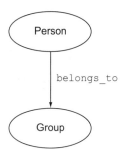

Here you can see that *nodes* are, roughly, the entities of the data model (in RDBMS terms) of a graph database, and *relationships* are, unsurprisingly, the relationships or connections between nodes. The plain English sentence that corresponds to this diagram is "A person belongs to a group."

Figure 2.2   A person belongs to a group.

Let's see how that looks with several people, and several groups (figure 2.3).

The pattern shown in figure 2.2 appears in the figure 2.3 diagram in several places; in fact, the whole diagram can be composed by overlaying copies of figure 2.2 on top of each other.

When it comes to querying the data in this model, there are two questions you might want to answer. First, for a given person, to what groups does that person belong? Second, for a given group, what people belong to that group? Both queries are easy to express in Neo4j's query language, Cypher:

```
MATCH (p)-[:belongs_to]->(g)
WHERE p.name = "Irene"
RETURN g.name
```

Matches all pairs of nodes "p" and "g" where there is a belongs_to relationship between "p" and "g", and the "p" node has the name "Irene".

Returns the name of each "g" node that matches the preceding conditions: "Cricket Club" and "Tennis Club".

```
MATCH (p)-[:belongs_to]->(g)
WHERE g.name = "Tennis Club"
RETURN p.name
```

Restricts the search to pairs of related nodes where the "g" node has the name "Tennis Club".

Returns "Irene" and "Jack".

It seems that this model is suitable for our use cases. By starting with a simple relationship, "a person belongs to a group," we've been able to generate a more complex graph by just repeating that relationship. Our initial graph fragment in figure 2.2 actually captures the entire model.

With more complex models, it sometimes makes sense to work in the opposite direction. You can do this by first drawing a diagram showing examples of all the different

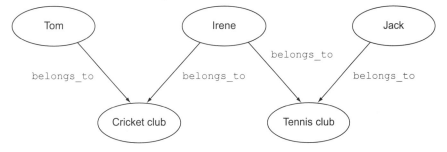

Figure 2.3   Three people in two groups

kinds of things in your system as nodes, then drawing arrows showing all the different kinds of relationships between them. Once you start seeing repeated patterns, you can pull those out into smaller graph fragments.

2.1.2   *Modeling with diagrams: a complex example*

Let's take a much more varied example, and see how it can be broken down into smaller patterns. In a large organization, users are given permissions to access different systems based on who they are, what roles they hold, and which groups they belong to. Here are examples of ways in which a user might have a permission.

- *Directly*—You have permission to access the files in your own personal folder on the shared filesystem.
- *Based on a role*—As a database administrator, you have permission to connect to the database-monitoring console.
- *Based on a group membership*—As a member of the group Sales and Marketing Team, you have permission to access the Contact Management System.
- *Based on the assignment of a role to all members of a group*—As a member of the group Developers, all of whom have the role Source Control Committer, you have permissions to check code out of the source repository and commit changes back in.

Figure 2.4 is an unconnected graph showing the entities in an access control system that enforces these permissions.

Figure 2.5 shows the same graph, with the possible relationships between these entities drawn in.

As you can see, there are several possible paths from a `User` to a `Permission`. In order to find out what permissions a user has, you need to find all the `Permission` nodes that a `User` node is connected to, via any path. In a traditional RDBMS, this would require a complex query expressing the union of each of the different kinds of paths:

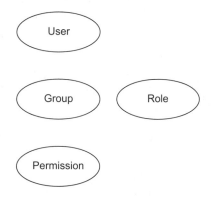

Figure 2.4   The entities in an access control system

- From `User` directly to `Permission` (one table join)
- From `User` to `Group` to `Permission` (two table joins)
- From `User` to `Role` to `Permission` (two table joins)
- From `User` to `Group` to `Role` to `Permission` (three table joins)

In Cypher, a single short query will suffice:

```
MATCH (u:User)-[*]->(p:Permission)
WHERE u.name = "User name"
RETURN DISTINCT p.name
```

This will match any pair of nodes where the first is labeled as a `User` having the specified name property value, the second is labeled as a `Permission`, and there is a path of

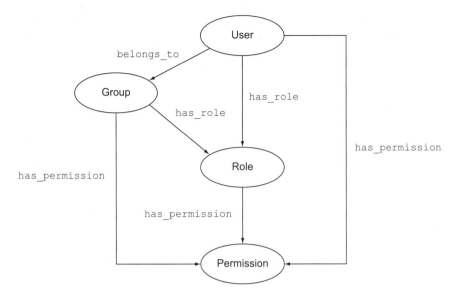

Figure 2.5 Relationships between entities in the access control system

any length between them. Finally, it returns the distinct names of all of the Permission nodes it has matched.

Now suppose you want to add a new feature to this model, reflecting the organization's hierarchical structure. Not only can users belong to groups, groups can be subgroups of larger groups—Testers, UX Designers, and Coders could be subgroups of the group Development, for example. Figure 2.6 shows the new model, extended with a subgroup_of relationship between groups.

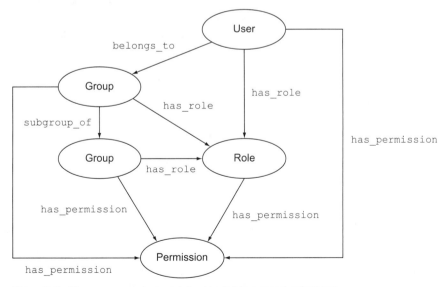

Figure 2.6 The access control model extended to support subgroups

Changing the RDBMS query to support this scenario would be a non-trivial task, but the Cypher query that worked with the initial model will work just as well with the extended one, because it is indifferent to *how* you get from a User to a Permission.

2.2   *Domain modeling*

In the model discussed in the previous section, the nodes carried very little extra information about themselves, besides their identifying names. It was intuitively clear how the domain entities—Users, Groups, Roles, and Permissions—should be represented by nodes in the graph. But not everything has to be a node; for example, there weren't any nodes for users' names, which were instead modeled as *properties* on User nodes.

Properties are an important part of Neo4j's data model, and they're also an important way in which it differs from the RDBMS model. In Neo4j, both nodes and relationships can have any number of properties, which are essentially key/value pairs (for example, name/"Irene"). They are normally used to store the specific properties of nodes and relationships.

Let's consider a scenario where the distinction between an *entity* (modeled with a node) and a *property* of an entity is less intuitively obvious.

2.2.1   *Entities and properties*

Sometimes when people first begin modeling with Neo4j, they come up with diagrams that look a bit like figure 2.7.

There may be some scenarios in which this is exactly the right way to model a user and their properties, but there are some warning signs here. If you see a relationship labeled has_property or similar, consider whether the node on the other end of the connection really needs to be a node. Unless, for some reason, you wanted to link users together based on their favorite colors, there's probably no need for Favorite-Color to be modeled as a node; it could be an property on the User node. The same is true for the name and age properties.

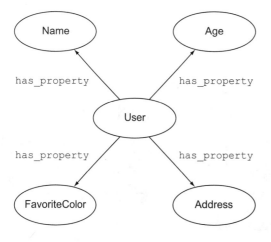

Figure 2.7   A User with some properties

If you convert these nodes into properties on the `User` node, and rename the remaining `has_property` relationship so that it more closely describes the relationship the `User` has with their `Address`, then the diagram will look like figure 2.8.

`Address` is different from `Name`, `Age`, and `Favorite-Color`, because you might be interested in using shared addresses to connect users to each other. A user who has moved house might have a current and a previous address, or a list of historical addresses. Accordingly, it may make sense to model addresses as entities, represented by nodes of their own.

Now suppose you want to distinguish between a user's current and previous addresses. One way to do this would be to attach an `is_current` flag to the address node as an property. But if two users had lived at the same address, and one was the current and the other a previous occupant, then whatever value this flag had would be false for one of them. Being a user's current address is not a property of the address itself, or of the user, but of the relationship between them—a relationship that may change over time, as users move from one address to another.

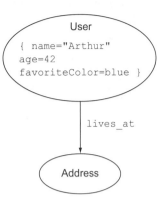

Figure 2.8 The user with some nodes converted to properties

There are at least three ways to represent the fact that an address is a user's current address. The first is to label the relationship itself differently, as in figure 2.9.

The second is to set an property on the relationship itself, as in figure 2.10. You might do this if you wanted to link users to addresses regardless of whether or not they currently live at them, and having different relationship types would complicate your queries.

The third way is to treat the user's occupancy of an address as a node in its own right. This is a technique called *reification* (literally, "making into a thing"), where a relationship between two nodes is broken into two relationships joined together by an intermediate node that represents the original relationship. This is useful when the relationship itself has relationships with other entities; for example, if a user's occupancy of

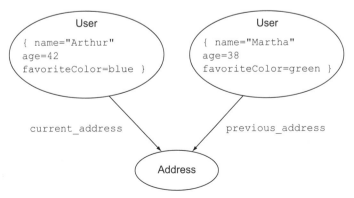

Figure 2.9 Two users with different relationships to the same address

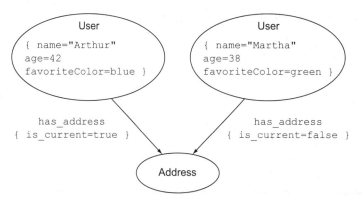

Figure 2.10 Two users with differently qualified relationships to the same address

an address is under a tenancy, managed by a letting agency. Figure 2.11 shows how this might work.

In this case, the flag indicating whether the occupancy is current has been added to the Occupancy node itself. But it could also be made a property of the has_held relationship, or two different relationship labels could be used for current or previous occupancies.

Another consideration when deciding whether to model the properties of entities using nodes is the efficiency with which the query engine can traverse the graph. It's usually not a good idea, for example, to extend a node's data by placing it in a relationship to another node whose only purpose is to hold additional properties, as in figure 2.12.

A better approach here would be to apply a *label* to the User node indicating that it has an extended property set, and place the extra properties directly on the User

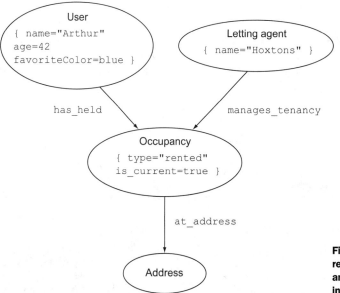

Figure 2.11 Reifying the relationship between a User and an Address in order to introduce other participants

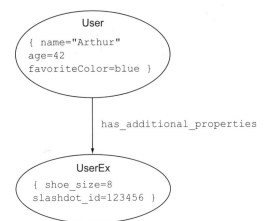

Figure 2.12 A User with additional properties stored in a related UserEx node

node itself. Labels are a powerful mechanism, introduced in Neo4j version 2.0, for assigning nodes to collections. A node can have multiple labels, so nodes can be treated as belonging to multiple, possibly overlapping, collections. By writing queries that target nodes with specific labels, you can do two things:

- Improve the performance of queries by reducing the number of nodes they have to consider when traversing the graph in search of pattern matches.
- Simplify queries by using labels to assert that nodes will have particular properties, so that queries don't have to handle the possibility of missing properties values.

You've seen labels used in the Cypher query examples given in this chapter: an expression like (u:User) matches a node with the User label, and it will ignore any other nodes.

Ultimately what should decide the representation you're going to use is the ease with which the patterns it contains can be queried and traversed. If it's difficult to see how two pieces of information are connected, but in reality their relationship is very straightforward, then consider linking them more directly in your graph. If you have nodes whose only purpose is to hold pieces of information belonging to other entities, consider moving that information into a property on that entity.

Don't be too worried, at this stage, about finding the right model. It's easy to refactor graphs using Cypher later on, to make explicit relationships that are only implicit in your current model. There's no such thing as a normal form for a graph database—only the form that best suits your application.

2.3   Further examples

We'll conclude this chapter with a couple of examples from different domains, both to illustrate the range of situations that can be modeled in Neo4j and to illustrate two pairs of opposing concepts: whether elements in the model are represented *implicitly* or *explicitly* in the graph, and whether data is generally *invariant* or *variable*.

To begin, let's revisit the underground stations example mentioned earlier.

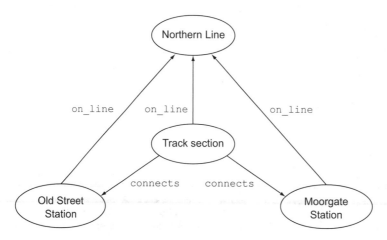

Figure 2.13 Two underground stations, with the connection between them reified as a single `Track Section`

2.3.1 Underground stations example

Our first example deals with the question of when you should model a particular aspect of your data *explicitly*, representing that aspect directly using nodes and relationships, and when you should allow that aspect to remain *implicit* in the data (but recoverable through querying). In this example, we'll model the stations, lines, and connections in the London underground system. We're interested in two things: which stations are directly connected to each other, and which stations are on which lines.

The big question here is whether or not to model underground lines directly as nodes, or implicitly as properties on relationships. If you model them as nodes, then you might have to connect every station and every section of track to the line it belongs to, as in figure 2.13.

This is quite a busy model, and your graph will quickly become very complex if you try to model multiple lines running through multiple stations. Alternatively, if you model underground lines as properties on relationships, then your graph is much simpler—figure 2.14 shows two stations connected by two different lines.

In order to know what lines Euston station is on, however, you now have to find out what connections it has to other stations. Fortunately, you can do this easily enough with a Cypher query:

```
MATCH (s1:Station)-[r:connected]-(s2:Station)
WHERE s1.name="Euston"
RETURN DISTINCT r.line
```
Finds all connections between the station named "Euston" and any other station, and returns their distinct line names

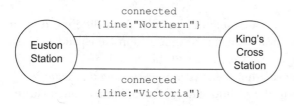

Figure 2.14 Two underground stations, with connections on two different lines

This will find all of the connections between Euston and any other station, and return the distinct line property values of all of those connections.

Both of these two ways of modeling the tube system are capable of containing exactly the same information. It would be possible to write queries to transform a graph modeled in the first way into a graph modeled in the second, and back again, without losing any detail. So how do you choose which way is best? The answer mainly depends on how you're going to populate your database, and how you're going to query it.

If, as in the first model, you have to create and manage explicit nodes and relationships to represent the existence of train lines and the fact that certain stations are on certain lines, then the database may be more unwieldy, and harder to visualize clearly, than one in which the only nodes are those representing stations, and the only relationships are those representing connections between stations. Running a query to find all of the stations that are on a particular line would be very quick, as the Neo4j database engine will only have to follow the relationships from a single node to all of its immediately connected nodes:

```MATCH (l:Line)<-[:on_line]-(s:Station)```
```WHERE l.name="Central"```
```RETURN s.name```
	Finds the node representing the line with the name "Central", and all of the station nodes immediately connected to it, returning the stations' names

This will run very quickly if you have an index on the name property of Line nodes, as the Neo4j query engine will be able to use that index to pick out its starting node.

The corresponding query against the second model will require a much more complex traversal of the graph in order to get its results.

```MATCH (s:Station)-[r:connected]-()```
```WHERE r.line="Central"```
```RETURN DISTINCT s.name```
	Finds all of the stations that are connected to another station by a connection on the "Central" line, and returns their names

In this case, the engine must consider *every* connected relationship between a pair of Station nodes, gather up all the nodes where the relationship has the required line property, and return all the unique Station names. If this is a query you're likely to want to run often, it may be worth considering surfacing the information it recovers by creating explicit nodes and relationships that represent that information.

What this example shows is that sometimes it makes sense to have some of the entities in your domain model remain *implicit* in the graph, rather than represent them *explicitly* with dedicated nodes. Conversely, it's sometimes worth surfacing implicit information and making it explicit so that it can be found more quickly by Neo4j's query engine.

2.3.2 *Band members example*

Our second example concerns modeling data to deal with information that changes over time, so that you can separate *invariant* aspects of the data from *varying* aspects.

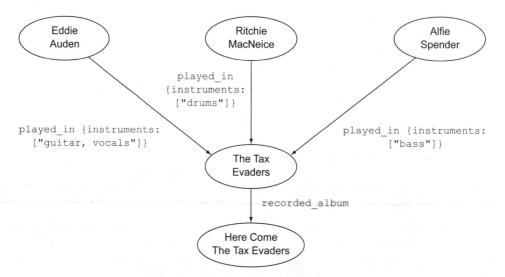

Figure 2.15   A simple model showing band members and a recorded album

Suppose you want to keep track of which musicians played which instruments on recordings by various rock bands. A simple model might look like figure 2.15.

One problem with this model is that bands sometimes change their members. In order to handle changes like this, you may need to create intermediate nodes that represent a state of affairs at a certain time. You could introduce lineup nodes representing the membership of a band at the point when a particular album was recorded, as in figure 2.16.

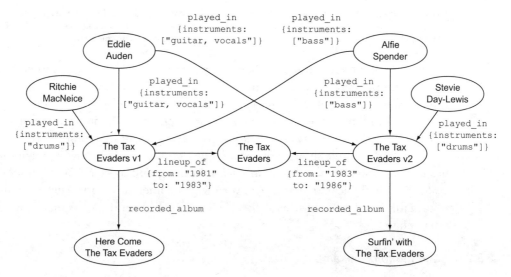

Figure 2.16   A more complex model showing two different lineups of the same band

With this model, you can easily find all of the albums recorded by (any lineup of) The Tax Evaders:

```
MATCH (a:Album)<-[:recorded_album]-(l:Lineup)-[:lineup_of]->(b:Band)
WHERE b.name="The Tax Evaders"
RETURN a.name
```

Returns "Here Come The Tax Evaders" and "Surfin' With The Tax Evaders"

But you could just as easily query for just those albums on which Ritchie MacNeice played drums:

```
MATCH (a:Album)<-[:recorded_album]-(l:Lineup)<-[:played_in]-(m:Musician)
WHERE m.name="Ritchie MacNeice"
RETURN a.name
```

Returns only "Here Come The Tax Evaders"

The *invariant* information in this graph is that there exists a band called The Tax Evaders—it keeps its identity even though its membership *varies*. You can represent variations in the composition of The Tax Evaders using nodes that represent its states at different moments in time, and use the lineup_of relationship to link these states to the central node, indicating that they are *different* states of the *same* thing. Likewise, the identities of the various musicians who have played in The Tax Evaders remain the same, even though their relationship to the band (and possibly other bands) will change over time.

This example demonstrates a use of *reification*—representing a relationship between entities, such as musicians and a band, as a node in its own right. The concept of a lineup as a thing representing the composition of a band at a particular moment in time turns out to be indispensable in the fast-moving world of rock and roll; reification is equally useful in less glamorous contexts, such as modeling the relationships between people and the addresses they live at, or software licenses and the computers they're activated on.

2.4 Summary

In this chapter you've seen how flexible data modeling for Neo4j can be, and how there may be several possible representations of the same domain. It's easy to start modeling with just pencil and paper, but you should be prepared to try putting the same data in different places—as properties on nodes, or on relationships, or pulled out into a node of its own.

We've considered some strategies for modeling data in a way that suits particular patterns of querying, choosing which data is to be *explicitly* represented by nodes and what can be left *implicit* and later inferred from queryable patterns within the data. We've also looked at data that changes over time and seen one pattern for modeling a mixture of *variable* and *invariant* data.

The examples you've seen in this chapter show the diversity of applications to which graph data modeling is suited. In the next chapter, you'll see how to traverse your model in order to retrieve data efficiently and powerfully.

Starting development with Neo4j

3

This chapter covers

- Modeling graph data
- Creating connected nodes using the Neo4j Java API
- Adding additional information to nodes and relationships using properties
- Strategies for differentiating between types of nodes

In chapter 1 we demonstrated the performance and scalability improvements available when using Neo4j as a database for graph data. We also discussed how data that's naturally modeled as a graph fits well with the Neo4j data model. Now it's time to get some hands-on practice.

In this chapter we'll introduce you to the Neo4j Core Java API by modeling and creating an example graph in the Neo4j graph database. We'll build on the social network example from chapter 1, but we'll make it slightly more complex by allowing users to rate movies they've seen.

The users in the social network can be friends. In addition, users can mark the movies they've seen and rate them with one to five stars based on how much they liked them.

32

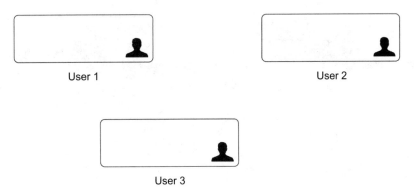

Figure 3.1   Users in a social network represented as boxes

In the first part of this chapter, we're going to model the requirements for this example using a series of diagrams, simulating the software design process. In the second part, we'll demonstrate how to create the same social network using the Neo4j Core Java API.

3.1   *Modeling graph data structures*

Before we dig into the world of Neo4j, let's model the social network domain as a generic graph. If you were doing modeling in your office, you'd probably draw the model on a whiteboard. We'll illustrate the whiteboard modeling with figures throughout this chapter.

First, you need a few users in your social network. The users are represented as boxes, as in figure 3.1.

Your goal is to build a social network of movie lovers, so the next natural step is to add the social element to the model. First, connect users who are friends using arrows. Say that User 1 has two friends, User 2 and User 3. Figure 3.2 illustrates the diagram with connections between friends.

NOTE   To be semantically correct, the friendship relationship should be bidirectional, but Neo4j's graphs are directed, which means that each relationship

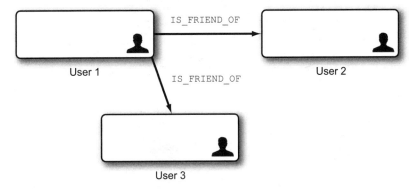

Figure 3.2   Simple social network graph with users connected as friends

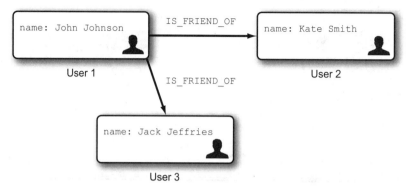

Figure 3.3   Richer model with a `name` property assigned to each user

must have well-defined start and end nodes. Bidirectional relationships in Neo4j can be modeled with two separate relationships, one in each direction. For simplicity, we've modeled friendships as single, directed relationships. As you'll see in later chapters, this will not affect our querying capabilities in Neo4j, because relationships can be followed in either direction, which will simplify our model significantly.

Okay, you have a few users, represented as boxes, who are friends in the social network. To differentiate between users, you can add a `name` property to each one, as shown in figure 3.3.

Figure 3.3 finally looks like a proper social network. But your goal is to build a social network of movie lovers, so the next step is to add a few movies to the model.

You can represent movies as boxes with a `name` property, as shown in figure 3.4.

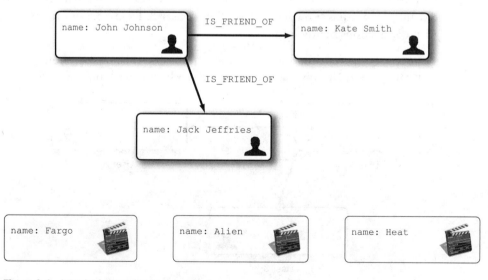

Figure 3.4   Introducing movies to the model

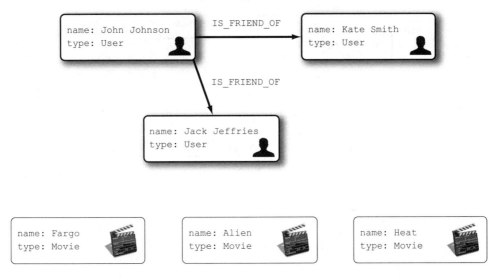

Figure 3.5 Introducing `type` properties to differentiate between `User` and `Movie` elements

There's one problem here: because both users and movies are represented as boxes with a name property, you don't have any way to differentiate between them. The easiest way to make a difference between user boxes and movie boxes is to introduce a type property, with a different value for different types of objects. Figure 3.5 illustrates the model with relevant types.

You're almost there—the final step is to add the movie-lovers element to the social network. Let's say that John liked *Fargo* and gave it five stars, Kate saw *Heat* and gave it three stars, and Jack liked *Fargo* and gave it four stars and *Alien* and gave it five stars. Figure 3.6 illustrates the modeling board after adding movie ratings.

And that's it—you have a model that represents the social network requirements, illustrated in the diagram, or the whiteboard if you're doing this exercise in the office.

This modeling process is typically performed in the initial stages of every software project. The drawings help you understand the requirements of the project and make the architectural decision-making easier and more transparent. The modeling exercise outcome often takes the form of documentation about the model, requirements, and architecture decisions and suggestions, along with diagrams.

After the model is ready, the development team would generally take over the project and start writing code to build the software product, based on the model and architecture. As part of that process, the model would be normalized and mapped to the persistence layer, which is typically a relational database.

Interestingly, the social network modeled in figure 3.6 represents a graph, with users and movies as nodes, and relationships connecting friends (`IS_FRIEND_OF`) and rated movies (`HAS_SEEN`). The same graph structure would typically be used in the code, using object-oriented programming (OOP) techniques. Yet the data would be

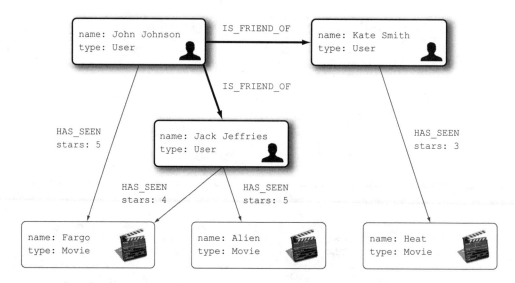

Figure 3.6   Complete model of a movie-lover's social network

stored in a number of tables, and accessed using the relational algebra. This "transla-tion" from a graph object model to a relational database and vice versa adds more complexity to the project and increases the number of lines of code you have to write, affecting efficiency and prolonging project delivery time. This is simply because you have to think about, implement, and configure a translation mechanism, using, for example, object-relational mapping (ORM) tools.

This is where Neo4j comes into play. Instead of storing graph-like structures in relational databases with the additional effort of creating a mapping mechanism, you can store graph objects like nodes and relationships natively in the Neo4j graph data-base. This allows you to model and code the software application at the same time, using the structure and terminology from the whiteboard more or less directly to drive your code.

3.2   *Using the Neo4j API*

When using Neo4j as underlying storage for the graph data structures, the modeling and coding can go hand in hand, as we'll demonstrate in the following sections.

3.2.1   *Creating nodes*

You can start by creating a node representing a user in the social network, using the instantiated graph database. Figure 3.1 (reproduced here as figure 3.7) illustrates the model drawing at this stage, containing three users.

You can write Java code that creates the graph in figure 3.7. The first two listings (3.1 and 3.2) create a single user node, using both the Java 6 (Neo4j 1.9.X) and Java 7 (Neo4j 2.0.X) idiomatic styles.

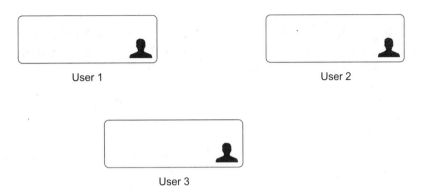

Figure 3.7 Graph with only node entities

The main difference between the two is in the handling of transactions. The APIs that create the node itself are identical, but as this is the first code we're presenting, we wanted to give you an initial taste of both versions upfront. Moving forward, this chapter and the remainder of the book will be using the Java 7 style of transaction management unless otherwise stated.

Listing 3.1 Creating a single user node in Neo4j (Java 6/Neo4j 1.9.X style)

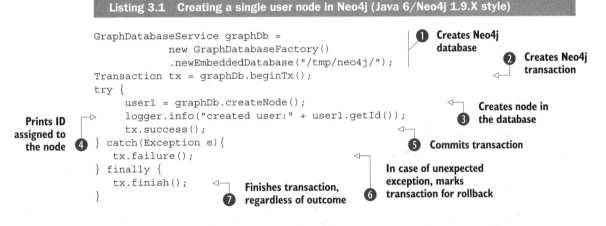

In both styles, the first step is to instantiate a Neo4j database ①. You provide the filesystem location where the data is located as the constructor argument. If this represents an existing Neo4j database, that database will be used; if the location doesn't exist, Neo4j will create an empty database at that location. The database should be created only once and reused for the application's lifecycle. In the following code examples, we'll assume that we're reusing an already configured, but empty, Neo4j database instance.

We mentioned before that Neo4j is a fully ACID-compliant graph database, supporting all standard transactional properties, as is expected from any other database. When using a Neo4j-embedded database, the transaction boundary is managed using the Neo4j Core Java API programmatically. Steps ❷ and ❺ in both listings (and ❻ and ❼ in listing 3.1) are part of the Neo4j API for transaction management. (Don't worry if you don't understand it all yet; we'll take an in-depth look at Neo4j transactions in chapter 7.) As all Neo4j operations must be executed within a transaction, you'll see these same lines of code in all code examples that write to Neo4j; without them, the code simply won't work. (In Neo4j 1.9 and below, transactions are only mandatory for operations that update the database, but from 2.0 onward, this includes read operations as well.) For now, all you need to note is that every block of code that accesses the Neo4j database is implemented within either a try/catch/finally block (Neo4j 1.9/Java 6) or a try (try with resource) block (Neo4j 2.0/Java 7), and that these patterns are used to handle the transaction boundary of the executed code.

In both approaches, the core part of the example is the code within the try block ❸, ❹. We'll include the transaction management code in all the examples throughout this chapter for consistency reasons, but we'll discuss Neo4j's transaction handling and API in more detail in chapter 7.

The GraphDatabaseService.createNode() method creates the node in the Neo4j database ❸. This method returns the created node itself, which you can use to inspect its properties or to manipulate the node further. In the preceding listings, you're using the returned node instance to print the internal ID of the node as generated by the Neo4j database ❹.

You've now seen the creation of a single user node, but because you're creating a social network, you'll need a few more users. The following listing creates three more users.

Listing 3.3 Creating multiple nodes in a single transaction

```
try (Transaction tx = graphDb.beginTx()) {
    Node user1 = graphDb.createNode();
    logger.info("created user:"+user1.getId());
    Node user2 = graphDb.createNode();
    logger.info("created user:"+user2.getId());
    Node user3 = graphDb.createNode();
    logger.info("created user:"+user3.getId());
    tx.success();
}
```

After the operations from listing 3.3, your graph will look exactly like figure 3.7, both in the object model and on disk, using the Neo4j graph database storage.

The next step is to connect the created user nodes using relationships.

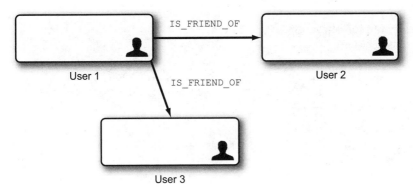

Figure 3.8   Simple social network graph with users connected as friends

3.2.2   *Creating relationships*

Before you start implementing relationships to connect users as friends, remind yourself of the model diagram in figure 3.2, shown again here as figure 3.8.

Relationships are the other main entity of the graph database, besides nodes. Every relationship has a name, which represents the label or type of relationship. In the Neo4j Core Java API, relationships are defined using the RelationshipType interface, which defines a single method that returns the relationship name, as illustrated in the following snippet:

```
public interface RelationshipType{
    public String name();
}
```

In the social network example, you're going to create friendship relationships between the users. For that, you need to implement the RelationshipType interface:

```
public class IsFriendOf implements RelationshipType{
    public String name(){
        return "IS_FRIEND_OF";
    }
}
```

◁─┤ **IsFriendOf class implements the RelationshipType interface**

◁─┐ **name() method returns the label of the relationship you'll use**

The RelationshipType interface has one interesting side effect: the signature of the only method it defines (String name()) looks exactly like the signature of the method available on all Java enumerations (enums). That gives you an option to implement Neo4j relationship types in a strongly typed, more expressive, and concise manner, using Java enums. The following snippet illustrates the same IS_FRIEND_OF relationship type implemented as a Java enum:

```
public enum MyRelationshipTypes implements RelationshipType{
    IS_FRIEND_OF;
}
```

The name of the enum represents the relationship name, as per the standard enum contract.

The DynamicRelationshipType class

If you know what relationship types are required at compile time, defining an actual class or (preferably) using the enum idiom to represent relationships is the recommended way to go. There may, however, be cases where you can only detect the relationship type at runtime and you still need a way to represent it. For these scenarios, the `org.neo4j.graphdb.DynamicRelationshipType` class can come in very handy.

The following snippet shows how the `IS_FRIEND_OF` relationship could be created with a `DynamicRelationshipType` class:

```
String runtimeVal = "IS_FRIEND_OF";
RelationshipType rel = DynamicRelationshipType.withName(runtimeVal);
```

Now that you've defined the relationship type you're going to use, you can create relationships between `user` nodes. To create relationships between two nodes, you need only call the `Node.createRelationshipTo(...)` method on one of the nodes, and pass in the target node and the relationship type.

> **NOTE** As we mentioned earlier, Neo4j's graphs are directed, with relationships having defined start and end nodes. When calling the `createRelationshipTo` method, the node on which the method is called will become the start node, and the node passed as an argument will become the end node. This will not affect the query flexibility or performance, as you'll see in the next chapters.

Like all write operations on the graph database, the creation of relationships requires a running transaction. The following listing shows how you can create the `IS_FRIEND_OF` relationship between the `user` nodes you created earlier.

Listing 3.4   Creating relationships between nodes using the Neo4j Core Java API

```
try (Transaction tx = graphDb.beginTx()) {        ⟵  Creates transaction for
    user1.createRelationshipTo(user2,                relationship creation
 ➥ MyRelationshipTypes.IS_FRIEND_OF);             Creates IS_FRIEND_OF relationship
    user1.createRelationshipTo(user3,             from node user1 to node user2
 ➥ MyRelationshipTypes.IS_FRIEND_OF);             Using same technique, connects
    tx.success();                                 user1 and user3 as friends
}
```

Next, we'll identify users in the graph using the `name` property.

3.2.3   Adding properties to nodes

Neo4j is a directed property graph. *Property graph* means that every graph entity can have a number of properties that describe it. Properties are stored as key-value pairs with the property name as the key referencing the property value. To illustrate the concept of properties, we're going to show you how to add the `name` property to the `user` nodes.

To add a property to a node, you need to call the `Node.setProperty(name, value)` method on the target node. The next listing shows how you can use the Core Java API to add names to all the users.

Listing 3.5 Adding name property to user nodes

```
try (Transaction tx = graphDb.beginTx()) {
    user1.setProperty("name", "John Johnson");        ◁─┐  Sets name property for
    user2.setProperty("name", "Kate Smith");            │  user1 (and later user2
    user3.setProperty("name", "Jack Jeffries");         │  and user3 as well)
    tx.success();
}
```

Now you have a richer graph model, where the users have names you can differentiate them by.

> **NOTE** In Neo4j, the property value must be set for every property added. In other words, properties with a `null` value are not permitted in Neo4j.

The property values in the preceding example are strings. But Neo4j supports a number of different types that can be set as node properties. Table 3.1 shows the property types that can be used, with their corresponding Java types.

Table 3.1 The property types in Neo4j

Description	Java type
Sequence of Unicode values	`java.lang.String`
Single Unicode value	`char`
True/false	`boolean`
8-bit integer	`byte`
16-bit integer	`short`
32-bit integer	`int`
64-bit integer	`long`
32-bit floating-point number	`double`
64-bit floating-point number	`float`
Arrays of any of above types	`[]`

Nodes with properties are schemaless, semi-structured elements. Each node can have any number of properties; the next listing illustrates how you can add different properties to different nodes.

> **NOTE** Properties can be added to relationships as well; that will be covered later in this chapter.

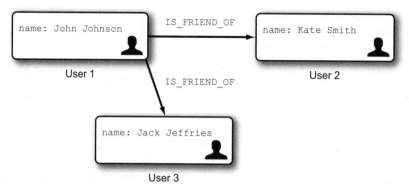

Figure 3.9   Rich property graph representing the social network

Listing 3.6   Adding different property types to nodes

```
try (Transaction tx = graphDb.beginTx()) {          Setting integer value
    user1.setProperty("year_of_birth", 1982);       as node property
    user2.setProperty("locked", true);
    user3.setProperty("cars_owned", new String[]{"BMW", "Audi"});    Setting Boolean
    tx.success();                                                     value as node
}                                                                     property
```

Setting (string) array as node property → (points to user3 line)

Setting integer value as node property → (points to user1 line)

Setting Boolean value as node property → (points to user3 line)

You've now made the graph model richer by storing additional information about nodes using properties. Figure 3.9 illustrates the social network after the enhancements from listing 3.5 (but not the example in listing 3.6) have been applied.

> **NOTE** As we mentioned before, Neo4j does not allow `null` properties. If you need to remove the property from a node, you have to do it explicitly using the Neo4j Core Java API: `Node.removeProperty(String propertyName);`.

Next you need to add a few more nodes representing the movies that the users watched and rated.

3.2.4   Node type strategies

The next step in the example is to add movies, which will be rated by the users, to the graph. You're going to add three `movie` nodes, following the same pattern used to add users earlier. The following listing illustrates the use of the Neo4j Core Java API to add nodes that represent movies.

Listing 3.7   Creating movie nodes using Neo4j Core Java API

```
try (Transaction tx = graphDb.beginTx()) {          Creates
    Node movie1 = this.graphDb.createNode();        movie node
    movie1.setProperty("name", "Fargo");
    Node movie2 = this.graphDb.createNode();        Add names property
    movie2.setProperty("name", "Alien");            to the newly created
    Node movie3 = this.graphDb.createNode();        movie node
    movie3.setProperty("name", "Heat");
```

```
tx.success();
}
```

Figure 3.10 illustrates the graph at this stage.

As you can see in figure 3.10, both `user` and `movie` nodes are represented as boxes. This is a very important point about Neo4j graph databases: there is no difference between `user` nodes and `movie` nodes from the Neo4j perspective. In Neo4j, by default, nodes are not typed, and determining the strategy for how each node is represented in the domain model is the responsibility of the developer.

In Neo4j 1.9 and below, the simplest strategy you can use is to add a `type` property to each node, with the value of the property determining the node type. This is a well-known strategy used in other NoSQL technologies (such as document databases) because it's easy to implement and understand. From Neo4j 2.0 onward, the recommended strategy is to make use of a new feature called "labels," which we'll cover in section 3.3. For now, we'll start with the Neo4j 1.9-compatible non-label strategies.

Using the `type` property strategy involves adding a `type` property to each node in the same way you previously added the `name` property to all nodes:

Listing 3.8   Adding a `type` property to determine node types

```
try (Transaction tx = graphDb.beginTx()) {
    user1.setProperty("type", "User");          Sets type property to value
    user2.setProperty("type", "User");          "User" for all user nodes
    user3.setProperty("type", "User");

    movie1.setProperty("type", "Movie");         Sets type property to value
    movie2.setProperty("type", "Movie");         "Movie" for all movie nodes
    movie3.setProperty("type", "Movie");

    tx.success();
}
```

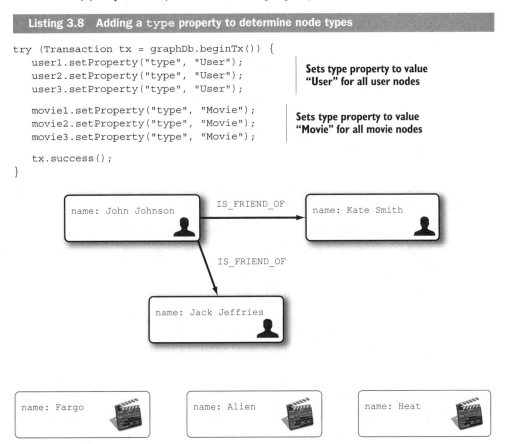

Figure 3.10   Graph with nodes representing users and movies

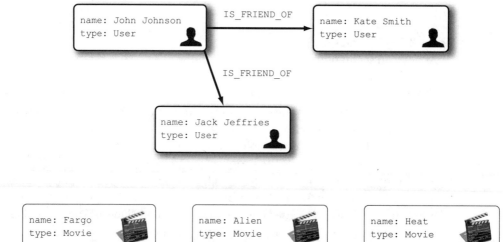

Figure 3.11 Nodes using the `type` **property strategy**

As in all previous examples, all graph database operations must be wrapped within the `try` transaction-handling block of code.

With the addition of node types, you can now determine the node type by simply checking the property value:

```
if("Movie".equals(node.getProperty("type"))){
    //this is a movie
}
if("User".equals(node.getProperty("type"))){
    //this is a user
}
```

> **NOTE** With this strategy, finding all nodes of a given type (such as all movies) by property requires using indexes, which we'll cover in chapter 5.

Figure 3.11 illustrates the graph with the `type` property set for each node.

You're almost there. All that's left to do is create relationships from users to the movies they like.

3.2.5 *Adding properties to relationships*

To make the social network graph complete, all you need to add is the relationship (called `HAS_SEEN`) between users and movies they rated. The `HAS_SEEN` relationship will start from the `user` node and be directed to the `movie` node, the same as the `IS_FRIEND_OF` relationship you used before.

There is one significant difference between the `HAS_SEEN` and `IS_FRIEND_OF` relationships: the `HAS_SEEN` relationship contains the additional information about how much the user liked the movie (represented by the number of stars the user gave to the movie). The number of stars is therefore not a property of the `user` node (because a user can rate multiple movies) or of the `movie` node (the movie can be rated by multiple users), but rather a property of the relationship between the user and the movie. You've seen how you can add properties to nodes, but adding properties to relationships is a new concept at this point.

We mentioned before that Neo4j is a property graph. In Neo4j, *property graph* applies to all graph entities—relationships as well as nodes. Adding a property to a relationship in Neo4j is as simple as adding a property to a node. We'll guide you through using the Neo4j Core Java API to add properties to relationships.

Before we proceed, you need to add a new relationship type to the relationship enum. The following snippet shows the updated `MyRelationshipTypes` enum with the new `HAS_SEEN` relationship:

```
public enum MyRelationshipTypes implements RelationshipType{
        IS_FRIEND_OF,
        HAS_SEEN;
}
```

The next step is to create named relationships between nodes, which is achieved in the same way that you added friendship relationships between users earlier in the chapter. The API call for the creation of a relationship will return the Neo4j `Relationship` object, and you can use it to add properties by calling the `Relationship.set-Property(String name, Object value)` method.

The following listing shows the code that creates the `HAS_SEEN` relationships and adds `stars` properties to them.

Listing 3.9   Creating relationships with properties

```
try (Transaction tx = graphDb.beginTx()) {
    Relationship rel1 =
        user1.createRelationshipTo(movie1,
 ➠ MyRelationshipTypes.HAS_SEEN);
    rel1.setProperty("stars", 5);
    Relationship rel2 =
        user2.createRelationshipTo(movie3,
 ➠ MyRelationshipTypes.HAS_SEEN);
    rel2.setProperty("stars", 3);
    Relationship rel3 =
        user3.createRelationshipTo(movie1,
 ➠ MyRelationshipTypes.HAS_SEEN);
    rel3.setProperty("stars, 4);
    Relationship rel4 =
        user3.createRelationshipTo(movie2,
 ➠ MyRelationshipTypes.HAS_SEEN);
    rel4.setProperty("stars, 5);

    tx.success();
}
```

> Creates HAS_SEEN relationship; the API call returns the Relationship object

> Adds stars property to relationship created on previous line

Once you've added the `HAS_SEEN` relationships to the graph, you've finally completed the social network using the Neo4j Core Java API. Figure 3.12 shows the final graph structure with all nodes, relationships, and properties.

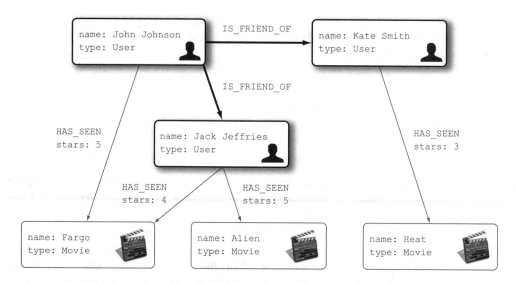

Figure 3.12   Complete model of a movie-lovers' social network

Figure 3.12 is the same as figure 3.6. You've managed to create the same graph in the Neo4j graph database using the Neo4j Core Java API.

3.3   *Node labels*

In the previous section we mentioned that nodes in the Neo4j database don't have types—they're just "boxes." In order to differentiate between movie nodes and user nodes, we added property types to each node, with corresponding values.

In version 2.0, Neo4j introduced the (built-in) concept of node labels, which can help you group similar nodes. Node labels are very similar to the relationship type names we discussed earlier.

Each node can optionally have one or more text descriptions, which we call node labels. Nodes with the same labels are stored in a specific manner so that they can be grouped and used together. Neo4j supports the following label-related operations out of the box in the Core Java API: loading all nodes by label and finding nodes by label and property. Schema indexes are also defined using labels.

> **NOTE**   Labels can be used for node lookup operations in Cypher queries as well. This use of labels will be discussed in chapter 6.

Just as in relationship types, node labels are defined using a simple interface with a single method, `String name()`:

```
public interface Label {
    java.lang.String name();
}
```

To create a new label, you can simply implement this interface, or, as with relationship types, use the Java enumeration idiom, which fulfills the `Label` interface contract:

```
public enum MyLabels implements Label{
    MOVIES, USERS
}
```

The following listing illustrates how you can create labels using the Neo4j Java API.

Listing 3.10   Adding labels to nodes

```
try (Transaction tx = graphDb.beginTx()) {
    movie1.addLabel(MyLabels.MOVIE);                    Adds label MOVIE
    movie2.addLabel(MyLabels.MOVIE);              ❶    to selected nodes
    movie3.addLabel(MyLabels.MOVIE);
    tx.success();
}

ResourceIterable<Node> movies =
        GlobalGraphOperations.at(graphDb)            ❷  Finds all nodes
        .getAllNodesWithLabel(MyLabels.MOVIE);           with MOVIE label
```

To add a label, you use the `addLabel()` method on the selected node ❶. To find all nodes with a given label, you can use the static `getAllNodesWithLabel(Label label)` method on the `GlobalGraphOperations` class ❷.

Figure 3.13 shows the graph with the added labels.

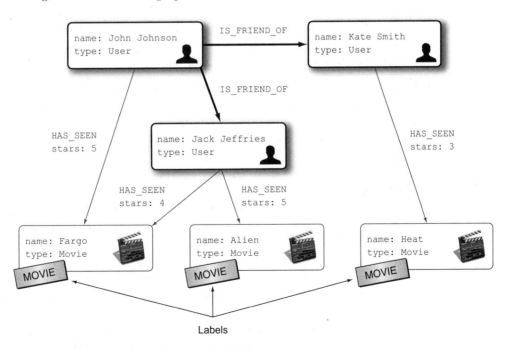

Figure 3.13   Movie nodes grouped using the label MOVIE

NOTE   In this example, the node labels supersede the type property for determining which nodes represent movies, so you can remove one of them. It's
recommended that you use labels wherever possible, simply because they're a
built-in feature of the Neo4j database, which allows greater flexibility with
querying and schema-based indexing.

In addition to finding all nodes with a given label, Neo4j Core Java API exposes
operations for finding all nodes with a given label and property, as is done in the following listing.

Listing 3.11   Finding nodes with a given label and property

```
ResourceIterable<Node> movies =                          Finds all nodes with the MOVIE
    GlobalGraphOperations.at(graphDb)                      label and name "Fargo"
    .findNodesByLabelAndProperty(MyLabels.MOVIE, "name", "Fargo");
```

By default, the lookup for nodes by label and property is performed by brute force by
the Neo4j engine (by iterating all through all nodes with the given label, and comparing the required property name and value). But if a schema index is defined on label
and property, the Neo4j engine will use the much faster index lookup. We'll discuss
using schema indexes in chapter 5.

NOTE   As you saw in listing 3.10, finding all nodes with a given label is considered a graph-global operation (as by design it can fetch large parts of the
graph), so the operation is available via the `GlobalGraphOperations` class. On
the other hand, finding all nodes by label and property (listing 3.11) is
exposed via the `GraphDatabaseService` interface, because it's expected to
return a small proportion of nodes in the graph.

Labels are a nice addition to Neo4j, and not only as a typing strategy. Because nodes
can have multiple labels, you can create labels to group nodes that are often used
together (even with different types), without the need to use properties. For example,
`RED_THINGS` (for all nodes that are red), `FLYING` (for all nodes that represent things
that can fly), and so on.

3.4   *Summary*

In the first part of this chapter, we showed how you could model the requirements for
a movie-lovers' social network example. You modeled the requirements using a set of
diagrams, or a virtual whiteboard, just as you'd approach application design in the
software development process.

  In the second part of this chapter, we demonstrated step by step how you could
create that same graph model in the Neo4j graph database using the Neo4j Core
Java API.

  What was interesting was that both sets of steps looked almost the same. Just as
drawing was the natural way to describe graphs for human understanding, the Neo4j
Core Java API allows you to follow the same pattern to describe the graph in the code.

Using the graph's natural language, you're able to implement the design with the Neo4j Core Java API and without any other tools or frameworks—no mapping or translation tools were required.

Graphs are indeed very powerful structures, and we use them daily to visualize models and problems related to software projects. Neo4j allows you to use clear and simple graphs as the programming model as well, making the transition from software design and requirements to programming easy and straightforward.

We scratched the surface of the Neo4j Core Java API in this chapter, showing how to create nodes in the graph, connect nodes using relationships, and to describe nodes and relationships using properties. In the next chapter, we're going to look at how you can use the power of graphs to query the data.

The power of traversals

4

This chapter covers

- Querying Neo4j using the Core Java API
- Traversing nodes and relationships using the Neo4j Traversal API
- Extending and customizing built-in Neo4j traversal operations

Chapter 3 introduced you to the Neo4j Core Java API and you created a graph representing a social network of users and the movies they like. In this chapter we're going to look at graph traversals—a powerful way of querying the graph data. *Graph traversal* is the process of visiting nodes in the graph by following the relationships between nodes in a particular manner.

We'll demonstrate the traversal options by showing you how to solve simple traversal problems, followed by more complex ones. In this chapter you'll get more familiar with the Neo4j Core Java API, as well as with the more advanced Neo4j Traversal Framework Java API (or "Neo4j Traversal API" for short).

Let's start with the simplest traversal, which follows relationships to find direct neighbors of the starting node using the Neo4j Core Java API.

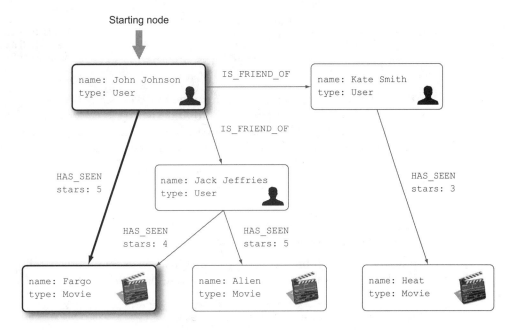

Figure 4.1 **The selected user and the movies he's seen are marked with a bold border.**

4.1 Traversing using the Neo4j Core Java API

The first traversal approach we'll look at makes use of standard methods available on the Neo4j Core Java API. We'll use the graph created in chapter 3 to perform the traversals.

The first traversal we'll look at can be described as "Starting from the node representing the user John Johnson, find all the movies that this user has seen." Figure 4.1 illustrates the part of the graph we're interested in.

To navigate to nodes representing movies John has seen, you'll start from the node representing John Johnson, then follow all of the HAS_SEEN relationships to the target movies. The nodes and relationships you want to visit as part of the traversal are marked with a dark border in figure 4.1.

The first task is locating the starting node for the traversal: user John Johnson.

4.1.1 Finding the starting node

Before you can proceed with the traversal, you need to find the node from which you're going to start the traversal, typically called the *starting node*. The Neo4j Core Java API has a single lookup method that can be used to load nodes from the graph database—GraphDatabaseService.getNodeById(Long id). This method loads the node by its internal identifier, which is represented as a java.util.Long number in Neo4j. We'll assume that the ID of the John Johnson user node is known and stored in the static variable JOHN_JOHNSON_NODE_ID:

```
public static Long JOHN_JOHNSON_NODE_ID = 3L;
private GraphDatabaseService graphdb;
public void getJohnNode(){
    return graphDb.getNodeById(JOHN_JOHNSON_NODE_ID);
}
```

Loads node object from Neo4j database by its identifier

> **NOTE** Ideally, you'd look up the starting node based on some property value instead of the node ID. For example, you'd find the user node by its name or email address. Ad hoc node lookup in Neo4j is performed using the index, which we'll cover in detail in chapter 5. In this chapter, node lookups will be performed using the node ID.

Now that you have the starting node, you can traverse the graph to find the movie nodes you're interested in.

4.1.2 Traversing direct relationships

To find all the movies John has seen, you first load John's node, then follow all the HAS_SEEN relationships from that node, as shown in the following listing.

Listing 4.1 Filtering movies by iterating through all relationships from the node

Uses Node.get-Relationships() to get all relationships that start or end at the given node ❶

Gets ending node of relationships, which represents movie in this model ❹

```
try (Transaction tx = graphDb.beginTx()) {
    Node userJohn = graphDb.getNodeById(JOHN_JOHNSON_NODE_ID);
    Iterable<Relationship> allRelationships = userJohn.getRelationships();
    Set<Node> moviesForJohn = new HashSet<Node>();
    for(Relationship r : allRelationships){
        if(r.getType().name().equalsIgnoreCase("HAS_SEEN")){
            Node movieNode = r.getEndNode();
            moviesForJohn.add(movieNode);
        }
    }
    for(Node movie : moviesForJohn){
        logger.info("User has seen movie: " + movie.getProperty("name"));
    }
    tx.success();
}
```

Finds starting node

Iterates through relationships using a typical Java for loop construct ❷

Filters HAS_SEEN relationships by checking each relationship type ❸

Prints resulting nodes in console

> **NOTE** Recall from chapter 3 that all Neo4j operations (including read operations from Neo4j 2.0 onward) need to be wrapped in a transaction. Listing 4.1 includes this initial boilerplate wrapping code, but we'll leave it out of future listings to reduce clutter and focus on the core aspects of the API under discussion. Don't forget about it, though, as the code won't work without it!

In listing 4.1, you use the Node.getRelationships() method call to get all relationships that either start or end at the selected node ❶. This method returns a java.lang .Iterable object that contains instances of org.neo4j.graphdb.Relationship, which you can iterate through using the Java for loop in the typical Java manner ❷. The userJohn.getRelationships() method will return all relationships starting or ending at the starting node, including the IS_FRIEND_OF relationships that you're not interested in (see figure 4.1). To identify only the relationships of type HAS_SEEN that you're interested in, you need to check the name of each relationship within the loop ❸.

To get the nodes that the relationship is associated with, the org.neo4j.graphdb .Relationship interface defines two methods: getStartNode(), which returns the starting node of the relationship, and getEndNode(), which returns the ending node of the relationship. We mentioned earlier that Neo4j incorporates a directed property graph model for its underlying graph storage. Every relationship in the Neo4j graph is directed, originating from the starting node to the ending node. For example, a HAS_SEEN relationship always originates from the user node to the movie node. As a result, the starting node will always be the node representing a user, and the ending node will be the node representing a movie.

In listing 4.1, this is exactly how you find the movies that John has seen: movie will always be an ending node of the HAS_SEEN relationship, so you get a reference to it by calling the Relationship.getEndNode() method ❹.

> **NOTE** Although all relationships must be directed, the actual traversal can go either way—down or up the relationship.

When the code in listing 4.1 is run, the resulting node is printed on the screen:

```
User has seen movie: Fargo
```

Based on the graph in figure 4.1, the result is correct. You performed a query of the graph data using the Neo4j Core Java API.

> **NOTE** The Node.getRelationships() method doesn't guarantee the order of relationships traversed. The order of the movies wasn't important for this example, but if you need ordered results, ordering would have to be performed as a separate step after traversal.

In the previous example, you filtered the relationships you're interested in by checking the name of every relationship connected to the starting node representing user John Johnson. Filtering relationships by name is a very common pattern in graph traversals. Neo4j provides an API that does exactly that, out of the box, so you don't have to repeat the if clause in the code that checks the relationship types. The following listing illustrates the improved code using Neo4j's built-in capabilities.

Listing 4.2   Filtering movies using the Neo4j Core Java API filtering capabilities

Uses the Node.get-Relationships-(Relationship-Type) method call to get all relationships with a given type that start or end at the given node

```
Node userJohn = graphDb.getNodeById(JOHN_JOHNSON_NODE_ID);
Iterable<Relationship> allHasSeenRelationships =
    userJohn.getRelationships(DynamicRelationshipType.withName("HAS_SEEN"));
Set<Node> moviesForJohn = new HashSet<Node>();
for(Relationship r : allHasSeenRelationships){
    Node movieNode = r.getEndNode();
    moviesForUser.add(movieNode);
}
for(Node movie : moviesForJohn){
    logger.info("User has seen movie: " + movie.getProperty("name"));
}
```

As you can see, the code doesn't have the if statement you used previously to filter relationships by required type. It's much more readable and concise, and it gives the same result as before:

```
User has seen movie: Fargo
```

If you need to be very specific, the Neo4j Core Java API allows filtering by relationship direction in addition to relationship type. To load only outgoing HAS_SEEN relationships for the starting user node, you could use the following snippet:

```
Iterable<Relationship> allOutgoingHasSeenRelationships =
    userJohn.getRelationships(Direction.OUTGOING,
    DynamicRelationshipType.withName("HAS_SEEN"));
```

As you can see, this code is improved by using the more advanced filtering features of the Neo4j Core Java API. But this is a very simple traversal, only looking at the direct neighbors of the selected node. In the next section, you'll go one step further and traverse the nodes beyond the direct neighbors by determining what movies John's friends like.

4.1.3   *Traversing second-level relationships*

Let's take the example to the next level and implement a simple recommendation engine that finds the movies that John's friends like, but that John hasn't seen.

Looking at the graph, John has two friends: Jack and Kate. Jack has seen *Fargo* and *Alien*, and Kate has seen *Heat*. But John has already seen *Fargo*, so you'd expect two movies to result from the traversal: *Alien* and *Heat*. Figure 4.2 illustrates the nodes and relationships you'll have to visit during the traversal.

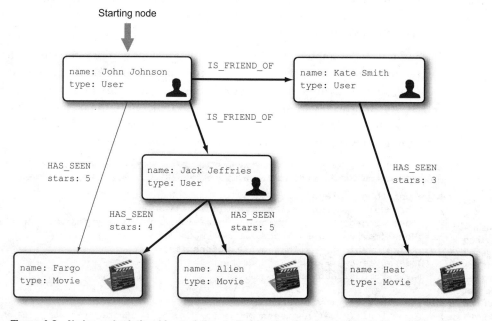

Figure 4.2   Nodes and relationships to follow to find movies that John's friends like

To solve this problem, we'll split it into several steps. First, you'll find all of John's friends by following the IS_FRIEND_OF relationships from the starting node. Next, you'll follow the HAS_SEEN relationships from the nodes representing friends to find the movies they've seen. The next listing shows the implementation of these two steps, again simply using the Neo4j Core Java API.

Listing 4.3   Finding movies that have been seen by John's friends

```
Node userJohn = graphDb.getNodeById(JOHN_JOHNSON_NODE_ID);
Set<Node> friends = new HashSet<Node>();
for (Relationship r1 :
    userJohn.getRelationships(IS_FRIEND_OF)) {
    Node friend = r1.getOtherNode(userJohn);
    friends.add(friend);
}
Set<Node> moviesFriendsLike = new HashSet<Node>();
for(Node friend : friends){
    for(Relationship r :
    friend.getRelationships(Direction.OUTGOING,
    HAS_SEEN)){
        moviesFriendsLike.add(r.getEndNode());
    }
}
for (Node movie : moviesFriendsLike) {
    logger.info("Found movie: " + movie.getProperty("name"));
}
```

Gets John's friend from the relationship ❷

Stores friend in local variable for later use ❸

❶ **Iterates through all IS_FRIEND_OF relationships**

❹ **Iterates through friends nodes stored earlier**

❺ **For each user-friend node, iterates through the outgoing HAS_SEEN relationships**

❻ **Adds movie node to collection**

❼ **Prints result on screen console**

The first part of this code stores the friends of John in the local variable friends ❶, ❷, ❸. First, you iterate through all the IS_FRIEND_OF relationships of the starting node, regardless of their direction ❶. Remember, although the IS_FRIEND_OF relationship has a starting and an ending node, you can go upstream as well as downstream to locate friends. But because you don't know whether John is the starting or ending node of the relationships, you can't use the Relationship.getStartNode() or Relationship.getEndNode() methods to determine the other participant in the friendship. Luckily, the Neo4j Core Java API has a solution for that: the Relationship.getOtherNode(Node node) method. This method, given a node on one end of the relationship, returns the node on the other end. In this case, because you know that the relationship has one end at the John node, you can use this method to find out John's friends ❷. Finally, you add the friend node to the local java.lang.Set variable friends ❸, which you'll use later.

In the second part of the code, you find all the movies John's friends have seen ❹, ❺, ❻. For each of the nodes stored in the temporary local variable ❹, you check all outgoing HAS_SEEN relationships ❺. Just as you did in the previous example, you load the ending node of the HAS_SEEN relationship (which you know represents a movie) and store it in the local Set variable moviesFriendsLike, which represents your result ❻.

Finally, you print the result to the console ❼. You should see something like the following:

```
Found movie: Fargo
Found movie: Alien
Found movie: Heat
```

Obviously, there's something wrong. Although all three movies have been seen by John's friends (*Fargo* and *Alien* by Jack and *Heat* by Kate), *Fargo* should not have been listed because John has seen it!

You have to make sure you remove the movies that John has seen from the list before you print it on the screen. To do that, you need to find all movies that John has seen (just as you did in section 4.1.2) and remove them from the result. The code in the following listing shows one way to do this.

Listing 4.4   Finding movies that have been seen by John's friends but not by John

```
Node userJohn = graphDb.getNodeById(JOHN_JOHNSON_NODE_ID);

Set<Node> friends = new HashSet<Node>();
for (Relationship r1 :
     userJohn.getRelationships(IS_FRIEND_OF)) {
    Node friend = r1.getOtherNode(userJohn);
    friends.add(friend);
}
Set<Node> moviesFriendsLike = new HashSet<Node>();
for(Node friend : friends){
    for(Relationship r :
        friend.getRelationships(Direction.OUTGOING, HAS_SEEN)){
            moviesFriendsLike.add(r.getEndNode());
    }
}
Set<Node> moviesJohnLike = new HashSet<Node>();
for(Relationship r :
    userJohn.getRelationships(Direction.OUTGOING,
    HAS_SEEN)){
    moviesJohnLike.add(r.getEndNode());
}

moviesFriendsLike.removeAll(moviesJohnLike);

for (Node movie : moviesFriendsLike) {
    logger.info("Found movie: " + movie.getProperty("name"));
}
```

❶ Finds all John's movies

❷ Removes all movies John has seen from the result

You've added another step to the traversal algorithm. First, you discovered which movies John has already seen ❶, then used the standard Java Collections API to remove John's movies from the original collection ❷. If you run the code from listing 4.4, you'll get two results, as expected:

```
Found movie: Alien
Found movie: Heat
```

You finally have code that works as a simple recommendation engine—recommending movies that have been seen by the user's friends, but not by the user.

Let's reflect on this implementation. You used a simple algorithm, implementing the solution in a series of steps: finding all friends, then movies friends have seen, and finally removing the movies the user has seen. While understandable and easy to read, this approach has one major flaw: it uses a lot of memory. After each step, you store the intermediate results in the local variable using Java heap space. This isn't a problem when dealing with few users and movies, but if your data set grows to hundreds of thousands, you'd most likely get the dreaded `OutOfMemoryError` exception while running the application. That's not a concern with this example, because you only have three users and three movies in total. But now is a good time to look at how Neo4j deals with large traversal results.

4.1.4 Memory usage considerations

You've seen that `Node.getRelationships(...)` methods return an `Iterable-<Relationship>` object. An `Iterable` interface allows the implementing class to be used in Java's `for` loop, which you did a few times in the previous examples. There are a lot of examples of classes implementing the `Iterable` interface throughout Java code—for example, all `java.util.Collection` classes, such as `java.util.Set` and `java.util.List` implementations, as well as `java.util.Vector` and `java.util.Stack`. But `Node.getRelationships(...)` methods don't return any of these well-known classes. They return Neo4j's `Iterable` implementation, `org.neo4j.kernel.impl.util` `.ArrayIntIterator`, which implements both Java `Iterable` and `Iterator` interfaces and is a thin wrapper around the `java.util.Iterator` class. No elements contained in the `Iterable` result are actually accessed before you iterate through the result. This implementation is lazily loaded on first access, and once used, it can't be used again—it becomes spent (this is the expected behavior for Java iterators).

This is very important when working with the Neo4j Core Java API. The `Iterable` allows Neo4j to return very large result sets, and it's the developer's responsibility to make sure elements are accessed in the correct manner. As we mentioned, if you load a large result from a Neo4j `Iterable` into a Java `List` or `Set` in your code, you have to be aware that your code will require a large amount of Java heap memory, and that you're in danger of generating `OutOfMemoryError` exceptions at runtime. This is why it's a good practice to use `Iterable` as much as possible in your code, without converting the code to memory-hungry structures whenever possible.

The following listing shows a solution to the same problem as before—finding movies that John's friends have seen but John hasn't—but this time using only the Java `for` loop constructs over the Neo4j `Iterable` implementation, without unnecessary memory consumption in local variables.

> **Listing 4.5   Using iterables to lower Java heap memory consumption**

```
Node userJohn = graphDb.getNodeById(JOHN_JOHNSON_NODE_ID);

Set<Node> moviesFriendsLike = new HashSet<Node>();
for (Relationship r1 :
    userJohn.getRelationships(IS_FRIEND_OF)) {
```

```
Node friend = r1.getOtherNode(userJohn);
   for (Relationship r2 :
→ friend.getRelationships(Direction.OUTGOING, HAS_SEEN)) {
      Node movie = r2.getEndNode();
      boolean johnLikesIt = false;
      for (Relationship r3 :
→ movie.getRelationships(Direction.INCOMING, HAS_SEEN)) {
         if (r3.getStartNode().equals(userJohn)) {
            johnLikesIt = true;
         }
   }
      if (!johnLikesIt) {
         moviesFriendsLike.add(movie);
      }
   }
}
for (Node movie : moviesFriendsLike) {
   logger.info("Found movie: " + movie.getProperty("name"));
}
```

NOTE While this solution looks better, there's a potential performance bottleneck for movies that have been seen by millions of users (because you check whether John has already seen the movie in each loop iteration). This won't have an impact on our limited data set, but it points out that for large data sets, it sometimes may be better to write simpler code, even if that means writing more of it. In this example, you could find all movies John has seen once up front, and then use that set to filter out movies in the for loop.

You've now managed to refactor your solution to use less memory and work better with potentially large data sets. And the results are as expected, so the solution is still correct. But the code in listing 4.5 is still not the prettiest we've ever seen. The Neo4j Core Java API allows you to access the low-level Neo4j structures to implement the required traversal, but at the price of writing more code and worrying about other aspects such as memory consumption. Luckily, Neo4j ships with a higher-abstraction API that can be used to describe the traversal requirements concisely and naturally. In the next section you'll refactor the traversal solution further to use the Neo4j Traversal API.

4.2 *Traversing using the Neo4j Traversal API*

You've implemented a recommendation engine using the Neo4j Core Java API, which allows you to use the low-level Neo4j data structures to achieve your goal. In this section you'll improve on this solution by using the expressive, and more fluent, Neo4j Traversal API.

4.2.1 *Using Neo4j's built-in traversal constructs*

The Neo4j Traversal API is a callback-based framework with a fluent builder API that allows you to expressively build the traversal rules in a single line of code. The main part of the Traversal API is the org.neo4j.graphdb.traversal.TraversalDescription interface, which defines builder methods for describing traverser behavior. You can think of a traverser as a robot that jumps from node to node via relationships, with a well-defined set of rules about the order of traversal, the relationship to follow, the nodes and relationships to include in the result, and so on. `TraversalDescription` is an immutable object that's used to define the traversal rules. Adding any new traversal rule (by invoking one of the builder methods on the `TraversalDescription` interface) always returns a new instance of `TraversalDescription`.

To illustrate how the Neo4j Traversal API works, let's refactor the traversal from the previous section to use the Neo4j Traversal API. In the following listing, the traversal that returns movies that have been seen by John's friends is implemented, without removing movies seen by John himself.

Listing 4.6   Using the Neo4j Traversal API to find movies seen by friends

Instantiates Traversal-Description **1**

Adds HAS_SEEN relationships to list of relationships to follow **3**

Starts traversal from node representing user John

```
Node userJohn = graphDb.getNodeById(JOHN_JOHNSON_NODE_ID);

TraversalDescription traversalMoviesFriendsLike =
          Traversal.description()
              .relationships(IS_FRIEND_OF)
              .relationships(HAS_SEEN, Direction.OUTGOING)
                  .uniqueness(Uniqueness.NODE_GLOBAL)
                  .evaluator(Evaluators.atDepth(2));
Traverser traverser = traversalMoviesFriendsLike.traverse(userJohn);
Iterable<Node> moviesFriendsLike = traverser.nodes();

for (Node movie : moviesFriendsLike) {
    logger.info("Found movie: " + movie.getProperty("name"));
}
```

2 Adds **IS_FRIEND_OF** relationships to list of relationships to follow

4 Sets uniqueness rule so each node in result is unique

Sets evaluator that matches only nodes at depth 2 **5**

Gets all nodes visited as a result

Neo4j provides a default implementation of the `TraversalDescription` interface, which you can instantiate using the static factory method `Traversal.description()` **1**. This will typically be your starting point when building a `TraversalDescription`, as you'll rarely need to provide your own implementation. Next, you define the relationships you want to include in the traversal **2**, **3**. `TraversalDescription` maintains the list of relationships added using the `TraversalDescription.relationships(...)` method, and only relationships that this list contains will be followed by the traverser. You can add the relationship type without specifying a direction, in which case both directions will be allowed **2**, or you can specify the allowed direction relative to the starting node **3**.

In the next line you specify how the traverser should behave with respect to the uniqueness of the nodes and relationships it encounters during the traversal. You want each node to be visited exactly once, so you set uniqueness to `Uniqueness.NODE_GLOBAL` **4**. Other allowed values are, for example, `Uniqueness.NODE_PATH`, which allows multiple traversals through the same node while the path from the starting node to the current node is unique; or `Uniqueness.RELATIONSHIP_GLOBAL`, which allows traversal through each relationship only once. We'll explain the differences between uniqueness values in more detail in chapter 8.

Finally, you add an evaluator to `TraversalDescription` ❺. The evaluator is responsible for two decisions as part of the Neo4j Traversal API:

- It determines whether or not the current node being visited should be added to the traversal result.
- It determines if the traversal should continue further down the current path of the graph, or if the path it currently evaluates should be abandoned, moving to the next path if possible.

The evaluators in Neo4j are defined using the `org.neo4j.graphdb.traversal` `.Evaluator` interface. Neo4j provides a number of convenient out-of-the-box implementations that you can use. The provided implementations are accessible via static factory methods in the `org.neo4j.graphdb.traversal.Evaluators` class. In listing 4.6, you use the `Evaluators.atDepth(int depth)` evaluator, which simply accepts all nodes at the specified depth, counting from the starting node. In addition, this evaluator stops any traversal at a depth higher than specified.

The other useful evaluator implementations provided by Neo4j are covered in chapter 8. Evaluators are one of the key concepts of the Neo4j Traversal API, and it's likely that you'll need to implement your own custom evaluators often. We'll look at a custom implementation of the `Evaluator` interface in the next section.

4.2.2 *Implementing a custom evaluator*

You now need to improve the previous section's code to exclude movies that John has seen from the result. To do that, you need to add a new rule to the traversal description. We mentioned earlier that Neo4j's `Evaluator` implementation defines which nodes to keep in the result and which to discard. In addition, it defines when the traverser should stop the traversal altogether. Based on that, you can implement an additional custom evaluator that will exclude the movies already seen by the user.

The `Evaluator` interface defines a single method that you need to implement, `public Evaluation evaluate(Path path)`. This method accepts a single argument of type `org.neo4j.graphdb.Path` that represents all nodes and relationships that were traversed until the current node. This interface defines a number of convenient methods for collecting information about the current state of traversal, such as all nodes traversed, all relationships traversed, the path starting node, the path ending node, and so on. Table 4.1 lists the methods that are available from the `Path` interface.

Table 4.1 The methods defined on the org.neo4j.graphdb.Path interface

Method signature	Description
`Node startNode();`	Starting node of the path, not to be confused with the starting node of the relationship
`Node endNode();`	Ending node of the path, which is the current node of the traversal, not to be confused with the ending node of the relationship

Table 4.1   The methods defined on the org.neo4j.graphdb.Path interface

Method signature	Description
`Relationship lastRelationship();`	Last relationship traversed
`Iterable<Relationship> relationships();`	All relationships traversed until the current node, in traversal order
`Iterable<Node> nodes();`	All nodes in the path, in traversal order
`int length();`	Returns the length of the path, which is actually the number of relationships traversed (or the number of nodes minus one)

NOTE   It's important not to confuse the path's starting and ending nodes with the starting and ending nodes of a relationship. Relationship starting and ending nodes depend on the direction of the relationship. Path starting and ending nodes depend on the traversal order. As Neo4j allows you to traverse relationships in any direction, this can sometimes lead to confusion if you're new to Neo4j.

The `evaluate(..)` method has the return type `org.neo4j.graphdb.traversal.Evaluation`, which is a Java enumeration with four possible values. Based on the returned `Evaluation`, the traverser decides whether to stop (or *prune* in Neo4j terminology) or continue with the traversal. In addition, the returned `Evaluation` is used to determine whether to keep the current node in the result (*include*) or to discard it (*exclude*). A combination of these two variables defines the four values of the `Evaluation` enumeration. Table 4.2 explains the different `Evaluation` values.

Table 4.2   The possible values of the Evaluation enumeration

Method signature	Description
`INCLUDE_AND_CONTINUE`	Include the current node in the result and continue traversing
`INCLUDE_AND_PRUNE`	Include the current node in the result but stop going further down this path
`EXCLUDE_AND_CONTINUE`	Discard the current node and continue traversing
`EXCLUDE_AND_PRUNE`	Discard the current node and stop traversing

Now that you understand the `Path` interface and the `Evaluation` enumeration, it's time to implement a custom evaluator. The following listing shows the code implementation.

Listing 4.7   Custom evaluator to exclude movies that the user has seen

Starting user node for the evaluator is provided in constructor.

```
public class CustomNodeFilteringEvaluator implements Evaluator {
    private final Node userNode;

    public CustomNodeFilteringEvaluator (Node userNode) {
        this.userNode = userNode;
    }
```

Class implements org.neo4j.graphdb.traversal.Evaluator interface.

If current node isn't a movie, discard it and continue.

```
public Evaluation evaluate(Path path) {
    Node currentNode = path.endNode();
    if (!currentNode.hasProperty("type") ||
        !currentNode.getProperty("type").equals("Movie")) {
        return Evaluation.EXCLUDE_AND_CONTINUE;
    }
    for (Relationship r :
        currentNode.getRelationships(Direction.INCOMING, HAS_SEEN)) {
        if (r.getStartNode().equals(userNode)) {
            return Evaluation.EXCLUDE_AND_CONTINUE;
        }
    }
    return Evaluation.INCLUDE_AND_CONTINUE;
}
}
```

Gets reference to current node in traversal.

Iterates through all incoming HAS_SEEN relationships of current movie node.

If starting node of relationship is same as user node, discard current node (as user has already seen it) and continue…

…otherwise, include current node in result and continue.

You can now include the implemented custom evaluator in the traversal definition. The next listing shows the improved traversal definition.

Listing 4.8   Improved traversal definition with a custom evaluator

```
Node userJohn = graphDb.getNodeById(JOHN_JOHNSON_NODE_ID);

TraversalDescription traversalMoviesFriendsLike =
        Traversal.description()
                .relationships(IS_FRIEND_OF)
                .relationships(HAS_SEEN, Direction.OUTGOING)
                .uniqueness(Uniqueness.NODE_GLOBAL)
                .evaluator(Evaluators.atDepth(2));
                .evaluator(new CustomNodeFilteringEvaluator (userJohn));
Traverser traverser = traversalMoviesFriendsLike.traverse(userJohn);
Iterable<Node> moviesFriendsLike = traverser.nodes();

for (Node movie : moviesFriendsLike) {
    logger.info("Found movie: " + movie.getProperty("name"));
}
```

❶ Existing evaluator is still used

Custom evaluator is added to Traversal-Description ❷

You'll remember that there's one evaluator already, which includes only nodes at depth level 2 ❶. The good thing is that you don't need to remove it, but simply add the new one ❷. In the Neo4j Traversal API, multiple evaluators can be composed together, so you can add many evaluators to the single TraversalDescription. If multiple evaluators are included during the traversal, then Boolean algebra applies: for the current node to be included in the result, all evaluators must return an Evaluation with an INCLUDE element (INCLUDE_AND_CONTINUE or INCLUDE_AND_PRUNE). Similarly, to continue the traversal down the same path, all evaluators must return a CONTINUE evaluator (INCLUDE_AND_CONTINUE or EXCLUDE_AND_CONTINUE).

If you run the improved application on the same data set, you'll see the expected output as before:

```
Found movie: Alien
Found movie: Heat
```

This time, however, you used the more fluent Neo4j Traversal API and managed to implement a solution in a more expressive manner. The Neo4j Traversal API has a declarative nature: you simply declare how you want the traverser to behave, and start it doing its job. If you're using the Java API, we recommend you use the Neo4j Traverser Framework API for graph traversals whenever possible, as it allows you to produce readable, maintainable, and performant code when dealing with complex graph traversals.

We'll come back to this topic in chapter 8, where we'll be covering more advanced traversal concepts.

4.3   *Summary*

In this chapter we introduced traversals as a powerful approach to querying interconnected data that's specific to graph databases.

In the first part of the chapter you learned how to use the Neo4j Core Java API to traverse the sample graph and find all movies a user's friends saw. The Neo4j Core Java API is powerful and flexible for traversing a graph, but for complex traversals the Neo4j Core Java API implementation could quickly become complex.

That's where the Neo4j Traversal API comes in, which we discussed in the second part of the chapter. Using the fluent Neo4j Traversal API, you can describe the traversal query in a simple and declarative manner, without sacrificing any of the power of graph traversal, and with minimal performance impact.

We'll prefer the Neo4j Traversal API for most of the examples throughout the book for its fluency and readability, but in some complex cases we'll also drop down to the Neo4j Core Java API—both approaches have their strengths and should be used to solve graph problems accordingly.

But before you start traversing a graph, you need to select one or more nodes as starting points. In this chapter you used a known node ID to find the starting node for traversal, but in practice it's unlikely you'll know specific node IDs—you're more likely to select a particular node based on one of its properties. To use that kind of "flat" node lookup, you need to use indexes, and that's exactly what we're going to explore in the next chapter. Read on!

Indexing the data

5

In the previous chapter you saw how easy it is to move between nodes in the Neo4j graph by traversing relationships. Moving between nodes allows you to quickly and easily find connected nodes, such as a person's friends and the movies they like. Neo4j is optimized to make graph traversal fast, but reducing the number of nodes that needs to be traversed by knowing where to start is important, and it becomes increasingly so as the size of the data set increases.

To determine where to start in the graph, Neo4j uses *indexing*. An index in a relational database provides the ability to quickly and easily find rows in a table by the values of particular columns. Similarly, Neo4j indexing makes it easy to find nodes or relationships with particular property values. Unlike a relational database, Neo4j requires your application code to create and maintain index entries.

Because the application code takes on the responsibility for indexing, you need to give careful thought to your indexing strategy. Poor decisions about indexing can lead to poor performance or excessive disk use. In this chapter we'll show you how to create, maintain, and use indexes with Neo4j. We'll then explore why you should index and discuss the inevitable trade-offs you'll need to make when creating an indexing strategy.

Before we start talking about the trade-offs, let's look at how to create index entries.

5.1 Creating the index entry

The most commonly used option when working with an index is explicitly creating the index, then adding entries as nodes are created. Each index entry typically identifies a node or relationship property value. The index entry contains references to one or more nodes having a particular value for the property you're indexing on.

Figure 5.1 shows that a node index such as this can be thought of as a value entry that relates to one or more pointers to nodes. In this case, we're expecting email addresses to be unique, so we expect one primary email address for each user.

In Neo4j, the `IndexManager` provides access to the index using a simple string as the index key. In our social networking application, a common starting point will be a user. To uniquely identify users, you'll have them use their email addresses to log in. The code in listing 5.1 shows the creation of a new user and the creation of an index entry. This means you can quickly find the node representing the user via the email address. All available index operations are defined on the `Index<Node>` interface, an instance of which is accessed from Neo4j's index manager component:

```
IndexManager indexManager = graphDB.index();
Index<Node> userIndex = indexManager.forNodes("users");
```

Note that you simply ask the Neo4j index manager component for the index with the required name. From the perspective of the code, it's irrelevant whether the index exists; if it doesn't exist, the index will be created when you ask for it.

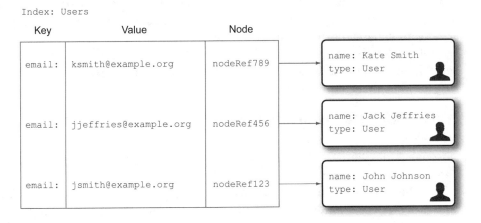

Figure 5.1 Index pointing to user nodes as values, using the `email` property as a key

---

Listing 5.1   Creating an index entry for a node using Neo4j API

Adds an entry to the usersindex for the email property with a value of the users email **5**

```
String johnSmithName = "John Smith";
String johnSmithEmail = "jsmith@example.org";
Node personOne = graphDB.createNode();
personOne.setProperty("name", johnSmithName);
personOne.setProperty("email", johnSmithEmail);

IndexManager indexManager = graphDB.index();
Index<Node> userIndex = indexManager.forNodes("users");
userIndex.add(personOne, "email", johnSmithEmail);
```

1 Creates a new blank node to represent the person

2 Sets the properties on the new node

3 Obtains a reference to the IndexManager

4 Looks up the index named users or creates one if not present

---

First up, you create nodes using the Neo4j Core API and add properties (**1**, **2**). Next, you create an index and give it the name users (**3**, **4**)—this name will become the unique identifier for this newly created index.

Finally, you add the node to the index **5**. To add a node to the index, you need to provide three parameters:

- The node you want to index (personOne)
- The index key ("email")
- The indexed value (jsmith@example.org)

The index key and value are then stored by Lucene (Neo4j's default indexing implementation), along with the reference to the person node, as illustrated in figure 5.1.

If you'd like to configure the Lucene index, Neo4j allows to you pass in various configuration options when the index is created. This can be done using the following method:

```
IndexManager.forNodes( String indexName, Map<String, String>
    customConfiguration );
```

Map customConfiguration can contain any valid Lucene setting. For a list of Lucene configuration settings, see the Neo4j/Lucene documentation at http://docs.neo4j.org/chunked/stable/indexing-create-advanced.html.

Of course, the real value of indexing a node is being able to find the right node quickly and easily. That's what we're going to look at in the next section, where you'll use the user email index to find user nodes.

5.2   *Finding the user by their email*

Having a network of users is great, but now it's time to start letting users interact through a full-blown web application that allows them to connect to friends as well as store movie information.

In this web application, one of the first things you want to do is display a list of the users' friends. Finding the friends of a user will involve traversing the friend relationships. But first you need to look up the node that represents the user that has logged in.

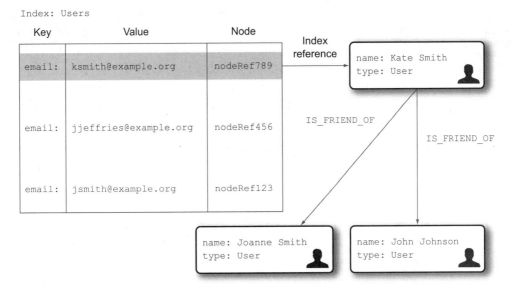

Index: Users

Figure 5.2   Looking up a user node from the index by using the `email` property

Since your users use their email addresses as login IDs and you index user nodes by email, it's easy to look up a user that has logged in. You can then traverse outbound friend relationships to find their friends, as figure 5.2 illustrates.

To find a user by email, you need to obtain a reference to the node index identified by the index's unique name; in this example you have an index called `users`. You can then get the index hits for a particular key and value. The next listing illustrates looking up the user node by `email` value.

Listing 5.2   Finding a single user by index lookup using the `email` property

```
String userEmail = "jsmith@example.org";

IndexManager indexManager = graphDB.index();
Index<Node> userIndex = indexManager.forNodes("users");
IndexHits<Node> indexHits = userIndex.get("email", userEmail);
Node loggedOnUserNode = indexHits.getSingle();

if (loggedOnUserNode == null) {
    throw new NoSuchUserException("No user with email "
    + userEmail + " found");
}
```

Gets the single result; throws a NoSuch-Element-Exception if more than one but not if none

Gets the index manager

Finds the user email index

Looks up known index key (email) for the user's email address and get hits

Checks that you found a matching node

Once you've found the logged-in user's node, it's easy to find their friends using a quick and simple traversal with the Core Java API:

```
Iterable<Relationship> outboundFriendRelationships =
        loggedOnUserNode.getRelationships(
    DynamicRelationshipType.withName("is_friend_of"),
    Direction.OUTGOING);
```

Gets outgoing relationships of type friend for the logged-on user returned by the index lookup

```
                      for(Relationship frRel: outboundFriendRelationships){
Iterates                  friends.add(frRel.getOtherNode(loggedOnUserNode));
through the           }
relationships
```

Iterates through the relationships (left annotation)

Stores the node at the other end of the relationship (right annotation)

In this section, we've demonstrated the typical pattern for working with indexes in Neo4j—find a node by index lookup, then perform the traversal as usual. The code in listing 5.2 assumes that you'll find at most one match for the user's email address. Let's now see how you can deal with multiple hits.

5.3 *Dealing with more than one match*

In the previous example, you indexed the `email` property for each user, and, assuming that email addresses are unique, you expected a single result from the index lookup operation.

That won't always be the case. Let's add another indexed property to the user nodes—age. Naturally, multiple user nodes can have the same value for the `age` property. The key in such an index can reference multiple user nodes as values, as figure 5.3 illustrates.

Earlier, we assumed that you'd always find at most one match for the provided user email address. If that's not going to be the case, you'll need to iterate over the index hits returned, as shown in the following listing, which retrieves all users who are 34.

Listing 5.3 Iterating through multiple results of an index lookup operation

```
IndexManager indexManager = graphDB.index();
Index<Node> userIndex = indexManager.forNodes("users");
IndexHits<Node> indexHits = userIndex.get("age", 34);
```
Calls get as you did for a single result

```
for (Node user : hits) {
    System.out.println(user.getProperty("name"));
}
```
Loops over one or more hits, printing the name

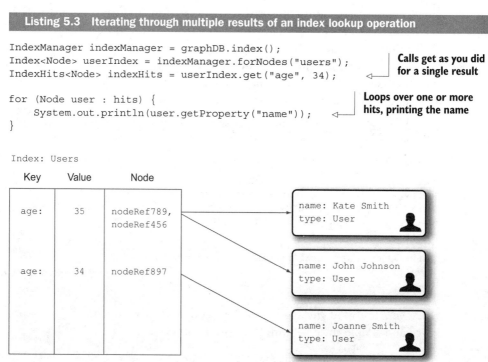

Figure 5.3 User nodes indexed by the `age` property, with each key potentially referencing multiple nodes

> **NOTE** IndexHits is one-time iterable. Once spent, you can't use it again. This is a constraint of Lucene. For more information, consult the Lucene documentation at http://lucene.apache.org.

There may be some cases where you want to find all the 34-year-old users; it's more likely that you'll want to find users in a range. Lucene supports range queries, and many other types of queries out of the box. Lucene details are beyond the scope of this book, but you can find all the details in the Lucene documentation (specifically at http://mng.bz/Lq6r).

> **NOTE** IndexHits should be closed after use. If you iterate through all the hits (as in the previous example), IndexHits will close automatically. If you don't fully iterate through *all* IndexHits values, you'll have to make sure you close it manually by calling IndexHits.close(). This is a constraint of Lucene; for more information, consult the Lucene documentation at http://lucene.apache.org.

Having seen how to create and query index entries, your next concern is how to deal with a change to the graph that requires a change to the index.

5.4 *Dealing with changes to indexed data*

The creation of index entries is rarely a case of create and forget. Even in this chapter's simple example, you'd need to deal with users changing their email addresses or wanting to delete their accounts.

Because the indexing strategies employed are entirely at the discretion of the application developer, Neo4j can't automatically update manually created indexes to reflect changes made to the graph itself. We'll see examples later on of how you can achieve this kind of flexibility via other mechanisms, but for now we'll concentrate on how you can deal with changes involving manually created indexes.

What happens when a user wants to update their email address? We already mentioned that all available index operations are defined on the Index<Node> interface:

```
Index<Node> userIndex = indexManager.forNodes("users");
```

The first thing you'll probably notice when looking at the Index<Node> interface is that there are no update methods, and no way of modifying an existing index entry once you have looked it up. The solution is quite simple: "remove then add" equals "update" when dealing with Neo4j indexes. The following listing shows how this can be done using the Neo4j Core Java API.

> **Listing 5.4 Updating the index using sequential remove and add operations**

```
String userEmail = "jsmith@example.org";
String updatedUserMail = "jsmith@shinynew.example.org"

IndexManager indexManager = graphDB.index();
Index<Node> userIndex = indexManager.forNodes("users");
IndexHits<Node> indexHits = userIndex.get("email", userEmail);   ⟵  Uses the index to get the existing person node
Node loggedOnUserNode = indexHits.getSingle();
```

```
if (loggedOnUserNode == null) {
    throw new NoSuchUserException("No user with email "
    + userEmail + " found");
}
userIndex.remove(loggedOnUserNode,"email", userEmail);
loggedOnUserNode.setProperty("email", updatedUserMail);
userIndex.add(loggedOnUserNode,"email", updatedUserMail);
```

Adds the new property value to the index

Removes the email entry for the given node

Updates the node with the new email property value

Indexing relationships

You've seen how to create index entries that allow you to quickly look up nodes in the graph, but it's also possible to index the relationships between nodes. This is much like indexing nodes, but you use relationship properties as index keys.

In our experience, it's less common for relationship indexes to be good solutions. We're not saying that relationship indexing is a poor practice, but if you find yourself adding lots of relationship indexes, it's worth asking why.

Usually a graph will represent entities of some form as nodes, such as people, movies, and cities. The relationships then represent the relationships between those entities. The questions you then usually ask are about who these entities are connected to. Who likes the movie, who is friends with a specific person, or what transport routes leave from a city.

It's not impossible to think of questions that might be answered by a relationship index, however. If you chose to represent the star ratings in the movie database with different relationships for different ratings, indexing the relationship would allow you to quickly find all the five-star reviews.

You can read more about relationship indexing in the Neo4j Manual: http://docs.neo4j.org/chunked/stable/indexing-relationships.html.

Later in this chapter we'll take a more detailed look at the trade-offs associated with indexing, but first we'll complete our tour of the indexing options by taking a look at auto-indexing.

5.5 Automatic indexing

So far in this chapter, we've focused on manually creating and maintaining index entries. If you're coming from an RDBMS world, you may wonder why the database can't do this work for you; after all, in the RDBMS world, you'd expect to declare which columns on a table you wanted indexed and to have the RDBMS then maintain the contents of that index as rows were inserted, updated, and deleted.

There are two ways that you can have Neo4j maintain indexes automatically—schema indexing and auto-indexing. Let's take a look at schema indexing first.

5.5.1 Schema indexing

In version 2.0, Neo4j introduced the concept of *schema indexing*. Conceptually, this is similar to the traditional index-handling approaches used by relational databases.

Schema indexing works closely with the concept of node labels, which we introduced in chapter 3. Each schema index is specific to a label and a set of properties. For example, you can define an index for users on their name property, or an index for movies on the title and production year properties. All you have to do is to define the index, and thereafter, Neo4j will take responsibility for maintaining it. This means that when you create a node with a label and a property that matches one or more indexes, all indexes will be updated for that value. When you delete a node, all entries for that node will be removed from all relevant indexes automatically. The same applies when you update node properties.

Let's take a look at a real example of this in the following listing.

Listing 5.5   Using schema indexes with Java API

```
Label movieLabel = DynamicLabel.label("MOVIE");        ◁┐  Creates labels
Label userLabel = DynamicLabel.label("USER");           │❶ you're going to use

Node movie, user;
                                                            ❷ Creates index for
// Create schema                                               movies on name
try (Transaction tx = graphDb.beginTx()) {                     property
graphDb.schema().indexFor(movieLabel).on("name").create();  ◁
    graphDb.schema().indexFor(userLabel).on("name").create(); ◁┐ Defines index for
    tx.success();                                              │ users on name
}                                                            ❸ property

// Add Labels and properties                             ❹ Defines node for movie
try (Transaction tx = graphDb.beginTx()) {                  "Michael Collins"
    movie = graphDb.createNode(movieLabel);             ◁
    movie.setProperty("name", "Michael Collins");

    user = graphDb.createNode(userLabel);               ◁┐ Creates node for
    user.setProperty("name", "Michael Collins");         │ user whose name is
    tx.success();                                        ❺ "Michael Collins"
}

// Verify results                                        ❻ Indexes lookup
try (Transaction tx = graphDb.beginTx()) {                  for movie by
    ResourceIterable<Node> result =                         name
        graphDb.findNodesByLabelAndProperty(           ◁
            movieLabel, "name", "Michael Collins");        ❼ Verifies that
    assertEquals(1, IteratorUtil.count(result));              it loaded the
    assertEquals(movie.getId(), result.iterator().next().getId()); ◁  right node
    tx.success();
}
```

This example uses two labels: one for movies, called MOVIE, and one for users, called USER. These are defined upfront ❶.

Now you need to define the schema indexes you're going to need. This is very similar to defining indexes in relational databases. The Java API for index creation is available under the GraphDatabaseService.schema() method. First, you create an index for the MOVIE label on the name property ❷, then you do the same for the USER label ❸. Note that this code is wrapped in its own transaction, separate from the remainder of the example. That's because this code would typically only be done once upfront in the application. More importantly, you'll get an exception if you try to do this all in one transaction—something along the lines of "org.neo4j.graphdb.Constraint-ViolationException: Cannot perform data updates in a transaction that has performed schema updates."

Having defined the indexes, you can now continue to create some nodes. First you create a node for the movie "Michael Collins" with the MOVIE label ❹. Because the movie's label and property name match the index you've already defined, this node will automatically be indexed and be searchable by its name. Next, just for fun, you create a user whose name is "Michael Collins", the same as the movie name ❺, then commit the transaction.

Provided all has gone according to plan, you can realistically now expect that your nodes have been indexed. You can verify that by searching for the "Michael Collins" movie. To search the schema index, you use the GraphDatabaseService.findNodes-ByLabelAndProperty(...) method ❻. As its name suggests, this method will perform the search across all nodes for the label and property values supplied. In this case, you want to search across the MOVIE label with a name property matching the value "Michael Collins". The returned result is a Java Iterable containing the matching nodes. You'd expect exactly one result from this search. You have two nodes with the same name, "Michael Collins", but only one has the MOVIE label, and this is the one you expect to get. The assertion proves that the result is correct ❼.

Every node can have one or more labels attached, each with an index defined. If the node has multiple labels, Neo4j will ensure that all relevant indexes are updated as required. Here is an illustration.

Listing 5.6 Updating multiple schema indexes

```
Label userLabel = DynamicLabel.label("USER");
Label adminLabel = DynamicLabel.label("ADMIN");

try (Transaction tx = graphDb.beginTx()) {
    graphDb.schema().indexFor(userLabel).on("name").create();
    graphDb.schema().indexFor(adminLabel).on("name").create();
    tx.success();
}

try (Transaction tx = graphDb.beginTx()) {
    Node user = graphDb.createNode(userLabel, adminLabel);
    user.setProperty("name", "Peter Smith");
    tx.success();
}

try (Transaction tx = graphDb.beginTx()) {
    ResourceIterable<Node> adminSearch =
            graphDb.findNodesByLabelAndProperty(
            adminLabel, "name", "Peter Smith");
    assertEquals(1, IteratorUtil.count(adminSearch));
```

❶ Creates index for both USER and ADMIN labels

❷ Creates user node with two labels (ADMIN and USER)

❸ Verifies that the index for ADMIN is updated correctly

```
ResourceIterable<Node> userSearch =
    graphDb.findNodesByLabelAndProperty(
        userLabel, "name", "Peter Smith");
assertEquals(1, IteratorUtil.count(userSearch));
tx.success();
}
```

④ Verifies that the index for USER is updated correctly

In this example, you define indexes for two labels, one for regular users, USER, and one for admins, ADMIN ①. Then you create a single node that represents both a regular user and an admin, using two labels ②. You'd expect that this user would be searchable across normal users as well as admins, and the next two steps confirm that this is the case (③, ④).

So far you've seen how the index gets populated on node creation. We've also mentioned that schema indexes get updated when a node is deleted. The following code snippet shows this:

```
try (Transaction tx = graphDb.beginTx()) {
    user.delete();
    tx.success();
}
```

Deletes node (in transaction)

```
try (Transaction tx = graphDb.beginTx()) {
    adminSearch = graphDb.findNodesByLabelAndProperty(
                    adminLabel, "name", "Peter Smith");
    assertEquals(0, IteratorUtil.count(adminSearch));

    userSearch = graphDb.findNodesByLabelAndProperty(
                    userLabel, "name", "Peter Smith");
    assertEquals(0, IteratorUtil.count(userSearch));
    tx.success();
}
```

Verifies that admin index is now empty

Verifies that user index is now empty

The schema indexing approach groups the indexed data by node label. This means that each index contains nodes with one label. If you need to automatically index all nodes on a given property (regardless of the node labels), you can instead use the auto-indexing feature.

5.5.2 Auto-indexing

To use auto-indexing, you need to tell Neo4j that you want to turn auto-indexing on for nodes, relationships, or both. But simply switching on auto-indexing doesn't cause anything to happen. In larger data sets, indexing everything may not be practical; you're potentially increasing storage requirements by a factor of two or more if every value is stored both in Neo4j storage and the index. There will also be performance overhead for every mutating operation because of the extra work of maintaining the index. As a result, Neo4j takes a more selective approach to indexing. Even with auto-indexing turned on, Neo4j will only maintain indexes of node or relationship properties it's told to index.

How you configure auto-indexing depends on whether you're running Neo4j in embedded mode or server mode (chapter 10 covers these two modes).

CONFIGURING AUTO-INDEXING IN STANDALONE MODE

To turn on auto-indexing for a standalone server, you'll need to modify its configuration file with additional properties. The configuration file can be found at $NEO4J_SERVER/ conf/neo4j.properties, and you'll need to add the following two lines:

```
node_auto_indexing=true
relationship_auto_indexing=true
```

Specifying what you want to index requires the addition of the following two neo4j.properties:

```
node_keys_indexable=name, dateOfBirth
relationship_keys_indexable=type,name
```

CONFIGURING AUTO-INDEXING IN EMBEDDED MODE

To turn on auto-indexing for Neo4j in embedded mode, you'll need to pass in additional values when you create the graph database instance. The following values need to be included as part of the java.util.Map argument containing configuration:

```
Map<String, String> config = new HashMap<String, String>();
config.put( Config.NODE_AUTO_INDEXING, "true" );
config.put( Config.RELATIONSHIP_AUTO_INDEXING, "true" );
EmbeddedGraphDatabase graphDb =
            new EmbeddedGraphDatabase("/var/neo4j/data", config );
```

Using the config map programmatically requires the addition of two properties, which contain a list of key names to index:

```
config.put( Config.NODE_KEYS_INDEXABLE, "name, dateOfBirth" );
config.put( Config.RELATIONSHIP_KEYS_INDEXABLE, "type, name" );
```

USING AN AUTOMATICALLY CREATED INDEX

Once you've added the appropriate configuration properties, the graph should be searchable through the auto-index. For example, given the preceding configuration, all relationships in the graph that have properties type or name, and all nodes in the graph that have properties name and dateOfBirth, should be searchable via the auto-index.

You've probably noticed that there's no way to specify an index name in the configuration, so you can't specify that you want to index node names in one index and date of birth in another. This is somewhat different from manual indexing, where an index name is always specified. This is because Neo4j has exactly one index for auto-indexed relationships and one index for auto-indexed nodes.

The following code shows how, having turned on auto-indexing of node properties with a key of name, you can access the index and use it to find nodes with a particular value for the name property:

```
AutoIndexer<Node> nodeAutoIndexer =
        graphDb.index().getNodeAutoIndexer();
    IndexHits<Node> nodesWithMatchingName =
        nodeAutoIndexer.getAutoIndex().get("name", "John");
    Node userNode = nodesWithMatchingName.getSingle();
```

Gets a reference to the node auto-indexer

Returns an iterable for IndexHits

Finds entries where name is "John"

Using the schema and auto-indexing facilities offered by Neo4j means less work for the application developer but also less control over what gets indexed. A naïve strategy of indexing all properties would have significant implications, for performance of graph mutation and also for disk space requirements. The following section will explore these trade-offs in greater detail.

5.6 *The cost/benefit trade-off of indexing*

Having seen the different approaches to indexing offered by Neo4j, we'll turn our attention to the trade-offs you need to consider when determining which indexing strategy is right for your application. You're probably starting to realize that Neo4j is extremely flexible when it comes to both indexing and the ways you can model your data.

For example, you could have modeled the social network data in a completely different fashion, which would have an impact on the indexing strategy. Figure 5.4 shows one alternative representation of the data, with intermediary nodes that represent Kate's movies and friends.

Is this a better way of representing the data for the social networking application? Unfortunately, the answer is that it depends on your application. Determining the best data representation and indexing strategy depends heavily on both the data that you want to store and the way that you want to interact with that data. Later in the book we'll discuss the trade-offs between different graph representations, but for the moment we'll focus on indexing.

The main trade-off when it comes to indexing is that the more indexing you have, the more disk space you'll need, the greater the performance hit you'll take on inserts and updates to the graph, and the more code you'll usually need to manage the creation and updating of indexes. The advantage is enhanced performance

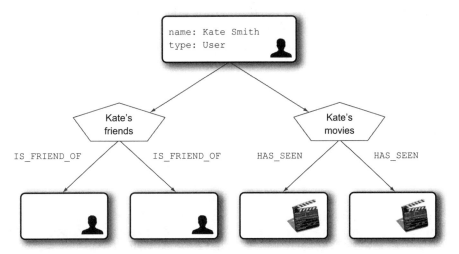

Figure 5.4 Graph of a social network using intermediate nodes to differentiate between relationships to user and film nodes.

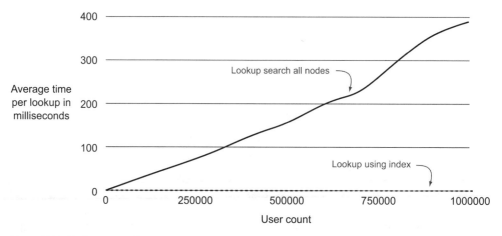

Figure 5.5   Performance of node lookup using index compared to iterating through all nodes

if your indexing strategy can eliminate large portions of the graph from consideration when querying.

5.6.1   *Performance benefit of indexing when querying*

The graph in figure 5.5 shows how marked the difference is between a simple search of all user nodes in the graph and the use of an index. This graph shows the average time to look up a random user node.

The solid line shows that the average time taken to find a node, if you simply search all nodes, is directly proportional to the number of nodes in the graph. This is not too surprising; the more nodes you have, the more you'll stumble blindly around the graph before you happen upon the user node you're looking for.

In marked contrast, the dotted line shows the time taken to find the user node using an email index. While this number varies a little, the variation is small, with an average of 0.1 to 0.3 milliseconds per search. When the test tops out at 1 million users, the search of all nodes is on average one thousand times slower than finding the user with an index.

Notes on the lookup benchmark

Note that it's considered bad practice to store the Neo4j ID externally for lookups because it's possible that this ID may change in some circumstances. The node ID should be treated as an internal implementation detail of Neo4j and shouldn't be stored in order to enable fast access.

The other way you can get at the nodes in the graph is via the `getAllNodes` method, which returns an `Iterable` that allows you to iterate through all the nodes in the graph. This can be a viable strategy for smaller datasets, but there's a performance overhead to loading large parts of the graph each time you need to find a particular node.

(continued)

The test uses `getAllNodes` to access all the user nodes. In a real application, this strategy would be even less performant than the test indicates, because it would encounter a significant number of nodes that were not of type `USER`.

As we keep saying, decisions around indexing are all about trade-offs. In the next section you'll see that the performance gains for lookups can easily be negated by the overhead of the index.

5.6.2 *Performance overhead of indexing when updating and inserting*

Having achieved close to constant times for finding a user by using an index, you might wonder what sort of performance overhead you're incurring for the extra index maintenance work you're doing.

The graph in figure 5.6 shows the average time taken to create the user node as the number of users in the dataset increases. The time doesn't grow much in relation to the number of users; however, the time taken to create a node and index for the email address takes roughly twice the time as creating the node alone.

An extra hundredth of a millisecond probably won't make much difference in this case, even with a million users, because it's likely that you'll create this user node once when the user registers and then update it infrequently. But this won't be the case in all applications. Where data is updated or created more frequently than it's read, thought should be given to the performance trade-off between fast updates and fast finds. It's also likely that you'll need to access your graph data in different ways, so you may have many indexes such as ZIP code, age, and sex, and each of these will further increase the performance overhead for inserts and updates.

In addition to the performance penalty of indexes, each index requires additional storage, and we'll look at that very briefly next.

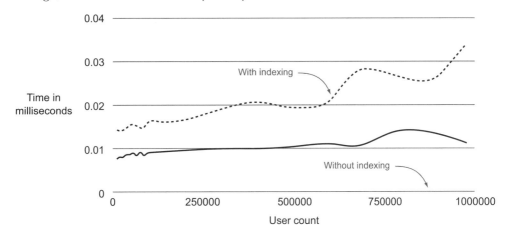

Figure 5.6   Average time for storing user node with and without indexing

5.6.3 *Storing the index*

The process of indexing essentially involves creating small lookup tables (small compared to the data set), which allow fast access to the right place in the graph. This means that in addition to the performance overhead of writing out the extra index data, you'll need more disk space to store all of this data.

5.7 *Summary*

In this chapter, you've seen that Neo4j provides flexible mechanisms that allow Neo4j applications to quickly focus in on the parts of the graph that are of interest. But with that flexibility comes the need to consider trade-offs when deciding what to index and what not to index.

This concludes part 1 of the book, in which we described all the basic concepts and techniques for dealing with graph data in the Neo4j database. In part 2, we're going to take an in-depth look at some key concepts in Neo4j. First we're going to learn about Cypher—Neo4j's human graph query language!

Part 2

Application
Development with Neo4j

In part 2 we'll cover aspects of building applications with Neo4j.

Chapter 6 introduces Cypher, the human graph query language. Cypher provides a language-independent way to both query and manipulate the graph, and this chapter explores how you can use it to interact with your graph domain model. With Neo4j being a fully ACID-compliant database, chapter 7 focuses on transactions, and how you can control and take advantage of this feature to ensure your application can query and store data in a consistent manner. Chapter 8 returns to the traversal API, with an even deeper dive to explore some more advanced options for navigating the graph via this dedicated API.

Chapter 9 introduces Spring Data Neo4j (SDN), a graph object mapping library which, for certain application use cases such as those manipulating a very rich domain model, can prove very useful for speeding up and simplifying development.

Cypher:
Neo4j query language

This chapter covers

- Explaining Cypher
- Executing Cypher queries
- Writing read-only Cypher queries
- Manipulating graph data using Cypher

In previous chapters we used the Neo4j Core Java API to manipulate and query graph data. This obviously required some Java skills to write and understand the implemented code. In addition, as the complexity of the queries increased, the code grew in both size and complexity, making it difficult to understand in some cases. This is where a query language comes in handy, allowing you to query and manipulate graphs using the power of expressive language structures that are also simple to read.

Neo4j's query language is called Cypher. In this chapter we're going to explain the nature of Cypher, demonstrate its basic syntax for graph operations, and cover some of the advanced features that can be useful in day-to-day development and maintenance of Neo4j databases.

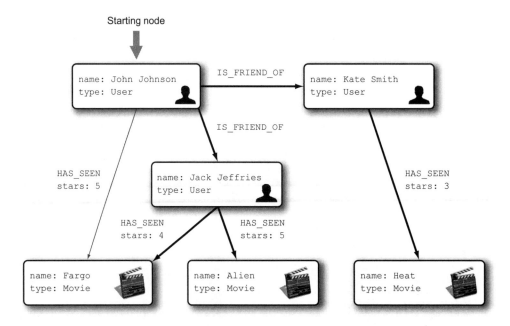

Figure 6.1   **A social network graph to be queried**

6.1   *Introduction to Cypher*

Cypher is a declarative query language for graphs that uses graph pattern-matching as a main mechanism for graph data selection (for both read-only and mutating operations). The declarative pattern-matching nature of Cypher means that you can query the graph by describing what you need to get from it.

To explain how Cypher works, let's take a look at Cypher in action.

6.1.1   *Cypher primer*

Figure 6.1 shows a simple graph representing a social network.

In chapter 4, when we discussed the Neo4j Traversal API, we demonstrated how to find all the movies a user has seen using Java code. As a reminder, the following listing shows the Java code used.

> **Listing 6.1   Traversing the graph using Java API to find all movies the user has seen**

```
try (Transaction tx = graphDb.beginTx()) {
  Node userJohn = graphDb.getNodeById(JOHN_JOHNSON_NODE_ID);
  Iterable<Relationship> allRelationships = userJohn.getRelationships();
  Set<Node> moviesForJohn = new HashSet<Node>();
  for(Relationship r : allRelationships){
      if(r.getType().name().equalsIgnoreCase("HAS_SEEN")){
         Node movieNode = r.getEndNode();
         moviesForJohn.add(movieNode);
      }
  }
```

```
for(Node movie : moviesForJohn){
    logger.info("User has seen movie: " + movie.getProperty("name"));
}
tx.success();
```

The traversal has three phases:

1 Find a starting node by ID.
2 Traverse the graph from the starting node by following the HAS_SEEN relationships.
3 Return the nodes that are at the end of the HAS_SEEN relationships.

Now let's see how you could write the same query using Cypher, following the same three phases of traversal:

```
start user=node(1)
match (user)-[:HAS_SEEN]->(movie)
return movie;
```

1 Finds starting node

Specifies match pattern that consists of starting node, HAS_SEEN relationship, and target movie node

Returns movie nodes

Just as in the Java code, you first need to find the starting node by using the node ID, which can be achieved in Cypher using the start and node keywords **1**. Note the name of the starting node—user—so that you can refer to it later in the same Cypher query.

Next, you set the pattern you need your result to match. The pattern is a description of all subgraphs you want to inspect within your data, and it consists of a number of nodes connected with relationships. Typical graph patterns consist of two nodes connected by a relationship, which is represented in the format ()-[]-(). Nodes are specified using parentheses, (), and relationships are specified using square brackets, []. Nodes and relationships are linked using hyphens. The node in the start clause (user in the preceding example) is used to fix the left side of the pattern. The whole pattern has two known elements (left-side node and the relationship), which you use to find all nodes that match the right side (nodes named movie in our example).

Finally, you're interested in all movies that match, so you use the return keyword to return them (again, referencing the node by the name introduced before). A semicolon is used to mark the end of the Cypher query.

When you run this Cypher query, you'll see exactly the same results as you did with the corresponding Java API solution, but with much simpler query syntax. Cypher is much simpler to read and understand for developers, operational staff, and anyone with enough domain understanding.

> **NOTE** From Neo4j 2.0, the start clause is optional. If the start clause is omitted, Neo4j will try to infer it from the node labels and properties in the match clause of the query. For clarity and compatibility with earlier Neo4j versions, all queries in this chapter will have explicitly defined start clauses. For more details on inferred start clauses, go to http://docs.neo4j.org/chunked/stable/query-start.html.

That said, how do you actually execute the Cypher query? Don't worry—we'll explain that in the next section.

6.1.2   *Executing Cypher queries*

There are a number of ways you can execute Cypher queries. Neo4j ships with a couple of tools that support Cypher executions, and Cypher can also be executed from Java code, much like SQL. Table 6.1 shows the Cypher execution options.

Table 6.1   Tools and techniques for executing Cypher queries

Tool	Description
Neo4j Shell	Command-line tool
Neo4j Web Admin Console	Web-based interface
Java	Programmatically
REST	Over HTTP using REST interface

Let's take a look at each of the first three options in more detail. The fourth option, using REST to execute Cypher queries, will be discussed in chapter 10.

EXECUTING CYPHER USING THE NEO4J SHELL

The Neo4j Shell is a command-line tool that's part of the Neo4j distribution. It can be used to connect to either of the following:

- *A local Neo4j database*—Connect by pointing the shell to the directory where the Neo4j data is stored.
- *A remote Neo4j server over RMI*—Connect by providing the shell with the host name and port to connect to.

The Neo4j Shell start script is located in the $NEO4j_HOME/bin/ directory, where $NEO4J_HOME is the directory where Neo4j binaries are installed.

Table 6.2 illustrates how to connect to a local or remote Neo4j instance on both Linux-based and Windows systems.

Table 6.2   Neo4j Shell startup script syntax for Linux and Windows environments

Database type	Linux command	Windows command
Local Neo4j database	`$NEO4J_HOME/bin/neo4j-shell –path=/var/neo4j/db`	`$NEO4J_HOME/bin/neo4j-shell.bat –path=/var/neo4j/db`
Remote Neo4j database	`$NEO4J_HOME/bin/neo4j-shell –host=localhost –port=1337`	`$NEO4J_HOME/bin/neo4j-shell.bat –host=localhost –port=1337`

Before you start running queries, you need to populate the graph database. For this example, we're going to use the same data set from chapters 3 and 4 (social network of movie lovers). The location of database files on disk we used is /var/neo4j/db because we used a Linux-based system, but you can replace it with the directory of your choice based on your OS (for example, c:\neo4j\db on Windows).

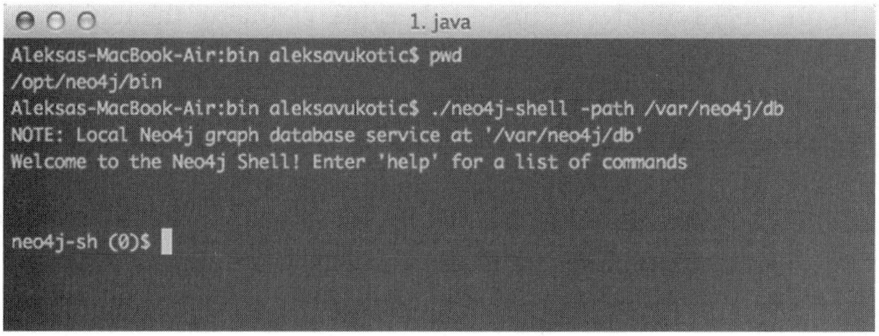

Figure 6.2   The Neo4j Shell ready to accept commands

Connect to the Neo4j database using the Neo4j Shell by running the following command from the $NEO4J_HOME/bin directory:

- `neo4j-shell -path=/var/neo4j/db` (Linux)
- `neo4j-shell.bat -path=/var/neo4j/db` (Windows)

After you press Enter, you should be inside the Neo4j Shell, as illustrated in figure 6.2, ready to run commands.

> **NOTE**   Make sure you have read permissions to the Neo4j data directory when starting the shell.

Cypher is natively supported by Neo4j Shell, so you don't need any special commands; just type the Cypher query in the console and press Enter. The results are returned in tabular format, very similar to the output of SQL queries run against a relational database. Figure 6.3 illustrates the output of a Cypher query that finds all movies that a particular user has seen.

As you can see, the result is just as you'd expect, based on the graph in figure 6.1. User 1 (John Johnson) has indeed seen only one movie: *Fargo*. You're returning `movie` nodes in the query, so the result is represented as such. `Fargo` is a node in the database, with an internal ID of 4 and two properties, `name` and `type`, with expected values, and the Cypher output illustrates that.

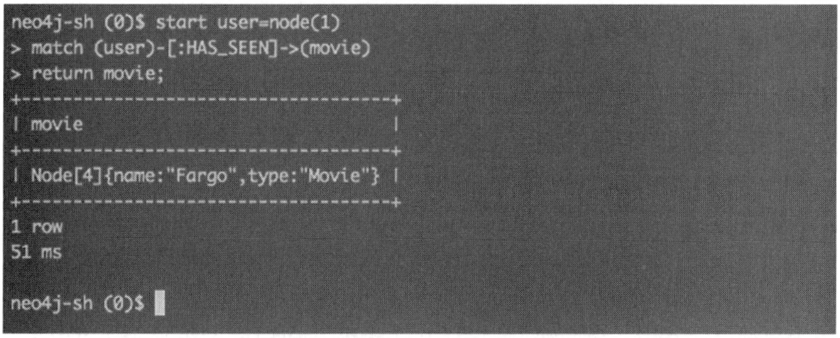

Figure 6.3   Cypher is executed in the Neo4j Shell natively, resulting in tabular output.

And that's it; you've executed your first Cypher query. You got the expected result by simply describing the subgraph you're interested in, without having to write any Java code and without worrying about transactions.

EXECUTING CYPHER USING THE WEB ADMIN CONSOLE

The Neo4j server comes with another useful operational tool, the Web Admin Console, a browser-based rich web interface to a Neo4j instance. It has plenty of features, allowing you to query, manipulate, and visualize Neo4j graph data, manage Lucene indexes, and maintain and monitor a Neo4j configuration. You can find more details about the Web Admin Console in chapter 11.

To access the Neo4j Web Admin Console, you need a running Neo4j server configured to point to your database location, such as /var/neo4j/db from the previous example. Follow these steps:

1   Install the Neo4j server by downloading the correct version and following the instructions detailed in appendix A of this book.
2   Edit the main Neo4j server configuration file, located at $NEO4J_HOME/conf/neo4j-server.properties. Locate the following line,

```
org.neo4j.server.database.location=data/graph.db
```

and replace the data directory so it points to the graph database you created in the previous section:

```
org.neo4j.server.database.location=/var/neo4j/db
```

3   Save the configuration file.
4   Start the Neo4j server using the following command:

```
$NEO4J_HOME/bin/neo4j start
```

With the server up and running (which can take a few seconds), you'll be able to access the Neo4j Web Admin Console by pointing your browser to http://localhost:7474. You should see the Web Admin Console homepage illustrated in figure 6.4.

The Web Admin Console embeds a fully functional Cypher execution engine running inside the browser (using some JavaScript wizardry). You can type your Cypher query in the text field at the top of the page, and as you press Enter, you'll see the result in the browser window. Figure 6.5 illustrates a Cypher query executing in the Web Admin Console.

Running Cypher inside the Web Admin Console is great when you don't have command-line access to the server running the Neo4j instance.

> **NOTE**   The Neo4j Web Admin Console has another nice feature—you can visualize the results of your Cypher query in the browser. To toggle between tabular and visual results, you can use the two buttons at the bottom-right corner of the browser.

So far you've run Cypher queries manually, using tools provided as part of the Neo4j distribution. We mentioned how easy it is to query the graph without writing a single

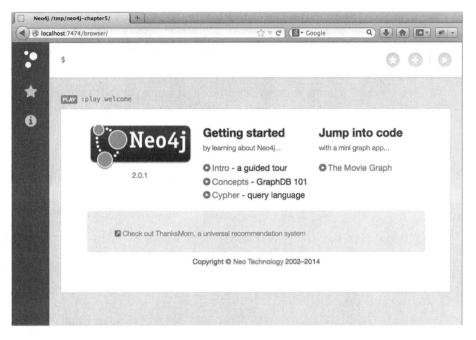

Figure 6.4 Homepage of the Neo4j Web Admin Console in the browser

Figure 6.5 Executing a Cypher query inside the Web Admin Console

line of Java code. But what about integrating Cypher with your custom application implemented in Java? Not to worry—the Neo4j Core Java API includes a Cypher API, making it easy to run Cypher queries from your Java code.

EXECUTING CYPHER FROM JAVA CODE

It's easy to query relational databases from Java using JDBC drivers and the JDBC API. Obtain the connection, create and execute the statement, iterate through the result set, and you have JDBC database queries in no time. You'll be pleased to know that executing Cypher queries in Java is even simpler!

The following code demonstrates the execution of the same sample Cypher query we executed in the Web Admin Console in figure 6.5, which finds all movies that a particular user has seen:

1 Instantiates ExecutionEngine by providing Neo4j database

Writes 2 Cypher query string

```
ExecutionEngine engine = new ExecutionEngine(graphDb);
String cql = "start user=node(1)" +
                    " match (user)-[:HAS_SEEN]->(movie)" +
                    " return movie;";
ExecutionResult result = engine.execute(cql);
System.out.println("Execution result:" + result.toString());
```

3 Executes query by passing it to the instantiated ExecutionEngine

Prints results

As you can see, all you need to do is instantiate Neo4j's `ExecutionEngine` for Cypher **1** and pass the valid Cypher query to it **2**, **3**. The `ExecutionResult.toString()` method creates the output in the same format as the Neo4j Shell, which makes it useful for debugging and troubleshooting.

To iterate over Cypher query results in Java, all you have to do is iterate over the `ExecutionResult` object returned by the `execute(...)` method:

```
ExecutionResult result = engine.execute(cql);
for(Map<String,Object> row : result){
    System.out.println("Row:" + row);
}
```

Each iterator element contains a single result row, represented as a Java `Map`, where the keys are column names and the values are actual result values.

The previous snippet iterates through Cypher query results row by row. Another option is to iterate through the results by a single column, which is useful if you're not interested in all columns returned, as the following code illustrates:

Gets all column names in result table

```
List<String> columns = result.columns();
    for(String column : columns){
        Iterator<Object> columnValues = result.columnAs(column);
            while(columnValues.hasNext()){
                System.out.println("Value:" + columnValues.next());
            }
    }
```

Locates results for a specified colum

Iterates through result values

CYPHER AND SCALA Although the core Neo4j graph engine is implemented in Java, the Neo4j Cypher engine is implemented in Scala, the popular, hybrid, functional programming language that runs on the Java virtual machine (JVM). For more information on Scala, see www.scala-lang.org/.

Alternatives to Cypher

Cypher isn't the only query language available for graphs. Another popular graph query language is Gremlin, which Neo4j also supports. Gremlin is actually a set of interfaces that define how the graph can be traversed and manipulated, and these interfaces must be implemented by every graph engine that wishes to be compatible. That means you can theoretically use the same Gremlin queries to work with data in any compatible graph database, making your code portable. Gremlin is an open source library and part of the popular Tinkerpop stack of graph libraries (https://github.com/tinkerpop/gremlin).

The main difference between Cypher and Gremlin is in their nature—Gremlin is an imperative language where users describe *how* to traverse the graph, Cypher is a declarative language that uses pattern matching to describe *what parts* of the graph data are required. This makes Cypher easier to read and understand. Gremlin is portable between different graph databases, but Cypher is developed by the Neo4j team and works only on Neo4j graph databases.

The Gremlin syntax and use are beyond the scope of this book, but you can find out more at https://github.com/tinkerpop/gremlin.

You now know how to execute a Cypher query, using both web-based and command-line utilities, and using the Java API. It's time to start writing some Cypher queries.

6.2 *Cypher syntax basics*

Cypher syntax consists of four different parts, each with a specific role:

- *Start*—Finds the starting node(s) in the graph
- *Match*—Matches graph patterns, allowing you to locate the subgraphs of interesting data
- *Where*—Filters out data based on some criteria
- *Return*—Returns the results you're interested in

Cypher's pattern-matching nature makes the graph patterns the key aspect of any query. That's why we're going to first take a look at Cypher's graph pattern-matching techniques.

6.2.1 *Pattern matching*

Pattern matching is the key aspect of Cypher that gives you great power to describe subgraph structures in a human-readable syntax. The following snippet illustrates matching the pattern of two nodes connected via a single named relationship:

```
start user=node(1)
match (user)-[:HAS_SEEN]->(movie)
return movie;
```

When describing a relationship, the relationship type is specified after a colon (`:`) within the square brackets. The type should appear exactly as it was defined when the relationship was created (syntax is case-sensitive). This simple query describes a single HAS_SEEN relationship using the [:HAS_SEEN] syntax.

The direction of the relationships is described using ASCII art in Cypher. The relationship is connected to its ending node using the ASCII arrow (a single hyphen character, followed by the greater-than or preceded by the less-than character, []-> or <-[]). The starting node of the relationship is connected using the single hyphen character ([]-). In the preceding example, the match (user)-[:HAS_SEEN]->(movie) pattern specifies the HAS_SEEN relationship from the user node toward the movie node.

If you don't care about the relationship direction, or you're not sure which is the starting or ending node of the relationship, you can use the single hyphen character on both sides, in which case it reads as "any." If you want to know if two users are friends, regardless of the direction, the following pattern can be used:

```
start user1=node(1)
match (user1)-[:IS_FRIEND_OF]-(user2)
return user2;
```

Let's now take a look at how the node and relationship identifiers are used in Cypher.

USING NODE AND RELATIONSHIP IDENTIFIERS

Both nodes and relationships in Cypher queries can be associated with identifiers, which are used to reference the same graph entity later in the same query. In the following example, the node named movie has been referenced in the return clause.

Relationships can be named as well, using slightly different syntax:

```
start user=node(1)
match (user)-[r:HAS_SEEN]->(movie)      ◁─── Names relationships by specifying the name
return movie;                                 before the colon and relationship type
```

To give a name to a relationship, simply specify the name you want to give it within the square brackets, before the relationship type.

Naming nodes and relationships can be very useful when creating complex patterns, because you can reference them later in other parts of a Cypher query. But if you don't need to reference the graph entity later, avoiding identifiers will make your query easier to read and understand.

In the preceding example, the nodes in the pattern were named (user is the starting node and movie is the node you want to return from the query), but not the relationship, because there was no plan to reference it anywhere else. To make the relationship anonymous, simply leave the relationship type within the square brackets, after the colon character, just as you did in the original query:

```
start user=node(1)
match (user)-[:HAS_SEEN]->(movie)        <-|  Unnamed (anonymous)
return movie;                               |  relationship
```

Nodes can similarly be anonymous. To make a node anonymous, use empty parentheses to specify the node, (). To illustrate this, let's write another Cypher query, where you want to return all HAS_SEEN relationships from the user node, without worrying about movie nodes:

```
start user=node(1)
match (user)-[r:HAS_SEEN]->()        <-|  Unnamed (anonymous) node
return r;                               |  used with named relationship
```

Using empty parentheses, you describe the fact that you expect a node, but you're not interested in any of its properties, nor do you want to reference it later, so you leave it unnamed.

> **NOTE**   Named nodes can be specified without parentheses in a Cypher match clause, such as start user=node(1) match user-[:HAS_SEEN]->movie return movie. In complex queries, you can remove the parentheses where possible, to declutter the query and make it more readable. Anonymous nodes must have parentheses.

All the patterns you've matched so far were quite simple, consisting of two nodes connected via a single relationship. Let's see how you can use more complex pattern matching with Cypher.

COMPLEX PATTERN MATCHING

Cypher supports quite complex pattern matching. Let's look at another example: finding all movies that User 1's friends have seen. You already solved this problem using the Neo4j Traversal API in chapter 4, so let's see how you can solve it using Cypher:

```
start john=node(1)                                        Complex graph pattern
match john-[:IS_FRIEND_OF]->()-[:HAS_SEEN]->(movie)  <-| connects three nodes via
return movie;                                             two relationships
```

Starting from the known node named john (with ID 1), you match the outgoing IS_FRIEND_OF relationship to another node (which is left anonymous), which in turn has a HAS_SEEN relationship to another named node, movie.

You don't need to name any relationships or intermediate nodes because you're not interested in them; all you want to return are nodes representing movies that John's friends have seen.

Running this query will return all movie nodes that any of John's friends have seen, whether or not John has seen them:

```
| Node[5]{name->"Alien",type->"Movie"} |
| Node[4]{name->"Fargo",type->"Movie"} |
| Node[6]{name->"Heat",type->"Movie"}  |
```

If you want this social network to recommend movies based on the taste of John's friends, then you should skip the movies that John has already seen. To get the result you want, filter the result you got in the previous example using a pattern that matches movies already seen by John. Using Cypher, you can match multiple patterns in the same query, referencing the same nodes in both patterns if required.

Look at the query in the following snippet:

```
start john=node(1)
match
john-[:IS_FRIEND_OF]->()-[:HAS_SEEN]->(movie),
john-[r:HAS_SEEN]->(movie)
return movie;
```

1 Matches movies that any of John's friends have seen

2 Matches movies that John has seen already

Multiple patterns in Cypher are differentiated using a comma (,) as a separator. The first pattern here is the one used in the previous example—matching movies that John's friends have seen **1**. The second pattern matches all movies that John has seen already **2**.

> **NOTE**   The resulting nodes will have to match *all* comma-separated patterns, acting effectively as a big AND clause.

The interesting bit here is that you use the same nodes as anchors in both patterns (both patterns start with the same john node, and both patterns match the same node named movie).

If you run this query, you'll get a single result, *Fargo*:

```
| Node[4]{name->"Fargo",type->"Movie"} |
```

Obviously, this isn't the result you wanted. You matched all movies John's friends have seen (resulting in all three movies), and then matched those to the movies John has seen, resulting in all movies that both John and some of John's friends have seen.

While this can be a useful query (if you want an answer to "What movies do John and his friends have in common?"), this isn't the answer you want here.

You need to replace the second pattern with a pattern that matches the nonexistence of the relationship: movies that John has *not* seen. The following snippet illustrates how you can use the NOT clause syntax to find all movies that John's friends have seen, but John hasn't:

```
start john=node:users(name = "John Johnson")
match john-[:IS_FRIEND_OF]->(user)-[:HAS_SEEN]->(movie)
where NOT john-[:HAS_SEEN]->(movie)
return movie.name;
```

1 Matches all movies John's friends have seen

2 Filters out movies that John has seen

The first pattern is exactly the same as before—matching movies John's friends have seen **1**. The second pattern, part of the where clause, filters out the movies returned by the first pattern, optionally connected via a HAS_SEEN relationship **2**.

```
neo4j-sh (?)$ start john=node:users(name = "John Johnson")
> match john-[:IS_FRIEND_OF]->(user)-[:HAS_SEEN]->(movie)
> where NOT john-[:HAS_SEEN]->(movie)
> return movie.name;
+------------+
| movie.name |
+------------+
| "Alien"    |
| "Heat"     |
+------------+
2 rows
293 ms
neo4j-sh (?)$ █
```

Figure 6.6   Result of the query execution in Neo4j Shell, finding movie recommendations for the user based on the movies their friends have seen

> **NOTE**   The `where` clause used in this example ❷ filters out the results of the query that you're not interested in, much like the SQL `where` clause in a relational database. We'll discuss the `where` clause in more detail later in this chapter.

The final result contains two movies (*Heat* and *Alien*), as you'd expect, given the data set illustrated in figure 6.1. Figure 6.6 shows the result after running the query in the Neo4j Shell.

You've now used Cypher to find movie recommendations for a user based on friends' ratings, but excluding the movies the user already watched. The solution to the same problem using Java APIs in chapter 4 resulted in over 40 lines of code. This time you did it in a 5-line Cypher query. The Cypher query is also much more readable and potentially understandable for anyone who understands the application domain, even if they don't have any programming skills.

> **NOTE**   In this chapter we're covering the basic Cypher concepts and syntax, and some advanced use of Cypher queries. For a full list of Cypher features and syntax, refer to the extensive online documentation in the Neo4j Manual: http://docs.neo4j.org/chunked/stable/cypher-query-lang.html.

Let's now take a more in-depth look at the anatomy of a Cypher query.

6.2.2   *Finding the starting node*

The querying of a Neo4j graph database follows a standard pattern: find the starting node(s) and run a traversal. You've followed this pattern in all your traversals so far, using the Neo4j Core API, the Traversal API, and Cypher. Starting nodes can be located by direct lookup by unique node ID, or, more typically, by using a Lucene index lookup, as you learned in chapter 5. Let's review the direct lookup by ID first.

NODE LOOKUP BY ID

As far as Cypher is concerned, starting nodes are specified at the beginning of the Cypher query, after the `start` keyword. In the examples so far, you've been loading the starting node with a direct ID lookup, as in the following snippet:

```
start john=node(1)
    return john;
```

① **Uses direct node lookup by ID to get the starting node in a Cypher query**

You can load the node by ID by simply specifying the ID in the parentheses right after the `node` keyword ①.

That works if you have one starting node, but sometimes you may need to apply the same pattern for multiple starting nodes and get all matching results—if, for example, you want to find all movies that either John or Jack have seen.

LOADING MULTIPLE NODES BY IDS

To use multiple IDs in the `start` clause, you need to list ID arguments as comma-separated values, as the following snippet demonstrates:

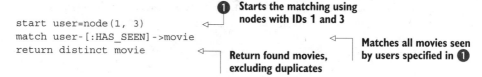

```
start user=node(1, 3)
match user-[:HAS_SEEN]->movie
return distinct movie
```

① **Starts the matching using nodes with IDs 1 and 3**

Matches all movies seen by users specified in ①

Return found movies, excluding duplicates

The `start` clause specifies two node IDs, using a single identifier: user ①. Next comes the pattern matching to find all movies that the user has seen. The `user` identifier references either nodes 1 or 3, so the pattern will match all movies that either User 1 (John, in this case) or User 3 (Jack) has seen. The resulting output looks like this:

```
|Node[5]{name->"Alien",type->"Movie"}|
|Node[4]{name->"Fargo",type->"Movie"}|
```

> **NOTE**   The `distinct` keyword in the `return` clause of the last query was used to eliminate duplicate results. `Distinct` works the same as in SQL queries—by excluding duplicated columns in the result set. Both Jack and John have seen *Fargo*, so if you didn't use the `distinct` keyword, *Fargo* would be returned twice in the result.

So far, so good. But most of the time you don't know the IDs of the nodes you're interested in—you know some other property, like a user's name, a movie title, or something similar. In the next section you'll learn how to use that information to load starting nodes.

USING AN INDEX TO LOOK UP THE STARTING NODE(S)

In chapter 5 we introduced indexing as a recommended way to look up starting nodes in a traversal. Cypher also supports direct access to Lucene indexes, so the typical traversal idiom in Neo4j becomes

1 Look up one or more nodes using the Lucene index.
2 Do a traversal starting from the node found in step 1.

How do you apply this pattern with Cypher? Cypher queries work by using pattern matching, so the typical usage would look like this:

1 Look up one or more nodes using the Lucene index.
2 Perform pattern matching by attaching the nodes you looked up in step 1 to the pattern.
3 Return the entities you're interested in.

The only question now is how to perform the Lucene index lookup in the `start` clause of the Cypher query instead of loading nodes by ID. It's very simple, as illustrated in this snippet:

```
start john=node:users(name = "John Johnson")
return john
```
Finds a node with the name property of "John Johnson" in index users

The `start` clause syntax is slightly different now. The `node:users` part specifies that you're interested in a node from the `users` index. The index name must match the index name you used when you added the node to the index. The arguments in parentheses specify the key-value pair you're looking for in the index; in this case, you're matching the property `name` with the value `"John Johnson"`. If such an index entry is found in the `users` index, that node will be loaded from the Neo4j database and used in the Cypher query.

This index lookup syntax requires an exact match of the key-value pair, and it is case-sensitive, so nodes with a `name` property of `"john johnson"` or `"John Johnso"` wouldn't be returned. At the same time, if multiple nodes are indexed with the same key-value pair (if you had more than one John Johnson in the database), all matching nodes would be loaded; it behaves similarly to the earlier example with multiple IDs.

If you want to use the full power of Lucene queries to look up start nodes, you can use a slightly different syntax with a native Lucene query:

```
start john=node:users("name:John Johnson")
return john
```
Uses native Lucene query for index lookup of nodes

This example will behave exactly the same as the previous one, with the only difference being in the argument to the index lookup. This time the entire index argument is passed within double quotes, and it contains a native Lucene query. This allows you to take advantage of the powerful Lucene query constructs, like wildcards or multiple property matching.

NOTE The documentation about native Lucene querying capabilities is available on the Lucene website: http://lucene.apache.org/core/3_6_0/query parsersyntax.html.

Here's an example of using a native Lucene query in Cypher:

```
start john=node:users("name:John* AND yearOfBirth<1980") return john
```

Index lookup for all nodes with name property starting with John (matching John Johnson, John Edwards, etc.) and born before 1980

NOTE   Automatic indexing, which we described in chapter 5, can also be used as part of a Cypher query in the same manner. All you have to do is use `node_auto_index` for the index name instead of `users` in the preceding query.

Next, let's take a look at how you can use schema-based indexes on labels to look up start nodes in a Cypher query.

USING A SCHEMA-BASED INDEX TO LOOK UP THE STARTING NODE(S)

In earlier chapters we discussed how you can type Neo4j nodes by assigning labels to nodes. We also mentioned how labels can be used as schema-based, built-in indexes for graph lookups. You can use the same indexes to look up nodes in Cypher.

Let's take a look at how you can use labels to find user nodes by name:

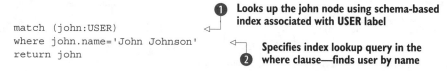

```
match (john:USER)
where john.name='John Johnson'
return john
```

❶ Looks up the john node using schema-based index associated with USER label

❷ Specifies index lookup query in the where clause—finds user by name

The label that specifies the schema index to use is defined as part of the node identifier, separated by a colon ❶. You must put the node identifier with the associated label inside parentheses. The index query is specified as part of the `where` clause, very similar to how it's done in SQL ❷.

NOTE   Label-based indexes can only be used for lookups on the full property values. For a full text search, you'll have to use manually created indexes as discussed in the previous section.

You now know how to use an index to look up nodes in the `start` clause of a Cypher query. But what if you want to fix multiple nodes on your graph pattern when executing a Cypher query and match them separately? What if you want to find all movies that both John and Jack have seen? Don't worry—this is also easy to achieve with Cypher, by specifying distinct multiple starting nodes as graph entry points.

MULTIPLE START NODES IN CYPHER

To specify multiple entry points to the graph, you can use a comma-separated list in the `start` clause of the Cypher query, as the following snippet illustrates:

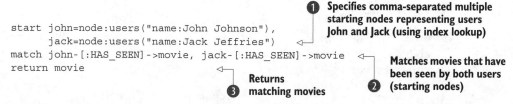

```
start john=node:users("name:John Johnson"),
     jack=node:users("name:Jack Jeffries")
match john-[:HAS_SEEN]->movie, jack-[:HAS_SEEN]->movie
return movie
```

❶ Specifies comma-separated multiple starting nodes representing users John and Jack (using index lookup)

❸ Returns matching movies

❷ Matches movies that have been seen by both users (starting nodes)

Starting nodes are presented as a comma-separated list, with each node having its own identifier that can be used throughout the query ❶. When you're matching patterns, all starting nodes can be part of a single pattern, or they can be used in separate patterns as in this example ❷. Both patterns in this example refer to the movie node (called by the same name in both patterns, so it represents the same node), which is the result of your Cypher query ❸.

6.2.3 *Filtering data*

Starting nodes and graph patterns are sometimes not enough to get the results you need using a Cypher query. In some cases, you'll need to perform additional filtering on nodes and relationships to determine what to return. Just as in SQL for relational databases, the query filtering in Cypher is performed using the where clause.

Typically, the where clause filters the results based on some property of a node or relationship. Let's look at an example that finds all friends of user John who were born after 1980. Let's assume that every user node has a yearOfBirth integer property holding the user's year of birth. The following snippet illustrates the solution:

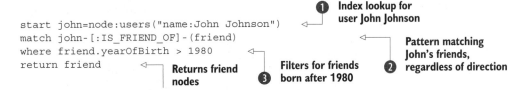

```
start john=node:users("name:John Johnson")
match john-[:IS_FRIEND_OF]-(friend)
where friend.yearOfBirth > 1980
return friend
```

❶ Index lookup for user John Johnson

❷ Pattern matching John's friends, regardless of direction

❸ Filters for friends born after 1980

Returns friend nodes

You find the starting node by performing the index lookup ❶, and you pattern match the friend nodes with an IS_FRIEND_OF relationship regardless of the direction ❷. Next, you filter only the matching friend nodes that have a yearOfBirth property greater than 1980 ❸. Because yearOfBirth is an integer property, you can perform a standard number comparison in the where clause.

For string properties, in addition to the standard equals (=) comparison, you can use regular expressions to filter out specific values. To find all friends who have an email address containing "gmail.com", for example, you could run the following query:

```
start john=node:users("name:John Johnson")
match john-[:IS_FRIEND_OF]-(friend)
where friend.email =~ /.*@gmail.com/
return friend
```

Filters user nodes by an email property matching a regular expression

As you can see, the regular expression comparison operator in Cypher is =~ (equals tilde). The regular expression is placed between two forward slashes (/). The expression itself follows the standard Java regular expression syntax (see http://docs.oracle.com/javase/tutorial/essential/regex/ for more information).

But what would happen if you don't have an email address stored for all users or nodes? As we discussed earlier, Neo4j allows for a semi-structured, schemaless data structure, so no two nodes have to have the same set of properties. The sample data set distributed with this book has an email property for some of the user nodes but not all. Let's see how to use Cypher to query for properties that aren't shared by all nodes.

To filter nodes that have a given property, regardless of the property value (for example, all friends who have a Twitter account), you need to use the Cypher function has:

```
start john=node:users("name:John Johnson")
match john-[IS_FRIEND_OF]-friend
where has(friend.twitter)
return friend
```

Filtering nodes that have the twitter property set using the has function

As you can see, filtering results in Cypher isn't difficult, and it looks very similar to the SQL where clause.

In the next section we'll take a look at the different types of results you can return from a Cypher query.

6.2.4 *Getting the results*

The results of a Cypher query are returned in the return clause. So far you've used it to return nodes you're interested in, but the return clause isn't limited to nodes only—you can also return relationships, properties of both nodes and relationships, and even entire paths of the subgraph.

> **NOTE**   A *path* in Neo4j represents the collection of nodes connected via relationships; for example, node1-[:relationship1]-node2-[:relationship2]-node3.

RETURNING PROPERTIES

In one of the earlier examples, you used Cypher to find all movies that John's friends have seen but John hasn't, and you returned matching movie nodes from the query. If you were using this data to display recommended movie titles on a web page, you'd be returning entire movie nodes with all properties—much more data than you need. The better approach would be to just return the node property you're interested in from the query.

The following snippet illustrates this:

```
start john= node:users(name = "John Johnson")
match
john-[:IS_FRIEND_OF]->(user)-[:HAS_SEEN]->(movie)
where not john-[:HAS_SEEN]->(movie)
return movie.name;
```

Returns only name property from Cypher query

If you run this query from Neo4j Shell, for example, you can see that the output is much less verbose than what you've seen previously:

```
| "Alien"   |
| "Heat"    |
```

> **NOTE**   If the property you're referencing isn't present on all entities in the result set, it will be returned as null for those entities that don't have the property.

RETURNING RELATIONSHIPS

Sometimes it makes more sense to query the graph for certain relationships. Suppose you want to display the ratings a user has given to the movies they've has seen. The rating is a property of a HAS_SEEN relationship (the actual property name is stars, referring to the number of stars awarded to the movie), so you need to return those relationships. The following snippet illustrates this:

```
start john=node:users("name:John Johnson")     ❶  Matches movies that John has seen;
match john-[r:HAS_SEEN]-(movie)                     identifier is set to HAS_SEEN relationship (r)
return r                                            Returns relationship
                                                    referenced by identifier
```

The query starts by looking up user John Johnson from the index and matching all movie nodes he has seen ❶. Then it returns the instances of the HAS_SEEN relationship. Note that to return a relationship, it needs to have an identifier (here r).

The output of this query would look like this:

```
| :HAS_SEEN[2] {stars->5} |
```

If you're only interested in the stars property of the relationship, you can return just that property from the query. Just like node properties, relationship properties can be referenced in the return clause. Here's a snippet that illustrates this:

```
start john=node:users("name:John Johnson")
match john-[r:HAS_SEEN]-(movie)              Returns stars property of
return r.stars                               HAS_SEEN relationship
```

This time, instead of the entire relationship entity, you're only returning the stars property you're interested in.

RETURNING PATHS

In addition to nodes and properties, you can return entire paths from the Cypher query. For example, when you're looking for movie recommendations based on the movies John's friends have seen, you may be interested in finding out how each movie is recommended by returning the full path from the starting user node, via all friends, to the recommended movie. The following snippet illustrates this:

```
start john=node:users(name = "John Johnson")                ❶  Gives the path the
match                                                           identifier recPath,
recPath = john-[:IS_FRIEND_OF]->(user)-[:HAS_SEEN]->(movie)     which can be used
where not john-[r:HAS_SEEN]->(movie)                            elsewhere in the query

return movie.name, recPath;                  Returns referenced path
                                             along with movie name
```

To return the path as a query result, you need to be able to reference it by giving it an identifier ❶. Then, you simply return the referenced path by specifying the identifier in the return clause.

The returned path output will contain all nodes and relationships that belong to it:

```
| "Alien"
| [
    Node[1]{
        name->"John Johnson",
        year_of_birth->1982,
        type->"User"
    },
```

```
        :IS_FRIEND_OF[1] {},
        Node[3]{
            name->"Jack Jeffries",
            cars_owned->[Ljava.lang.String;@3927ff0d,type->"User"
        },
        :HAS_SEEN[5] {stars->5},
        Node[5]{
            name->"Alien",type->"Movie"
        }
    ] |
    | "Heat"
    | [
        Node[1]{
            name->"John Johnson",
            year_of_birth->1982,
            type->"User"
        },
        :IS_FRIEND_OF[0] {},
            Node[2]{
            name->"Kate Smith",
            locked->true,type->"User"
        },
        :HAS_SEEN[3] {stars->3},
        Node[6]{name->"Heat",type->"Movie"}
    ] |
```

NOTE In the previous example you returned both a node property and a path from the Cypher query. All returnable graph entities discussed here can be specified in any desired combination.

When displaying data on a screen or printing on paper, you usually won't want to display all results at once, but rather split them into pages for better readability and usability. In the next section you'll learn how to page the results of a Cypher query.

PAGING RESULTS

If your result set contains a lot of entries, you may need to page the results for rendering on a web page. To page Cypher query results, Neo4j has three self-explanatory clauses:

- *order*—Orders the full result set before paging, so that paging returns consistent results regardless of whether you're going forward or backward through the pages
- *skip*—Offsets the result set so you can go to a specified page
- *limit*—Limits the number of returned results to the page size

Suppose one of the users in your database is a real movie buff, who has seen and rated hundreds of movies. If you were to display all of that user's movie ratings (stars awarded) on a single page, the type would be unreadably small (or it wouldn't fit).

You could decide to display only 20 movies per web page, ordered by movie name. To query the graph to get such paged results, you'd use the order, limit, and skip clauses. The following query returns the third page (entries 21–30):

```
start john=node:users("name:John Johnson")
match john-[:HAS_SEEN]->(movie)
return movie
order by movie.name
skip 20
limit 10
```

❶ Orders results by movie name

❷ Skips first two pages (2 × 10 = 20 entries)

Returns 10 results (page size)

After matching the movies the user has seen, as we've discussed, you order the results by the name property ❶. Because you're interested in the third page of the results, you skip two pages' worth (20) of entries ❷. Finally, you limit the returned result set to the page size (10 in this example).

> **NOTE** The Neo4j online documentation includes an easily printable Cypher reference card with common syntax and query details: http://neo4j.org/resources/cypher.

Cypher performance

In simple queries, you can see that the performance of Cypher queries roughly matches that of the Neo4j Traversal API or Core Java API. But when running more complex queries, with complex pattern matching or intensive filtering, Cypher will not perform as well as the Traversal API or Core Java API. In some cases the difference can be an order of magnitude or more greater.

As Cypher is relatively young, its developers have concentrated on adding all required functionality to it first; performance has not been the priority. As of Neo4j 2.0, however, Cypher binds to the Neo4j engine lower on the stack than the Traversal API. This will make it possible to fine-tune Cypher performance to be better than the Traversal API. Once the feature set becomes stable, you can expect performance tuning of the Cypher parser and execution engine to produce much better results.

Given its simplicity and expressiveness, Cypher is the best option for most graph queries, but for very complex traversals or inserts of big data sets, you may want to use the Core Java API and Traversal API. We covered the basics of the Core Java API in chapters 3, 4, and 5. For in-depth coverage of the Traversal API, see chapter 8. In future versions of Neo4j, you can expect Cypher to become the most efficient and fastest way to interact with Neo4j.

We've come to the end of the Cypher syntax section. You've learned how to perform pattern matching in Cypher, how to filter out results, how to return not only nodes but other graph entities directly, and how to order and limit returned result sets.

Our discussion so far has been related to reading data from Neo4j. In the next section we'll show you how to create, update, and delete graph data using Cypher.

6.3 *Updating your graph with Cypher*

From Neo4j version 1.7 on, you can use Cypher to run mutating operations against your graph database to create, update, and delete nodes and relationships and their properties.

The syntax for mutating operations is very intuitive, so let's take a look at a few examples.

> **NOTE**   Cypher graph mutating operations are a relatively new feature of the Neo4j database, so the syntax for mutation may be subject to significant changes in future releases. This book is based on the Neo4j version 2.0 Cypher syntax. You're advised to consult the Neo4j Manual for the latest syntax (http://docs.neo4j.org/chunked/stable/query-write.html).

Let's start with creating nodes and relationships.

6.3.1   Creating new graph entities

To create a node with properties, you can use the following syntax:

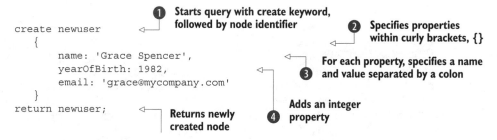

The command that creates graph entities is, unsurprisingly, `create`, followed by the node identifier ❶. Following that, you specify a comma-separated list of properties to be added to the node, enclosed with curly brackets ❷. Each property is specified by its name, followed by a colon, followed by a property value ❸. String property values are enclosed in single quotes, but numeric and Boolean properties don't need any quotes ❹. Finally, you return the newly created node using its identifier, just like in the previous Cypher examples.

Okay, you've created a node, so how about creating a relationship? Let's make the newly added user Grace a friend of John:

```
start john = node:users(name = "John Johnson"), grace = node(10)
create john-[r:IS_FRIEND_OF]->grace
return r;
```

❶ Uses start clause to specify existing nodes that participate in the relationship

❷ Creates the path between nodes and the relationship

You want to create a relationship between the existing two nodes, so you need to somehow reference them first. This is done exactly the same way as specifying start nodes in a read-only query, using the `start` clause and node lookup ❶. Next, in the `create` clause, you simply specify the graph path as a pattern referencing starting nodes by their identifiers and setting the relationship you want to create between them ❷.

> ## Cypher and transactions
>
> When running Cypher from a command line or web interface, each query execution is wrapped in a single transaction. You don't have to worry about starting or finishing transactions or dealing with their failure—everything will be taken care of by the Neo4j engine. If the query succeeds, the transaction will automatically commit. If the query fails, the transaction will be rolled back.
>
> In an application context, Cypher queries will execute with the existing transaction context. If you create a transaction programmatically, you can use multiple queries within the same transaction and commit or roll back everything at the end.
>
> Because we're using Neo4j Shell or the Web Admin Console to run the Cypher examples throughout this chapter, each query is automatically wrapped in a single transaction, so no additional setup is necessary.
>
> For in-depth information about Neo4j transactions, read chapter 7 on Neo4j transactions.

So far you've created a node with some properties and a relationship. But you could have done all that in a single command, as the following snippet illustrates:

```
start john = node:users(name = "John Johnson")
create john
        -[r:IS_FRIEND_OF]->
        (grace {
    name: 'Grace Spencer',
    yearOfBirth: 1982, email: 'grace@mycompany.com'
})
return r, grace;
```

1 Specifies start node representing John

2 Creates new node and relationship between node John and new node

In this example, you fixed an existing `john` node **1**. In the `create` clause, you specified the pattern from `john`, via a non-existent `IS_FRIEND_OF` relationship, to a non-existent node `grace`, with the same properties as before **2**. Cypher is smart enough to recognize which nodes and relationships are fixed (`john` from the `start` clause), and which are new and should be created in the database (the `IS_FRIEND_OF` relationship and `grace` node). This is a very powerful approach for creating full paths of new nodes and relationships with properties.

The Cypher `create` clause will create all elements in the matching pattern regardless of whether or not they exist. If you ran the previous node snippet, which creates John's friend Grace Spencer, twice, you'd end up with two Grace Spencer nodes and two `IS_FRIEND_OF` relationships from John's node. This is probably not what you'd want. To create only graph entities that don't already exist, you should use the `create unique` Cypher command, illustrated in the following snippet:

```
start john = node:users(name = "John Johnson")
create unique john
        -[r:IS_FRIEND_OF]->
        (grace {
```

```
    name: 'Grace Spencer',
    yearOfBirth: 1982, email: 'grace@mycompany.com'
})
return r, grace;
```

The only change from the previous example is the use of the create unique command. Running this snippet multiple times will not multiply the number of entities—you will always have one Grace Spencer node and one IS_FRIEND_OF relationship between the John and Grace nodes.

Now you know how to create new nodes, relationships, and properties, but how about deleting them? The next section will discuss deleting data from Neo4j using Cypher.

6.3.2   Deleting data

To delete a node, Cypher provides a delete command. Let's delete the user Grace you just created:

```
start grace = node(10)          Uses start clause to
                                select node to delete
delete grace            Uses delete command to
                        delete selected node
```

But if you run this command, you'll get an error, warning you that the node has relationships. In Neo4j, you can only delete a node if it doesn't have any relationships (either incoming or outgoing). To make sure you can delete a node, you need to delete its relationships at the same time, as shown in the following snippet:

```
start grace = node(10)      ❶ Matches all relationships to selected
match grace-[r]-()            node, regardless of direction
delete grace, r      Deletes relationship and
                     ❷ node at the same time
```

Here you use the standard pattern to match all relationships coming into or going out of the grace node ❶, and delete all relationships that start or end at the specified node ❷.

The output of the delete query doesn't contain any data, but it will show the number of deleted nodes and relationships:

```
Nodes deleted: 1
Relationships deleted: 1
```

Finally, let's take a look at how you can update properties on existing nodes using Cypher.

6.3.3   Updating node and relationship properties

Let's say you made a mistake with John's year of birth, and you need to update it. The command to do that would look like this:

```
start john=node:users(name = "John Johnson")  ❶ Selects node to update
set john.yearOfBirth = 1973          Sets properties to update
```

You can see that the syntax is very simple: first you select the node to update ❶, then you use the set command to set the selected property of the node to the new value. If the property you're setting doesn't already exist, it will be created by this command.

You can specify multiple nodes to add the same property to all of them:

```
start user=node(1,2)
set user.group = 'ADMINISTRATOR'
```

Neo4j doesn't allow null property values on graph entities. In effect, a null property value is treated as a non-existent property. So if you want to remove a property, you would use the delete command. This is demonstrated in the following snippet:

```
start n=node(1)
delete n.group;
```

Graph-mutating operations in Cypher are a relatively new feature of Neo4j at the time of writing. We've demonstrated some useful examples that should get you going. For more detailed and up-to-date information on the evolving Cypher syntax, see the Neo4j Manual at http://docs.neo4j.org/chunked/stable/cypher-query-lang.html.

Schema indexing in Cypher

In chapter 5 we introduced the concept of schema indexing, and the improved automatic indexing feature of Neo4j, where indexes are fully maintained by the Neo4j engine as part of a node's lifecycle. You also learned how to use schema indexing from Java code. It's possible to perform all schema-indexing operations from Cypher as well.

The detailed description of the Cypher syntax required to achieve this is out of scope for this book, but you can consult the Neo4j Manual for all the details (http://docs.neo4j.org/chunked/stable/query-schema-index.html).

Note that graph-mutating operations in Neo4j *don't* support updates to manually created indexes. If you need to index your newly created nodes using custom indexes (not schema indexes), you'll have to use the Neo4j Core Java API, language bindings, or REST API.

We've covered a lot about Cypher so far, but there's much more to it under the surface. In the next section we'll look at some of the other Cypher goodies.

6.4 Advanced Cypher

You've learned how to write and execute fairly complex Cypher queries so far, but there's much more to Cypher than that. In this section we're going to take a look at some of the advanced features in Cypher, like data aggregation, Cypher functions, and chaining multiple queries together. Let's start with data aggregation.

6.4.1   *Aggregation*

Just like GROUP BY in SQL, Cypher supports aggregating functions in queries. Instead of using a dedicated GROUP BY clause, the grouping key in Cypher is defined as all non-aggregating results of the query. Here's how you could count the number of friends for each user in the graph:

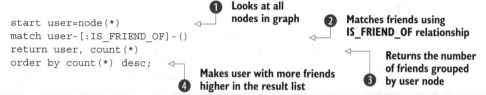

```
start user=node(*)
match user-[:IS_FRIEND_OF]-()
return user, count(*)
order by count(*) desc;
```

❶ Looks at all nodes in graph

❷ Matches friends using IS_FRIEND_OF relationship

❸ Returns the number of friends grouped by user node

❹ Makes user with more friends higher in the result list

You're looking at the entire graph in this example, so all nodes are used as starting nodes ❶. For each user node, you match their direct friends by following one level of the IS_FRIEND_OF relationship ❷. The return clause contains one non-aggregating entry (user node) and one aggregated function (count) ❸. This means that you're using the user node to group the counts by, getting one result row per user. You can use the aggregated values to order the entire result set in the order by clause as well ❹.

In addition to the count function, Cypher supports all the usual aggregation functions from SQL: SUM for summing numeric values, AVG for calculating averages, and MAX and MIN for finding the maximum or minimum values of numeric properties.

To find the average age of all John's friends, you can use the following query:

```
start john=node:users(name = "John Johnson")
match john-[:IS_FRIEND_OF]-(friend)
where HAS(friend.yearOfBirth)
return avg(2014-friend.yearOfBirth);
```

❶ Makes sure that node has yearOfBirth property

❷ Uses AVG function to return average age

Here you're checking that the node has a year of birth property set, before using it in mathematical calculations ❶. Then you return the calculated average value ❷.

> **NOTE**   To get the age of the user, you subtract the year of birth from the current year. We're using this book's publication year of 2014 in this example.

Let's now have a look at Cypher's built-in functions.

6.4.2   *Functions*

Cypher supports a number of functions that you can use to evaluate expressions in your query. Let's look at some of them.

Cypher functions are used to access internal attributes of graph entities, such as node and relationship IDs and relationship labels (types). In the count example, you've seen the ID(node) function used to retrieve the internal ID of a given node. In addition, you can use the TYPE(relationship) function to find the type for a relationship.

To demonstrate the use of the TYPE function, let's find an answer to the following question: "How many relationships of each type start or finish at user John?" The following snippet shows the required Cypher query:

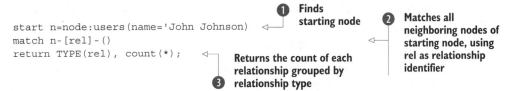

```
start n=node:users(name='John Johnson)
match n-[rel]-()
return TYPE(rel), count(*);
```

❶ Finds starting node

❷ Matches all neighboring nodes of starting node, using rel as relationship identifier

❸ Returns the count of each relationship grouped by relationship type

The first two steps in the example are very familiar: find the starting node using the index lookup ❶, and find all its neighboring nodes using the match clause ❷. The identifier rel is used to reference every relationship later in the query. Finally, you return the type of each relationship using the TYPE function, along with the count ❸. As TYPE is a non-aggregating function, the results will be grouped by relationship type.

Cypher also supports functions that allow you to easily work with iterable collections within the query. As an example, let's solve the following problem: John would like to be introduced to Kate on Facebook. He doesn't know Kate and would like to find out which of his friends, and friends of his friends, know her, up to the third level. Because he needs to use Facebook, he's only interested in people who are on Facebook already (who have the facebookId property set). The following snippet shows the required query:

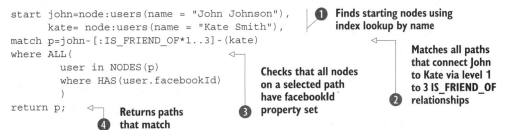

```
start john=node:users(name = "John Johnson"),
      kate= node:users(name = "Kate Smith"),
match p=john-[:IS_FRIEND_OF*1..3]-(kate)
where ALL(
        user in NODES(p)
        where HAS(user.facebookId)
      )
return p;
```

❶ Finds starting nodes using index lookup by name

❷ Matches all paths that connect John to Kate via level 1 to 3 IS_FRIEND_OF relationships

❸ Checks that all nodes on a selected path have facebookId property set

❹ Returns paths that match

You start the query by locating known starting nodes representing John and Kate in the Neo4j database ❶. In the match clause you find all paths that connect John and Kate by following the IS_FRIEND_OF relationships up to the third level ❷. You're using the identifier p to reference the matching path later in the query.

The smart bit comes in the where clause ❸. You use the NODES(p) Cypher function to extract the collection of all nodes in the given path. You check that each node has the facebookId property by using the HAS function. Then you use the ALL function to apply the HAS predicate to every element of the collection of nodes. The function ALL will return true if every element in the given iterable matches the predicate, so if one of the nodes on the path p doesn't have a facebookId property, the path will be discarded.

Finally, you return the paths that fulfill all criteria ❹. The path will contain all people John will need to contact so he can be introduced to Kate on Facebook.

You've seen quite a few functions in action in this example:

- `HAS(graphEntity.propertyName)`—Returns `true` if the property with a given name exists on a node or relationship.
- `NODES(path)`—Transforms a path into an iterable collection of nodes.
- `ALL(x in collection where predicate(x))`—Returns `true` if every single element of `collection` matches the given `predicate`.

Neo4j supports a lot more functions with similar purposes to the ones we described here. For example, like the `NODES(path)` function, the `RELATIONSHIPS(path)` function returns a collection of all relationships on the given path.

In addition to `ALL`, Neo4j supports other predicate-based Boolean functions:

- `NONE(x in collection where predicate(x))`—Returns `true` if no elements of the supplied collection match the predicate; otherwise it returns `false`.
- `ANY(x in collection where predicate(x))`—Returns `true` if at least one element matches the predicate; if none matches, it returns `false`.
- `SINGLE(x in collection where predicate(x))`—Returns `true` if exactly one element of the collection matches the predicate; if no elements or more than one element matches, this function returns `false`.

NOTE   There is simply not enough space in this book to cover all the Neo4j functions in detail. For more information, please read the comprehensive Neo4j Manual (http://docs.neo4j.org/chunked/stable/query-function.html).

6.4.3   *Piping using the with clause*

In Cypher you can chain the output of one query to another, creating powerful graph constructs. The chaining (or piping) clause in Cypher is `with`.

To illustrate its use, let's build on a previous example where you used Cypher to count the number of relationships of each type from the `john` node. Let's add a requirement to include only relationships that occur more than once: if John has seen two movies, that `HAS_SEEN` relationship would be included, but if he has seen just one movie (or no movies at all), the relationship wouldn't be included.

The problem involves filtering on an aggregated function. In SQL, filtering on aggregate functions is done using the `HAVING` clause, but Cypher doesn't support that. Instead, in Cypher you can use `with`, as the following snippet illustrates:

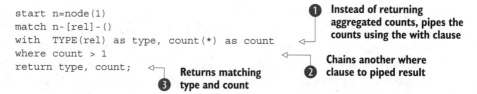

```
start n=node(1)
match n-[rel]-()
with  TYPE(rel) as type, count(*) as count
where count > 1
return type, count;
```

1 Instead of returning aggregated counts, pipes the counts using the with clause

2 Chains another where clause to piped result

3 Returns matching type and count

The query starts with the index lookup of the starting node, then matches all relationships connected to it. But, instead of returning the aggregated result as before, you chain it using the with clause ❶. In the with clause, you rename the output that will be used as input in the chained command (type and count). After chaining, the output defined using the with clause acts as input to the new where clause ❷. Finally, you return the matching result ❸.

> **NOTE** It's mandatory to name the output fields of the with clause before they're used in a chained query.

If Cypher is evolving that quickly, will you have to rewrite your Cypher queries every time you upgrade to the next Neo4j version? We'll look at how you can deal with different versions of Cypher syntax next.

6.4.4 *Cypher compatibility*

We've already mentioned that Cypher is a quickly evolving language, and its syntax is subject to frequent change. To add valuable new functionality to Cypher, its developers sometimes need to introduce breaking changes, which will make queries written for earlier Neo4j versions fail when they're run against a Neo4j database with a newer version.

Fortunately, there's a simple configuration that will allow you to run queries against any of the supported Neo4j Cypher engines. You can specify the exact version of Neo4j your query syntax conforms to just before you query:

```
CYPHER 1.8 start n=node(1)
match n-[rel]-()
with  TYPE(rel) as type, count(*) as count
where count > 1
return type, count;
```

❶ Specifies the exact Cypher parser version at the start of the query

You can specify the required Neo4j version using the CYPHER keyword followed by the Neo4j version at the beginning of your query, just before the start clause ❶.

> **NOTE** The Cypher examples in this chapter have been tested with Neo4j version 2.0.

In addition to applying the Cypher parser version to all queries, you can set the global configuration option to cypher_parser_version. This option is set in the neo4j .properties file. For the location of this file in both the server and embedded modes, look at chapter 10, where we discuss different configuration options.

6.5 *Summary*

You've now been introduced to Cypher, Neo4j's query language. You've learned how to execute Cypher queries against your graph database, how to write efficient Cypher queries to extract data from your graph, and how Cypher makes your queries simpler and more readable, without sacrificing the performance of the traversals too much. The graph data-manipulation feature also makes Cypher useful for all maintenance tasks in Neo4j.

In the next chapter, we're going to take a deep dive into Neo4j transactions.

Transactions 7

This chapter covers

- Why transactions are important
- How Neo4j handles transactions
- How to integrate Neo4j with other transaction management systems
- How to take advantage of transaction events

Neo4j differs from some other NoSQL technologies by being fully ACID-compliant (ACID being an acronym for atomic, consistent, isolated, durable). Being fully ACID-compliant means Neo4j offers the same guarantees you'd have if you were working with a traditional relational database system.

It's important to have ACID guarantees when you work with Neo4j because it's commonplace to mutate a number of graph entities (nodes, relationships, and index entries) within the same transaction. It's also easier to reason about the behavior of systems that are ACID-compliant compared to eventually consistent systems, where you have no real guarantees about when your changes will be visible across a cluster, and compared to technologies where there are no transactions and therefore partial results of a larger business operation may become temporarily visible to competing transactions. The durability aspect of ACID transactions also provides a high degree of confidence that once your transaction is committed, the data won't be lost.

You've seen transactions being called in other chapters in this book. In this chapter we'll explore transactions in more detail.

7.1 *Transaction basics*

First, let's examine the idiomatic way of programmatically creating transactions in Neo4j, as shown in the following snippet:

```
try (Transaction tx = graphDatabaseService.beginTx()) {
    //do something with the database
    tx.success();
}
```

This code begins by making use of the Java 7 *try-with-resource* statement to create a new transaction and define a block of code against which this transaction will apply. Any statements that interact with the database and are executed within this block will all operate against the same transaction. The call to the `success` method at the end of the `try` block signifies that a commit should occur when the transaction finishes (or the resource "closes," in try-with-resource terminology). The transaction finishes (or closes) when the code block completes. Neo4j will then ensure that this transaction is committed (having detected that the `success` method was previously called). If an exception is thrown while "doing something with the database," the `success` method won't be called, and the transaction will be rolled back when it finishes. Neo4j's decision logic regarding whether to commit or roll back a transaction is based on whether the `success` or `failure` method was previously called. If you want to roll back a transaction explicitly, such as from a conditional code block, you can invoke the `failure` method, and the transaction will be unconditionally rolled back at the end of the block. Calling neither the `success` nor `failure` method will also result in the transaction being rolled back (default).

> **Transactions before Neo4j 2.0**
>
> In older versions of Neo4j (1.9 and earlier), managing transactions was a bit more complicated, mainly because of the lack of auto-closable resources before Java 7, which Neo4j complies with since version 2.0.
>
> If you're using an older version of Neo4j, the idiomatic way to handle transactions is as follows:
>
> ```
> Transaction tx = graphDatabaseService.beginTx();
> try {
>     //do something
>     tx.success();
> } finally {
>     tx.finish();
> }
> ```
>
> This style is still available but has been deprecated in Neo4j 2.0.

Neo4j 2.0 requires a transaction to be initiated for any read or write operation on a graph object including nodes, relationships, schemas, and indexes. Note that in previous versions of Neo4j, there was no such requirement for read operations.

The following listing shows code that first reads a node representing a person, then attempts to set an age property on it.

Listing 7.1   Attempting to update without a transaction

```
Node userNode = graphDatabaseService.index()
    .forNodes("byName").get("name", "John").getSingle();
userNode.setProperty("age", 34);
```

Finds the starting node. This will fail with Neo4j 2.0. ❶

Sets the age of the user without first starting a transaction. ❷

NOTE   Examples in this chapter deliberately assume a very simple data model that consists of two nodes, John and Bob, representing two people with age properties set on them. This data model will be sufficient to demonstrate the transactional behavior of Neo4j.

When executing this code with a pre-2.0 version of Neo4j, line ❶ will pass but line ❷ will result in a NotInTransactionException. This is because mutating operations in Neo4j 1.X required a transaction, while read-only ones did not. In Neo4j 2.0 and later versions, both ❶ and ❷ will fail with a NotInTransactionException.

7.1.1   Adding in a transaction

The following listing shows the code from listing 7.1 but with transaction management added. For the rest of this chapter, we'll assume the transactional style and requirements of Neo4j 2.0.

Listing 7.2   Attempting to update with a transaction

```
try(Transaction tx = graphDatabaseService.beginTx()) {
    Node userNode = graphDatabaseService.index()
        .forNodes("byName").get("name", "John").getSingle();
    userNode.setProperty("age", 34);
    tx.success();
}
```

Starts the transaction

Sets the age of the user

Marks the transaction as successful

This listing represents the general pattern of starting a transaction, carrying out some operations, and assuming they complete without exception. After the success method is called and the code block completes, the changes are committed to the database.

> **Schema-based operations and transactions**
>
> If you're performing any schema-related activities within the graph, this code will need to be in a separate transaction from all other Neo4j transactional code; otherwise, an exception of the form ConstraintViolationException will be thrown with the message "Cannot perform data updates in a transaction that has performed schema updates."

(continued)

Schema indexing was covered in chapter 5, and the following snippet is a partial copy of listing 5.5 to demonstrate this case. To recap, you're defining name as a schema-indexable property on the USER label in one transaction, and then using a separate transaction to actually set the value on a real user node:

```
Label userLabel = DynamicLabel.label("USER");

// 1. Do schema related work in one transaction.
try (Transaction tx = graphDb.beginTx()) {
    graphDb.schema().indexFor(userLabel).on("name").create();
    tx.success();
}

// 2. Do other work in a separate transaction.
Node user = null;
try (Transaction tx = graphDb.beginTx()) {
    user = graphDb.createNode(userLabel);
    user.setProperty("name", "Michael Collins");
    tx.success();
}}
```

7.1.2 Finishing what you start and not trying to do too much in one go

Creating a transaction in a try block, as we said previously, guarantees that transactions are finished appropriately in a timely manner. The stateful nature of transactions requires that you give consideration to the amount of work you attempt to do in a single transaction. This only really becomes an issue for very large transactions, including large inserts or updates, such as the one shown in the following listing. When executed, this code will likely fail with an out-of-memory exception, depending on the amount of memory available for the JVM.

Listing 7.3 A really big transaction can run out of memory

```
try(Transaction tx = graphDatabaseService.beginTx()) {
    for (int i = 0; i < 100000000; i++) {
        Node n = this.graphDatabaseService.createNode();
        n.setProperty("number", i);
    }
    tx.success();
}
java.lang.OutOfMemoryError: Java heap space
    at java.util.HashMap.addEntry(HashMap.java:766)
    at java.util.HashMap.put(HashMap.java:402)
    at java.util.HashSet.add(HashSet.java:217)
    at org.neo4j.kernel.impl.api.DiffSets.add(DiffSets.java:98)
    at ....
```

In order to avoid out-of-memory exceptions in very large transactions, the work should be broken down into a number of smaller transactions. It's not, however, generally advisable to create a large number of nodes using a separate transaction for each new node because the computational cost of the transaction will have a significant impact on performance. A better strategy would be to do some hundreds or perhaps thousands of creation operations in a batch with one transaction. The exact number will depend on the amount of data involved in creating each node.

The previous example conflates the server's and the client's behavior, because of its use of the embedded mode. In a more traditional client/server scenario, the pressure of handling large transactions mainly affects the server, because it's the server that needs to keep track of all uncommitted transactions started by a potentially large number of clients.

Batch inserter and transactions

It's worth noting that Neo4j does in fact provide batch insertion functionality to allow for speedy batch inserts. This class, however, is optimized for speed and doesn't support transactions, instead writing changes to disk as it goes. Such functionality can often be useful in situations where you have a large dataset that needs to be loaded once, but you need to be fully aware of the implications of using this facility. For more information, please see the "Batch Insertion" chapter of the Neo4j Manual: http://docs.neo4j.org/chunked/stable/batchinsert.html.

In this section, you've seen how to programmatically manage transactions when your code needs to interact with the graph. This allows you to define atomic units of work and to have confidence that a successful finish means your changes are durable and that the graph remains in a consistent state at all times. In the next section, we'll dive a bit deeper into transactions, including how to use locks as a way of controlling the isolation level of read transactions. Although this is not required, it's something you may do in certain circumstances.

Nested transactions

Neo4j supports flat nested transactions, which means that it's possible to nest transactions, but inner and outer transactions will ultimately share the same context. If all transactions call the `success` method, then all their modifications will be committed to the database.

If you need to signal failure explicitly from an inner transaction, you can call the `failure` method, which will mark the whole transaction as failed. In this case, the transaction will be rolled back and a `TransactionFailureException` will be thrown at the end of the outermost transaction.

7.2   *Transactions in depth*

We've covered the basic workings of transactions in Neo4j, and that should give you enough knowledge to handle the most common transactional requirements. But if you need to achieve higher isolation guarantees than the default isolation level, or to write code that's robust and isn't likely to generate deadlocks, you'll need some understanding of Neo4j's transaction management model.

We'll start by examining how transactions work and the default isolation level offered by Neo4j. After that we'll look at how you can use explicit locks to obtain stronger isolation guarantees.

7.2.1 Transaction semantics

Let's examine some of the guarantees that ACID transactions offer and how they're handled in Neo4j.

> **Transactions and thread locality**
>
> Each new transaction in Neo4j is bound to the current thread. For that reason, it's absolutely essential to ensure that each transaction finishes properly and that each transactional context is properly cleaned up. Otherwise, the next transaction to run on the same thread could potentially be affected by the stale context, resulting in erroneous and inconsistent outcomes. The coding idioms shown in this chapter will help you avoid such problems.

DURABILITY

Durability refers to writing data to permanent storage in a way that survives restarting the database. If a transaction succeeds, you can assume that the data has been persisted to the disk in a durable manner.

Under the covers, though, Neo4j maintains a transaction log that gets updated and persisted for each successful transaction with mutating operations. When it reaches a certain size, or when the database shuts down, the transaction log gets flushed and the appropriate store files get updated on the disk. Chapter 11 discusses the role of the transaction log.

ISOLATION LEVELS AND NEO4J LOCKS

A number of database management systems implement locking mechanisms to manage concurrent access to the same database resources. Neo4j transactions are governed by distinct read and write locks on each graph resource (nodes and relationships).

Read locks are useful because they ensure that the resources you're interested in are consistently locked and can't be modified unexpectedly while you're reading them. More precisely, read locks can *optionally* be acquired on any graph resource if there is no write lock currently active on the same resource. Read locks are *not* mutually exclusive; multiple read locks can be acquired on the same resource by multiple threads at the same time. Only one write lock can be acquired on a resource at any given moment, and only if there are no other active locks, either read or write, on the resource in question. The distinction between read and write locks and the way they interact allows developers to flexibly trade off consistency for performance, depending on what's acceptable for the situation at hand.

By default Neo4j transactions don't try to acquire read locks automatically. Reads therefore see the latest committed state of nodes, relationships, and index entries, except within their own transaction, where local modifications (even if not committed yet) are visible. Figure 7.1 provides an example that demonstrates this situation.

Conversely, write locks are acquired automatically for any graph resource you try to mutate at the point when the mutation occurs, and they're held for the full duration of the transaction. Every transaction makes sure to release any acquired lock automatically when it completes.

This default behavior is very similar to the Read Committed isolation level in relational databases, which removes the potential for dirty reads, but still allows phantom reads and non-repeatable reads to happen.

What exactly is locked?

Which graph resources are locked and when? When you try to modify a graph object (that is, when you create, delete, or update a property on a node or a relationship), Neo4j has to acquire a write lock on the object in question to protect it against concurrent modification. Equally, when you create a new relationship between two existing nodes, both nodes are locked by the transaction.

A *phantom read* is the situation in which one transaction can potentially see a different number of nodes and relationships at different times if some entities were added or deleted by another transaction in the meantime.

In *non-repeatable reads*, a transaction can read the same property of a node or relationship twice and get different values if that property was updated simultaneously by another transaction.

Figure 7.1 illustrates the default isolation level in Neo4j. In the figure, two threads are competing to access the same graph resources, resulting in a Read Committed isolation level.

It's possible to achieve higher transactional guarantees by managing locks explicitly, as you'll see in the next section.

Transactions in High Availability mode

The transactional behavior described in this chapter focuses mainly on what happens within a single instance of Neo4j. In High Availability (HA) mode, there are two types of Neo4j instances, master and slaves, and transactions ensure that writes are always consistent and durable. Although technically you can target any Neo4j instance for a write operation, writes are first pushed to the master and are eventually propagated to slaves. This behavior is automatic and can be configured to achieve a suitable trade-off between performance and durability. For more details on Neo4j HA and its use in production, see chapter 11.

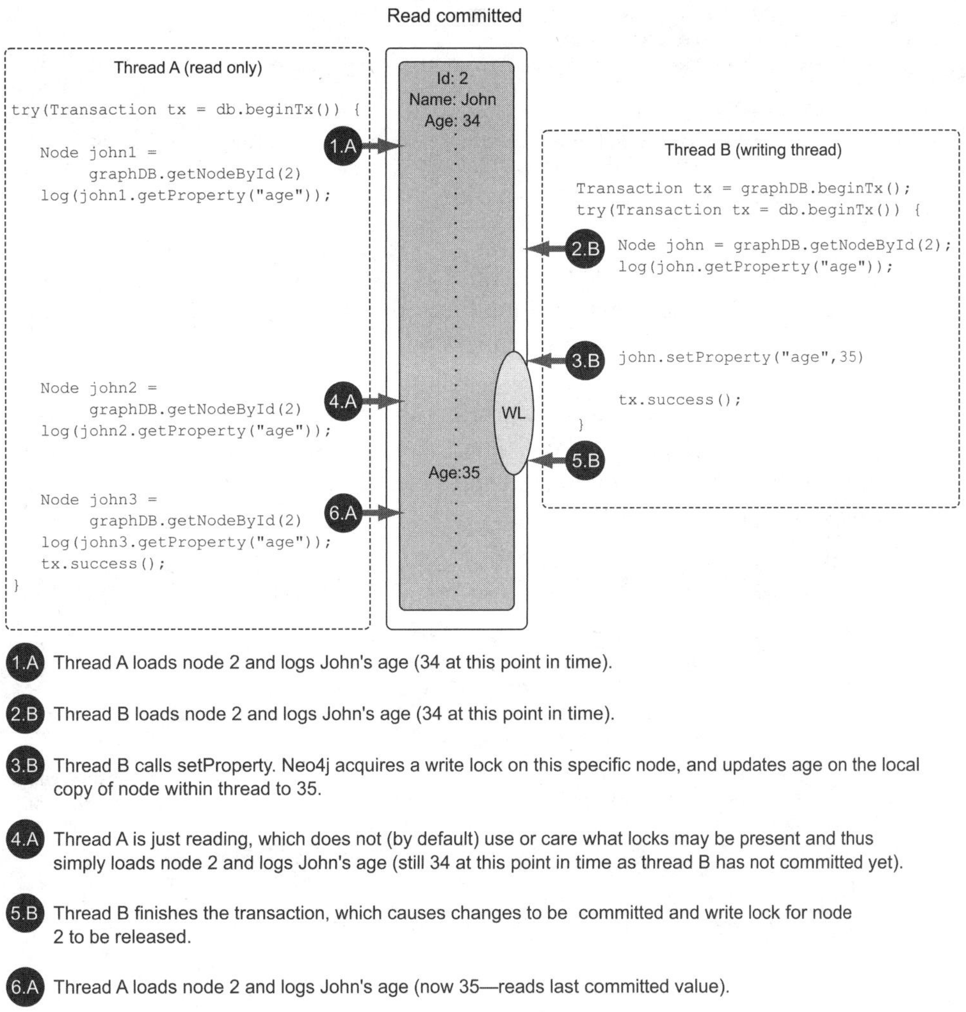
Read committed
Thread A (read only)
try(Transaction tx = db.beginTx()) {
Node john1 =
graphDB.getNodeById(2)
log(john1.getProperty("age"));
Node john2 =
graphDB.getNodeById(2)
log(john2.getProperty("age"));
Node john3 =
graphDB.getNodeById(2)
log(john3.getProperty("age"));
tx.success();
}
Id: 2
Name: John
Age: 34
Age:35
WL
Thread B (writing thread)
Transaction tx = graphDB.beginTx();
try(Transaction tx = db.beginTx()) {
Node john = graphDB.getNodeById(2);
log(john.getProperty("age"));
john.setProperty("age",35)
tx.success();
}
1.A
2.B
3.B
4.A
5.B
6.A
1.A Thread A loads node 2 and logs John's age (34 at this point in time).
2.B Thread B loads node 2 and logs John's age (34 at this point in time).
3.B Thread B calls setProperty. Neo4j acquires a write lock on this specific node, and updates age on the local copy of node within thread to 35.
4.A Thread A is just reading, which does not (by default) use or care what locks may be present and thus simply loads node 2 and logs John's age (still 34 at this point in time as thread B has not committed yet).
5.B Thread B finishes the transaction, which causes changes to be committed and write lock for node 2 to be released.
6.A Thread A loads node 2 and logs John's age (now 35—reads last committed value).

Figure 7.1 Default isolation level

7.2.2 Reading in a transaction and explicit read locks

As you saw previously, reading values from the graph returns the latest committed value (or the current modified state), which is equivalent to the Read Committed isolation level. The following listing shows some code that reads a property on the node twice—the user's age in this case—as part of a business operation, doing additional reading between the reads.

Listing 7.4 Reading the same thing twice without a transaction

```
try(Transaction tx = graphDatabaseService.beginTx()) {
    Node n = graphDatabaseService.index().
        forNodes("byName").get("name", "John").getSingle();
```

Reads the age from the user node

```
int age = (Integer) n.getProperty("age");
//do a different operation
int secondAge = (Integer) n.getProperty("age");

    if (age != secondAge) {
        throw new RuntimeException("surely some mistake");
    }
    tx.success();
}
```

Does further processing

Reads the age again, but with potential for an updated value

Depending on the time taken to do that other processing, there may be a significant window during which external modifications might occur. If your code mixes a high number of reads and writes, this might become an issue.

If you need a higher level of isolation to ensure that others can't change graph resources you're reading, Neo4j offers the potential for the explicit acquisition of read locks on graph resources. The following listing shows the same code, but this time with the addition of an explicit request to acquire a read lock on the node prior to any property reading.

Listing 7.5   Reading the same thing twice with increased isolation

```
try(Transaction tx = graphDatabaseService.beginTx()) {
    Node n = this.graphDatabaseService.index()
        .forNodes("byName").get("name", "John").getSingle();
    // acquire a read lock on n. The lock will be released automatically
    // when the transaction completes
    tx.acquireReadLock(n);
    int age = (Integer) n.getProperty("age");
    //do something else
    int secondAge = (Integer) n.getProperty("age");

    if (age != secondAge) {
        throw new RuntimeException("should now never happen");
    }
    tx.success();
}
```

Begins a transaction

Requests a read lock on the node

Figure 7.2 illustrates how using read locks can help you achieve better isolation.

There are two good reasons you should avoid acquiring locks systematically when reading. As previously mentioned, this will generate transactional state, and that uses memory. Second, the main trade-off here is write concurrency, because threads wishing to update any node or relationship where there is an explicit read lock will be blocked until the lock is released or the transaction finishes.

7.2.3   *Writing in a transaction and explicit write locks*

As discussed previously, the current transaction will acquire individual write locks automatically for you on each resource when you try to mutate it. These locks, however, do not necessarily all get acquired at the same time. There may well be cases where your business logic will need to modify a collection of nodes or relationships in

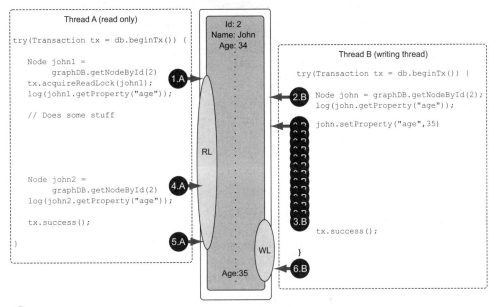

1.A Thread A loads node 2 and explicitly requests a read lock. Logs John's age (34 at this point in time).

2.B Thread B is just reading, which does not (by default) care what locks may be present and thus simply loads node 2 and logs John's age (still 34 at this point in time).

3.B Thread B calls setProperty. Neo4j detects that a read lock already exists for this node and blocks until it is able to acquire a write lock.

4.A Thread A gets a local copy of node info and logs John's age (still 34 at this point in time).

5.A Thread A finishes the transaction, which by default will release all of its locks, including the explicitly requested read lock.

3.B Thread B gets unblocked and can now acquire its own write lock against the node and update its local copy of John's age to 35.

6.B Thread B finishes, which commits the change and releases the write lock.

Figure 7.2   Explicit read locks

a consistent way, and you want to guarantee that no other transaction is able to modify them concurrently. If your application requires such a high transaction isolation level, which is very similar to the Serializable isolation level in RDMS, you can acquire write locks on a set of graph resources explicitly at the beginning of a transaction, before you mutate the data. As usual, those locks will be released automatically when the transaction completes.

In the following listing, you acquire write locks explicitly on two nodes to guarantee they're updated collectively in a serializable fashion.

Listing 7.6   Acquiring write locks explicitly

```
try (Transaction tx = graphDatabaseService.beginTx()) {
   Index<Node> nodeIndex = graphDatabaseService.index().forNodes("byName");
   Node n1 = nodeIndex.get("name", "John").getSingle();
   Node n2 = nodeIndex.get("name", "Bob").getSingle();
   tx.acquireWriteLock(n1);
   tx.acquireWriteLock(n2);
   n1.setProperty("age", 35);
   n2.setProperty("age", 37);
   tx.success();
}
```

Again, in doing this you need to be very careful and weigh consistency against performance and resource consumption.

7.2.4   *The danger of deadlocks*

Although the locking techniques discussed earlier allow you to manage isolation levels flexibly, locks inevitably introduce the possibility for deadlocks to happen. *Deadlocks* are a sort of "chicken or egg" situation that can happen if two or more transactions are competing to acquire the locks on the same graph resources. If transaction A tries to lock nodes 1 and 2 in that order, while transaction B tries to acquire the locks for the same nodes in the reverse order, then potentially each transaction could lock one node and wait indefinitely for the other node to be released, thus creating a deadlock.

Neo4j has a built-in mechanism to detect deadlocks when they happen, in which case a `DeadlockDetectedException` will be thrown and the transaction will be rolled back. Deadlock detection is only possible when locking is exclusively managed by Neo4j; that is, by relying on Neo4j's automatic default locking mechanism, or by only using the Neo4j API locking-related methods (`acquireReadLock` and `acquireWrite-Lock`) that we discussed previously. If any other locking mechanism is used, such as using the Java `synchronized` keyword, deadlocks won't be detected if they happen, and your application is likely to appear to hang.

To deal with deadlocks effectively, there are a number of simple things you can do. The first is to stick to the core API provided by Neo4j and not to use any external locking mechanism. This will ensure Neo4j's deadlock-detection mechanism will kick in, ensuring your application doesn't completely lock up, and that data will remain consistent. All operations in the core Neo4j API (unless otherwise specified) are thread-safe, so you should generally have no need for external synchronization. The other simple thing you can do is avoid deadlocks altogether by making sure that graph resources are consistently accessed in the same order.

We've now covered Neo4j transactions in detail. In the next sections, we'll focus on issues related to integrating Neo4j transactions with other transaction management systems.

7.3 *Integration with other transaction management systems*

The transaction-handling code we've looked at so far has exclusively used Neo4j's core API to initiate and complete transactions; it didn't make any assumptions about the nature of the environment that the code is executed from.

If you're building a typical enterprise application, though, it's likely that you'll need to integrate with an existing transaction manager, such as a JTA transaction manager provided by the application server. The `org.neo4j.kernel.impl.transaction` package contains a number of classes to support this use case.

Equally, if the application is built on top of the popular Spring Framework, you can benefit from Spring's declarative transaction support to make your code more robust. The following listing creates a Spring JTA transaction manager, wired into the Neo4j `TransactionManagerService` and `UserTransactionService`.

Listing 7.7 Configuring Spring transaction manager

```
<beans>
    <tx:annotation-driven transaction-manager="neo4jTransactionManager"/>

    <bean id="pretendService" class="org.neo4jia.tx.APretendService">
        <property name="graphDatabaseService" ref="graphDatabaseService"/>
    </bean>

    <bean id="graphDatabaseService"
class="org.neo4j.kernel.EmbeddedGraphDatabase" destroy-method="shutdown"
        scope="singleton">
        <constructor-arg value="target/spring-test"/>
    </bean>

    <bean id="neo4jTransactionManagerService"
class="org.neo4j.kernel.impl.transaction.SpringTransactionManager">
        <constructor-arg ref="graphDatabaseService" />
    </bean>

    <bean id="neo4jUserTransactionService"
class="org.neo4j.kernel.impl.transaction.UserTransactionImpl">
        <constructor-arg ref="graphDatabaseService" />
    </bean>

    <bean id="neo4jTransactionManager"
class="org.springframework.transaction.jta.JtaTransactionManager">
        <property name="transactionManager" ref="neo4jTransactionManagerService"
        />
        <property name="userTransaction" ref="neo4jUserTransactionService" />
    </bean>
</beans>
```

Annotations to the listing:
- Enables declarative transactions
- Configures the graph database service
- Configures Neo4j Transaction-ManagerService and User-Transaction-Service
- Configures the graph database service
- Configures a standard Spring JTA transaction manager and injects the Neo4j TransactionManagerService and UserTransactionService

This configuration gives the `APretendService` bean the ability to annotate its public methods with Spring's `@Transactional` annotation and therefore to avoid the need to manage transactions manually.

The next listing shows what `APretendService` looks like, including declarative transaction management using annotations.

```
public class APretendService {

    private GraphDatabaseService gds;

    @Transactional
    public Node createNodeViaAnnotatedMethod(String name, int age)  {
        Node node = gds.createNode();
        node.setProperty("name", name);
        node.setProperty("age", age);
        return node;
    }

    public void setGraphDatabaseService(GraphDatabaseService gds) {
        this.gds = gds;
    }
}
```

You've seen how you can integrate Neo4j with a typical Spring application. For a more object-oriented programming model, chapter 9 discusses Spring Data Neo4j, which provides a mapping solution between domain classes and Neo4j.

Next, let's look at how you can add custom logic around Neo4j transactions using transaction events.

7.4   *Transaction events*

Some databases implement triggers to enable custom code execution around database transactions. Neo4j has transaction event handlers to fulfill this functionality.

The `TransactionEventHandler` interface contains three methods, `beforeCommit`, `afterCommit`, and `afterRollback`, that when implemented and registered with the database will be invoked at these key points for each transaction. The `beforeCommit` method can optionally return an object that will be passed on to the other two methods if any context or state needs to be communicated.

The following listing shows the skeleton of a transaction event handler created from the `GraphDatabaseService` object.

```
graphDatabaseService.registerTransactionEventHandler(new
    TransactionEventHandler<Object>() {
    @Override
    public Object beforeCommit(TransactionData data) throws Exception {
        // do some work

        // no need to return state
        return null;
    }

    @Override
    public void afterCommit(TransactionData data, Object state) {
        // do some work
    }
```

```
@Override
public void afterRollback(TransactionData data, Object state) {
    // do some work
 }
});
```

The `TransactionData` objects will inform you about the changed graph resources within the transaction. Typical use cases for event handlers include auditing and integration with external systems. For example, you could publish an event to update a dashboard every time a new user is added to the system.

Be extra careful with the code that you run from a transaction event handler, though, as it will be running from the same thread as your transaction—slow-running code will have an impact on the performance of your system. Also, an exception thrown from an event handler will cause the transaction to fail.

Transactions and Neo4j server

This chapter has focused on demonstrating the use of programmatic transaction handling for an embedded Neo4j setup. Neo4j can also be run in server mode, where clients access the Neo4j server via a well-established HTTP REST-based API, and chapter 10 provides details about what's required to do this. It's important to understand the considerations and the way in which transactions are handled when running in server mode in order to be able to build robust, performant applications. This sidebar aims to highlight some of the key points relating to transactions that you should look out for when running in server mode, without going into explicit details. Please see section 10.4.3 for more information.

By default, every request made to the Neo4j server is done via a REST API call, and each call will occur within its own transaction. But making a lot of fine-grained REST calls will likely have a negative impact on the performance of your application. Besides the overhead added by creating a new transaction for each request, the multiple network calls alone could prove catastrophic for performance. In order to help address some of these issues, the following options for handling transaction scenarios in a server context should be considered:

- *Using the REST Cypher endpoint*—Provides the ability to execute a single Cypher statement, which may result in multiple nodes and/or relationships needing to be updated. All affected nodes/relationships will be updated as part of the single HTTP request.
- *Using the REST transactional endpoint*—Provides the ability to execute a series of Cypher statements within the scope of a transaction, but unlike the Cypher endpoint, over multiple HTTP requests.
- *Using the REST batch endpoint*—Provides the ability to define a job—a set of low-level REST API calls to be executed as a single transaction when sent to the batch REST endpoint.
- *Using server plugins or unmanaged extensions*—Provides the ability to define Java code that can be run within the Neo4j server itself as a result of a REST call, providing full programmatic control (including transaction handling).

7.5   *Summary*

Transactions can be a complicated topic, but hopefully you now understand how Neo4j allows you to take full advantage of ACID-based transactions to manage concurrent access to graph resources.

We've covered how transactions work in detail: the default transaction behavior is satisfactory for most common cases, but we've examined the implications of transactions trying to access the same graph resources at the same time and how higher isolation levels can be achieved by using read and write locks explicitly.

Enterprise applications are often built on top of a framework such as Spring, and we've covered how Neo4j transactions can be integrated with Spring's transaction management system, taking advantage of Spring's declarative approach.

Finally, we've covered transaction event handlers, which are useful for adding custom behavior around your transactions, like triggers in traditional RDBMSs do.

Now that you know how to use transactions, the next chapter will teach you more about traversal operations, so that you can query the data in more sophisticated ways.

Traversals in depth

This chapter covers

- How traversal ordering impacts performance and memory footprint
- Using expanders during traversal
- Controlling the number of visits to each node using the `uniqueness` property
- Improving graph query performance using bidirectional traversals

Writing efficient traversals is the key to successfully querying graph data. You learned the basic concepts of the Neo4j Traversal API in chapter 4. In this chapter we're going to dig a little deeper into the inner workings of the Traversal API so you can learn how to solve the most complex graph problems in an efficient manner.

8.1 Traversal ordering

Every time a traverser visits a node, it needs to make a decision about which relationship to follow and which node to visit next, repeating the process until the traversal completes. By selecting an optimal path through the graph, the traversal can complete more quickly and use less memory. There are two main ordering

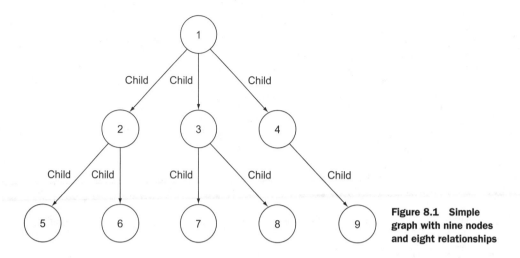

Figure 8.1 Simple graph with nine nodes and eight relationships

algorithms in graph theory, and they're used for most traversals in Neo4j: *depth-first* and *breadth-first* algorithms.

To see how traversal efficiency and performance can depend on the selected ordering, look at the graph in figure 8.1.

The graph in figure 8.1 has nine nodes. It represents a tree, which is a graph type where each two nodes are connected via a single path. In other words, a tree is a graph without any cycles. To make our illustration of traversal ordering simpler, we'll use the tree graph as an example. (For an example of a graph with cycles, and therefore not a tree, see figure 8.4.)

The root node of the graph is marked as 1. Nodes directly connected to the root node (branches) are marked 2, 3, and 4. The rest of the nodes (leaves) are two relationships away from the root node (nodes 5–9).

Let's look at the differences between walking this graph using the depth-first and breadth-first traversal orderings. Our goal is to walk the graph so that we visit each node in the graph exactly once.

8.1.1   *Depth-first*

Every time you visit a node, you need to decide which relationship to follow next, or which nodes to hop to next. Depth-first ordering says that you should first hop to the first child of the node you're currently on that hasn't been visited before. If all descendant nodes have already been visited, you should go backwards to the first node that has a child you haven't yet visited. Figure 8.2 illustrates the order of visits to each node using depth-first traversal.

You start the traversal at node 1. Node 1 has relationships to three other nodes (2, 3, and 4) and you're going to visit the first child node you haven't visited before—in this case, node 2. You can imagine the traverser as a little robot that jumps from node 1 to node 2 via relationship *a*.

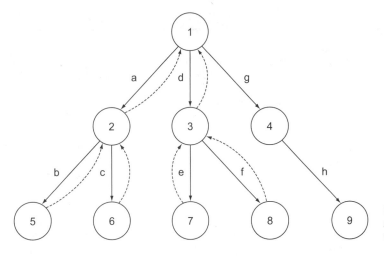

Figure 8.2 Walking the graph using depth-first ordering

Once you inspect node 2, you have to decide where to go next. Remember the depth-first rule: visit a child of the node that hasn't been visited before, if one is available. So you'll make the next hop from node 2 to node 5 (via relationship *b*). In only two hops, you've made it to the deepest point in the graph—from the root node (node 1) to node 5. This is why the depth-first algorithm is named that: you're traversing the graph so that you go as deep as you can, as soon as you can.

Now that you're on node 5, you should go to its child node, but node 5 is a leaf in the graph, so it doesn't have any child nodes to hop to. In that case, the depth-first algorithm has a rule that says to go backwards to the first node that has a descendant that hasn't been visited before. You return to node 2 and then apply the original rule. Node 2 has two descendants (nodes 5 and 6), and you've already visited node 5, so the next stop is node 6 (via relationship *c*).

Using the same rules, you'll end up walking the graph in the following order of nodes:

$$1 \to 2 \to 5 \to 6 \to 3 \to 7 \to 8 \to 4 \to 9$$

If you're looking at figure 8.2, you've hopped via relationships *a, b, c, d, e, f, g,* and *h* during the traversal, in that order.

It's interesting to realize that you visited node 4 next to last, although that node is very close to the root node, the starting point. You'll also notice that you visited the nodes in the left part of the graph (nodes 1, 2, 5, and 6) much sooner than the nodes in the right part of the graph (nodes 4, 8, and 9). This is a consequence of the depth-first traversal, and you should use it to your advantage when modeling a graph and designing the traversals. We'll discuss this again when we compare the depth-first and breadth-first orderings.

The question now is how we can make use of the depth-first algorithm in the Neo4j Traversal API. Let's do just that: implement the traversal we just described using the Neo4j Traversal API. You can see the solution in the following listing.

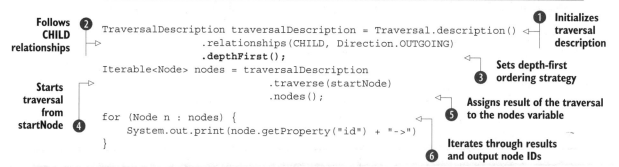

Listing 8.1   Walking the entire graph depth-first using the Neo4j Traversal API

First, you need to initialize a traversal description, just like you did when you used the Neo4j Traversal API in chapter 4 **1**. Then you configure the traversal to follow only outgoing relationships of type CHILD **2**. Next, you set the traversal ordering to depth-first. To do so, you use the dedicated method depthFirst() as part of the Traversal-Description builder **3**.

Once the description is complete, you start the traversal by specifying the starting node **4**, and return all nodes you visit during the traversal **5**. Remember, the return type of the traversal result is a lazy Java Iterable instance. Just specifying the starting node and calling nodes() on the traverser won't visit any nodes at that point. You need to start iterating through the results for the traverser to start moving through the graph, which is exactly what you do here **6**. During iteration, you can process the visited nodes as you wish, depending on your software requirements. In this example, you simply print the node property "id" to the console.

The resulting output will prove that you've indeed used depth-first algorithm rules when walking the graph:

```
1 -> 2 -> 5 -> 6 -> 3 -> 7 -> 8 -> 4 -> 9 ->
```

NOTE   Depth-first is the default branch-ordering strategy in Neo4j. If you don't specify the traversal ordering when building your traversal description, depth-first will be used.

Let's now take a look at the other built-in branch selector strategy: breadth-first.

8.1.2   *Breadth-first*

As its name suggests, the breadth-first algorithm tries to go as wide in the graph as possible, before visiting nodes more distant from the starting node. As part of the breadth-first algorithm, the traversal will first visit all siblings of the current node before moving on to their children. *Siblings* in this sense means nodes the same distance from the root node as the node you're currently visiting. Figure 8.3 shows the breadth-first traversal order for the same graph used earlier.

You start from root node 1, as before, and continue by visiting its first descendant, node 2 (via relationship *a*). Next, you visit the siblings of node 2, moving to nodes 3

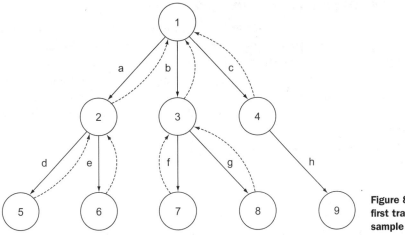

Figure 8.3 Breadth-first traversal of the sample graph

and then 4. Once you visit node 4, there are no more nodes the same distance from the root node to visit, so you move to the nodes on the next depth level, starting with the descendants of node 2, visiting nodes 5 and 6, in that order. Then you continue to nodes 7 and 8, and finally you visit the descendant of node 4 (node 9). The order of nodes you visited using the breadth-first algorithm is as follows:

$$1 \rightarrow 2 \rightarrow 3 \rightarrow 4 \rightarrow 5 \rightarrow 6 \rightarrow 7 \rightarrow 8 \rightarrow 9$$

In breadth-first traversal, you visit nodes closer to the root node earlier, leaving nodes further away from the root node for later.

Let's now update the traversal implementation to use the breadth-first strategy. The traversal description builder in the Neo4j Traversal API has a dedicated method to do just that, as the following listing illustrates.

Listing 8.2 Breadth-first traversal using the Neo4j Traversal API

```
TraversalDescription traversalDescription = Traversal.description()
                    .relationships(CHILD, Direction.OUTGOING)
                    .breadthFirst();
Iterable<Node> nodes = traversalDescription
                    .traverse(startNode)
                    .nodes();
for (Node n : nodes) {
    System.out.print(node.getProperty("id") + "->")
}
```

Initializes traversal description ⟶

Assigns result of the traversal to the nodes variable ⟶

Follows CHILD relationships ⟵

Sets breadth-first ordering strategy ❶ ⟵

Starts traversal from startNode ⟵

Iterates through results and processes them

As you can see, the code is very similar. The only difference is that you use a different method to specify the traversal ordering when building a traversal description ❶. The console output will match the order established earlier in this section:

```
1 -> 2 -> 3 -> 4 -> 5 -> 6 -> 7 -> 8 -> 9 ->
```

8.1.3   *Comparing depth-first and breadth-first ordering*

As you've seen in the last two sections, a depth-first traversal will favor searches with the solution in the left part of the graph. A breadth-first traversal will be faster when the result is closer to the starting node than if it's a longer distance from the starting node. These two characteristics are very important when designing the graph and the traversal you need to execute.

Take node 4 in figure 8.1, as an example. If you start to traverse the graph from root node 1 using depth-first ordering, the traversal will need to walk almost the entire graph before node 4 is found, because it's visited next to last. If you do the same using breadth-first ordering, node 4 will be visited fourth from the start, with half as many nodes visited on its path. As traversal speed is directly proportional to the number of hops (or nodes visited on the path), you could find the result in half the time if you used breadth-first ordering rather than depth-first ordering.

If you're looking for node 5, the depth-first algorithm would yield the result in three hops, and the breadth-first algorithm would need five.

The larger the graph gets, the bigger the impact of traversal ordering on traversal performance. To illustrate, create a graph where each node has exactly three descendants. Create a starting node and connect it with three child nodes. Then take each of the three child nodes and add three descendants to each of them. Then continue like that up to depth level 12. The resulting graph will have 797,161 nodes and 797,160 relationships.

Now run a traversal to find a particular node at a specific depth level. As a measure of performance, we'll use the number of nodes visited until the solution is found.

> **NOTE**   The number of hops and nodes visited is directly related to the time needed to perform the traversal. Using actual times to measure performance would make the results dependent on available hardware resources as well as the state of the caches, which we're trying to avoid in this simple experiment. Neo4j can visit between tens of thousands and millions of nodes per second, depending on the hardware, caches, and traversal complexity.

Table 8.1 illustrates the results of the experiment.

Table 8.1   The performance of a traversal depending on the location of node searched for and the traversal algorithm used

Depth level	Node location	Depth-first	Breadth-first
3	First on left side	3	13
3	Last on right side	767,637	39
6	First on left side	6	364
6	Last on right side	796,068	1,092
9	First on left side	9	9,841

Table 8.1 **The performance of a traversal depending on the location of node searched for and the traversal algorithm used**

Depth level	Node location	Depth-first	Breadth-first
9	Last on right side	797,121	29,523
12	First on left side	12	265,720
12	Last on right side	797,160	797,160

As you can see from the table, when the result is close to the starting node, breadth-first ordering will generally yield better performance. But further away from the starting node, breadth-first ordering is always slow, and depth-first ordering can be extremely efficient, depending on whether the resulting node is located in the left or right part of the graph.

In the worst-case scenario, where the entire graph needs to be traversed (when the resulting node is in the bottom-right corner of the graph), both depth-first and breadth-first ordering need to visit all nodes. But due to the larger memory footprint of breadth-first traversals, it's better to use depth-first ordering in this case.

In addition to speed, another aspect you need to consider when deciding on the traversal ordering is memory consumption of the traversals. Imagine once again that the traverser is like a little robot that jumps from node to node via relationships. This robot will have to remember some state about which node it came from, and which nodes it has yet to visit. The larger the graph, the more memory is needed to store that state. But the selected traversal ordering affects the memory it needs. Let's see how.

When using depth-first ordering, you try to go deep into the graph as soon as you can. As soon as you come to the bottom of the graph (visit a node that has no descendants that have not been visited before), you can completely forget about that branch of the graph—from the traversal perspective, it's considered complete. In the Neo4j Java world, that means you can dereference that path from memory and leave it for garbage collection cleanup. Because some of these paths will be visited early during the traversal, you can start deallocating memory as soon as you start traversing.

Breadth-first traversal tries to go as wide as it can in the graph, before starting with the nodes on the next depth level. As a result, during traversal you need to remember all the nodes you've visited and which descendants you haven't yet visited. The larger and more complex the graph, the more nodes you have to remember, resulting in a larger memory footprint.

In general, the more relationships there are per node, the more memory is needed for breadth-first traversal.

How do you choose between depth-first and breadth-first ordering? You have to realize that you, as an application architect and developer, have one big advantage: you know and understand the domain model you operate on. Based on your domain insight, you can determine which ordering to use for each of your traversals (and it can vary from case to case on the same graph).

If the solution is close to the starting node, breadth-first ordering would probably be better. But if the graph is very dense (that is, has a lot of relationships per node), breadth-first ordering may use too much memory to be practical.

An understanding of traversal ordering and insight into your problem domain will give you a good starting point, but to determine the best traversal overall, you'll need to experiment with different options. If Neo4j's built-in ordering options don't match your requirements, you can implement your own ordering by using the org.neo4j .graphdb.traversal.BranchSelector interface, which is part of the Neo4j Traversal API. Custom traversal implementations are out of scope for this book, but you can find useful information by looking at the Neo4j Manual (http://docs.neo4j.org/) and visiting the Neo4j Google Groups (https://groups.google.com/forum/#!forum/neo4j).

Let's look at the Neo4j mechanisms that can help you decide how to follow relationships from the current node during traversal: path expanders.

8.2   *Expanding relationships*

The expander is the component of the Neo4j Traversal API that's responsible for deciding which relationships should be followed from any node visited during the traversal. In addition to selecting relationship types and directions, the expander is responsible for the order in which relationships are followed.

Neo4j provides a number of expander implementations out of the box. The default implementation, which is the one most commonly used, is StandardExpander.

8.2.1   *StandardExpander*

The standard expander is encapsulated in the StandardExpander class, and it provides a collection of built-in expanders that allow you to specify the relationships you want to follow, including their direction. The relationships will be expanded in the order they were added to the graph.

> **NOTE** StandardExpander is the default implementation used by the Neo4j Traversal API.

To illustrate the use of StandardExpander, consider the following example: in a social network, people who work with each other are connected via a WORKS_WITH relationship, and people who are close friends are connected via an IS_FRIEND_OF relationship. In addition, users in the network can link to the films they liked (a LIKES relationship). Figure 8.4 shows the sample graph we'll be using.

What we want to do now is find all movies that John's direct contacts (both friends and work colleagues) like. Looking at figure 8.4, you'd expect the result to contain the movies *Fargo* and *Alien*. *Top Gun* shouldn't be part of the result as it's liked by John himself. *Godfather* and *Great Dictator* shouldn't be part of the result because only John's friends' friends like them (and you only want the movies liked by John's direct contacts).

The following listing illustrates the traversal implementation.

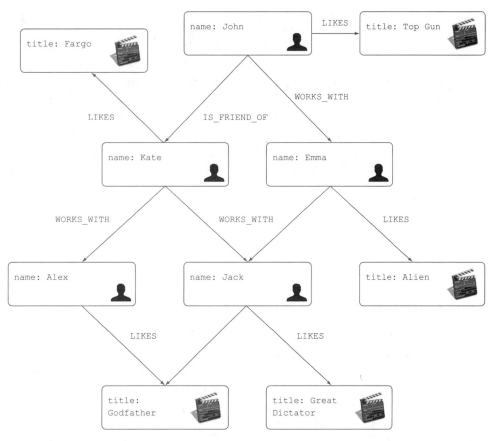

Figure 8.4 A social network of users and movies they like

Listing 8.3 Finding all movies John's friends and colleagues like

```
TraversalDescription traversal = Traversal.description()
        .expand((PathExpander)StandardExpander.DEFAULT
            .add(WORKS_WITH)
            .add(IS_FRIEND_OF)
            .add(LIKES))
    .evaluator(Evaluators.atDepth(2))
    .evaluator(new Evaluator() {
        @Override
        public Evaluation evaluate(Path path) {
            if (path.endNode().hasProperty("title")) {
                return Evaluation.INCLUDE_AND_CONTINUE;
            }
            return Evaluation.EXCLUDE_AND_CONTINUE;
        }
    });
```

Uses factory method to access instances of Standard-Expander ❶

❷ Adds relationship types to expand

❸ Only considers nodes at depth 2 for end result; end traversal after depth 2

Includes only movies in the result ❹

```
Iterable<Node> nodes = traversal.traverse(john).nodes();
for (Node n : nodes) {
    System.out.println(n.getProperty("title"));
}
```
❺ **Runs traversal and print movie title to console**

You use the `TraversalDescription.expand(...)` method to set the expander you want to use for the traversal ❶. You instantiate `StandardExpander` using the static factory method, then add the relationships you'd like to follow ❷. Because you're looking at movies that John's direct contacts have seen, you want to include only nodes at depth 2 and stop the traversal after that ❸. To make sure you're only returning movie nodes in the result (and not user nodes, for example), you add another evaluator to check the `title` property on the nodes, because only movie nodes have this property ❹. Finally, you execute the traversal starting from the node representing John, and print the movie titles to the console ❺.

Once the query is executed, the expected result is printed to the console:

```
Fargo
Alien
```

In the code, you passed the expander built into the `StandardExpander` class to the `TraversalDescription.expand(...)` method to select which relationships to follow from each node. But because `StandardExpander` is the default expander used by the `TraversalDescription` builder, you can conveniently use its shortcut methods to select which relationships to expand, resulting in code that's much clearer and more concise. The following snippet shows how you can update the traversal from listing 8.3 to use this syntax. A portion of the code from listing 8.3 has been omitted for clarity:

```
TraversalDescription traversal = Traversal.description()
                .relationships(WORKS_WITH)
                .relationships(IS_FRIEND_OF)
                .relationships(LIKES)
        . . .
```
Uses the Traversal-Description.relationships(...) method to add required relationships ❶

In this snippet, you use the `TraversalDescription.relationships(...)` method to add the relationship types you want to expand ❶. Because `StandardExpander` is used by default, this will result in exactly the same code being executed under the hood as for the code in listing 8.3, with slightly more concise syntax.

The code in listing 8.3 looks much more like the code you used for traversals earlier in the book, but you now know that behind it is the `StandardExpander` in action. Using the `TraversalDescription.expand(...)` method, you can have control over which expander is used for any traversal, which is the flexibility we'll be taking advantage of in the following sections.

In the next two sections, you're going to learn how to use nondefault expander implementations in your traversals. First, let's start with ordered relationship expanders.

8.2.2 *Ordering relationships for expansion*

As you've seen, `StandardExpander` has a limitation—the order of the relationships to be expanded is fixed, and it uses the order in which the relationships were created. In most cases this is a reasonable limitation, as most traversals treat each relationship type the same way. But in some scenarios it would be preferable to expand relationships in a particular order. Let's use the same graph as in the previous section (figure 8.4) to demonstrate the use case for ordering relationships.

Just as in the previous section, we'll find all movies that any of John's direct contacts liked (including both friends and work colleagues). This time, we'll prefer the movies liked by John's close friends, putting them at the top of the result list. You'd expect the same traversal results as before, but in a specific order (different than before):

1 *Alien* (as recommended by John's friend Emma)
2 *Fargo* (as recommended by Kate, who is John's work colleague)

You can easily order relationships by type prior to expansion by using `OrderedByType-Expander` instead of the default `StandardExpander`, as the next listing shows.

Listing 8.4 Expanding relationships in the order of relationship types

```
PathExpander expander =
        new OrderedByTypeExpander()            Instantiates OrderedBy-
                .add(IS_FRIEND_OF)          ❶ TypeExpander
                .add(WORKS_WITH)
                .add(LIKES);                   Adds relationships to follow,
        TraversalDescription traversal =    ❷ in the required order
                Traversal.description()
                .expand(expander)              Uses configured
                .evaluator(Evaluators.atDepth(2))  OrderedByTypeExpander
                .evaluator(new Evaluator() {    ❸ for the traversal
        @Override
        public Evaluation evaluate(Path path) {
            if(path.endNode().hasProperty("title")){
                return Evaluation.INCLUDE_AND_CONTINUE;
            }
            return Evaluation.EXCLUDE_AND_CONTINUE;
        }
    });
Iterable nodes = traversal.traverse(john).nodes();
for(Node n: nodes){
    System.out.println(n.getProperty("title"));
}
```

You instantiate the new expander using its default constructor ❶; then you add the relationship type to follow ❷. The specified relationship types are guaranteed to be expanded in the same order as they're added to the expander, for every visited node. Because you want the `IS_FRIEND_OF` relationships to always be traversed first, you add it first in your code.

To use the newly created expander, you specify it using the `TraversalDescription` `.expand(...)` method ❸. The rest of the code is the same as before.

When you execute this traversal, the result will be exactly as expected:

```
Alien
Fargo
```

`OrderedByTypeExpander` gives you more power when you're designing traversals. In some cases, however, none of Neo4j's built-in traversals provides the functionality that the problem requires. In that case, you can implement your own custom expanders using the Neo4j Traversal API; that's what we're going to show you in the next section.

8.2.3   *Custom expanders*

Neo4j has an extension point readily available for when you need to build a custom expander that meets your requirements. The extension API is defined with the `Path-Expander` interface, which is part of the Neo4j kernel library.

The `PathExpander` interface defines two methods you need to implement:

- *Iterable<Relationship> expand(Path path, BranchState<STATE> state);*—This method contains the logic that determines which relationships the traverser should follow (and in which order) from the current node of the traversal. The argument `path` contains the full path (including nodes and relationships) that was traversed up to the current point in the graph. You can use all available methods of the `path` object as usual. For example,

  - `Path.endNode()` gets the node you're currently visiting.
  - `Path.startNode()` gets the node from which the traversal started.
  - `Path.lastRelationship()` retrieves the last relationships traversed before you reached the current point in the graph.

  In addition to the traversal path, you have access to another method argument, `BranchState`, which represents the state associated with the current branch of the traversal. It's optional, and typically expanders won't use it.

- *PathExpander<STATE> reverse();*—This method returns the expander with the same expanding logic, but with reversed direction, and it's typically used in bidirectional traversals (which we'll discuss later in this chapter). Think of the `reverse` method as the expander you'd need to use to get from the current node back to the starting node of the traversal.

Let's now implement a sample custom expander. Based on the same social network graph used earlier in this section (see figure 8.4), we'll design a traversal that will again find all movies that John's direct contacts like. But instead of using the standard Neo4j Traversal API components, including custom evaluators, we'll use the custom `PathExpander` implementation.

The main challenge with this query is to avoid any movies John likes, and also any movies liked by John's friends' friends. To do this, we'll use a custom expander with the following characteristics:

- Follow only the IS_FRIEND_OF and WORKS_WITH relationships from the start node (representing John).
- For all nodes visited at depth 1 (representing John's friends and work colleagues), follow only the LIKES relationships.

Using built-in TraversalDescription methods and StandardExpander, it's not possible to build a traversal with these characteristics. But you can implement a custom PathExpander that does just that. The following listing shows the implementation of such an expander.

Listing 8.5 Expanding relationships based on distance from the starting node

```
public class DepthAwareExpander implements PathExpander{          ← Implements
                                                                      PathExpander
    private final Map<Integer, List<RelationshipType>>                interface ❶
                           relationshipToDepthMapping;

    public DepthAwareExpander(Map<Integer, List<RelationshipType>>
                           relationshipToDepthMapping) {              ❸ Implements
        this.relationshipToDepthMapping = relationshipToDepthMapping;    expansion
    }                                                                    logic in
                                                                         expand(...)
    @Override                                                            method
    public Iterable<Relationship> expand(Path path, BranchState state) { ←

        int depth = path.length();                         ← Finds current
        List<RelationshipType> relationshipTypes =         ❹ depth of traversal
               relationshipToDepthMapping.get(depth);
        return path.endNode()                                       ←
                .getRelationships(
                relationshipTypes.toArray(new RelationshipType[0])
                );
    }                                            Expands all relationships of
                                             configured types of current node ❻
    @Override
    public PathExpander reverse() {
        //omitted for clarity
    }
```

❷ Uses java.util.Map object to store mappings between traversal depth and relationship types to follow

❺ Finds relationships to follow for current depth (from mappings)

The DepthAwareExpander implements the PathExpander interface from the Neo4j kernel API ❶. To map the distance from the starting node (or depth) to the relationship types, you use a simple java.util.Map ❷.

The key method to implement is expand(...), which expands the relationships you should follow from the node you're currently visiting ❸. The depth of the currently visited node can be found with the Path.length() method ❹. Next, you look up the relationships for the given depth from the configured mappings ❺. Finally, you return the expanded relationships of specified types from the current node ❻. The current node is located using the Path.endNode() method.

The next step is to use the custom expander in the actual traversal. The following listing shows a traversal that prints query results to the console (titles of all movies John's direct friends like).

Listing 8.6   Finding all movies John's friends like using a custom expander

```
HashMap<Integer, List<RelationshipType>> mappings =
                new HashMap<Integer, List<RelationshipType>>();
mappings.put(0, Arrays.asList(
                new RelationshipType[]{IS_FRIEND_OF, WORKS_WITH}
                ));
mappings.put(1, Arrays.asList(                       ❶ Configures depth/
                new RelationshipType[]{LIKES}));        relationships mappings

TraversalDescription traversal =
            Traversal.description()                  ❷ Uses DepthAwareExpander
            .expand(new DepthAwareExpander(mappings))  as traversal expander
            .evaluator(Evaluators.atDepth(2)
);                                                   ❸ Returns only
Iterable<Node> nodes = traversal.traverse(john).nodes();   nodes at depth 2
for(Node n: nodes){
    System.out.println(n.getProperty("title"));      Starts traversal from
}                                                     John, and prints
                                                    ❹ results to console
```

The first step is to configure which relationships to follow at each depth ❶. The mappings are to follow the IS_FRIEND_OF and WORKS_WITH relationships directly from the starting node (depth 0) and the LIKES relationships from nodes at depth 1. The key point in the traversal implementation is to configure the traversal description to use the custom expander ❷. As you're only interested in the nodes up to depth 2, you use the atDepth evaluator to stop the traversal at the specified depth ❸. Finally, you start the traversal from the node representing John and iterate through the results in the usual manner ❹.

When you execute the traversal, the console output will display the expected movies, *Alien* and *Fargo*, which are liked by John's direct contacts. The full demo, including all the code in this section, is available as part of this book's sample code.

The next advanced Neo4j Traversal API topic we'll cover is uniqueness, so read on to learn how to control how many times the traverser can visit any node or relationship.

8.3   *Managing uniqueness*

The uniqueness aspect of the traversal determines how many times you can visit a node over the duration of the traversal. There are a few different uniqueness settings in the Neo4j Traversal API that you can apply to your traversals, and in this section we're going to demonstrate their uses and behavior. All available uniqueness options are accessible as constants in the Uniqueness class in the Neo4j Java library.

8.3.1   *NODE_GLOBAL uniqueness*

The most typical uniqueness setting in Neo4j traversals is NODE_GLOBAL. It basically means that each node can be visited once and only once during the traversal.

> **NOTE**   NODE_GLOBAL is the default traversal setting, so if you don't specify the uniqueness, this setting will be applied to your traversals.

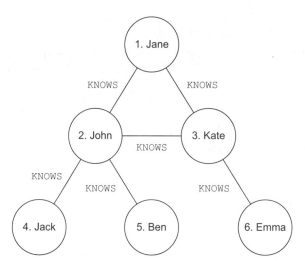

Figure 8.5 A simple social network graph

NODE_GLOBAL is a common requirement for traversals, so let's illustrate it with an example. Let's look at a simple social network graph, with six nodes representing users, and KNOWS relationships between users who know each other. Figure 8.5 illustrates this.

Let's implement a traversal to find the solution to the following problem: who of user 1's (Jane's) direct connections can introduce her to user 5 (Ben)?

The following listing shows the implementation of the required traversal using the NODE_GLOBAL uniqueness.

Listing 8.7 Finding Jane's direct connections who can introduce her to Ben

```
TraversalDescription description =
    Traversal.description()                                    ❶ Creates traversal by
            .relationships(KNOWS)                                 following KNOWS
            .evaluator(new Evaluator() {                          relationships
                @Override
                public Evaluation evaluate(Path path) {
                    Node currentNode = path.endNode();
                    if (currentNode.getId() == ben.getId()) {   ❷ Stops traversal
                        return Evaluation.EXCLUDE_AND_PRUNE;        when target node
                    }                                              (Ben) is reached
                    Path singlePath = GraphAlgoFactory
                        .shortestPath(
                        Traversal.expanderForTypes(KNOWS), 1)    ❹ If direct
                        .findSinglePath(currentNode, ben);          path exists,
                    if (singlePath != null) {                       includes
                        //direct link exists                        the node in
                        return Evaluation.INCLUDE_AND_CONTINUE;     the results
                    } else {
                        return Evaluation.EXCLUDE_AND_CONTINUE;
                    }
                }
            })
```

❸ Finds direct path between current node and target node (Ben)

❺ If direct path doesn't exist, skips the node and continues

```
                              .uniqueness(Uniqueness.NODE_GLOBAL);
              Iterable<Node> nodes = description.traverse(jane).nodes();
```

Sets uniqueness to
6 NODE_GLOBAL

Starts traversal from jane node
and returns all nodes 7

You create the traversal in the usual manner, and configure it to follow the KNOWS relationships in any direction **1**. You then implement the custom evaluator to determine whether or not each visited node should be included in the results. The first step in the evaluator is to stop the traversal if the target node (Ben, in this case) is reached **2**—there is no point in checking who can introduce Jane to Ben after she meets him! Next, you try to find a direct path between the current node and the target node representing Ben **3**. You're using Neo4j's built-in graph algorithm to calculate the direct path (using the GraphAlgoFactory class). If a direct path exists, that means you found a node that can introduce Jane to Ben, so you include the current node in the result **4**. If there's no direct link, skip the node and continue with the traversal **5**.

The main reason for this experiment is to demonstrate uniqueness, so you set it to the required NODE_GLOBAL setting using the uniqueness() method of the traversal description builder **6**. Finally, start the traversal from the node representing Jane and return all collected nodes **7**.

If you run the traversal and output the result to the console, you'll see a single result:

```
John
```

You can confirm, by looking at the graph in figure 8.5, that John is the only person in Jane's network who can introduce her to Ben.

So far, so good. Let's expand this experiment to the NODE_PATH uniqueness setting.

8.3.2 *NODE_PATH uniqueness*

The NODE_PATH uniqueness setting specifies that no path from the starting node to the current node can be traversed twice. Multiple visits to the same node are allowed, but only if they belong to different paths.

Let's update the code in listing 8.7 by changing the uniqueness for the traversal to NODE_PATH, and, keeping all other traversal settings exactly the same, run the query again. The code will look very similar, as the following listing shows. A portion of the code has been omitted for clarity.

Listing 8.8 Making connections using NODE_PATH uniqueness

```
TraversalDescription description =
            Traversal
            .description()
            .relationships(KNOWS)
            .evaluator(new Evaluator() {
                    @Override
                    public Evaluation evaluate(Path path) {
                        //… omitted for clarity
                })
```

```
                .uniqueness(Uniqueness.NODE_PATH);
Iterable<Node> nodes = description.traverse(jane).nodes();
...
```

❶ Uses **NODE_PATH** uniqueness

The only difference in the code is the different constant used to configure the uniqueness: NODE_PATH ❶.

If you run this query, the output will look like this:

```
John
John
```

John is printed twice—you have two entries in your result, although both represent the same node. Why did this happen? Take a careful look at the graph in figure 8.5. Jane is indeed connected to Ben via John. But there is another path that connects Jane and Ben—one via Kate and John! These are different paths in the graph, and because you're using NODE_PATH uniqueness, both represent valid results.

Previously, you only had one result because both paths (Jane–John–Ben and Jane–Kate–John–Ben) go via the john node, and since you used NODE_GLOBAL uniqueness, the second path was never realized.

To illustrate this further, let's change the traversal query slightly, and find what paths Jane has to Ben via her direct contacts.

To answer this, you must understand that you're not only interested in the users who know Ben, but rather in all nodes on paths between Jane and Ben. All you have to do is change the result of your traversal, as the next snippet shows:

```
TraversalDescription description = Traversal.description()
            .relationships(KNOWS)
            .evaluator(new Evaluator() {
                @Override
                public Evaluation evaluate(Path path) {
                    ...
                }
            })
            .uniqueness(Uniqueness.NODE_PATH);
Iterator<Path> paths = description.traverse(jane).iterator();
```

❶ Uses **NODE_PATH** uniqueness as before

❷ Returns all paths from traversal

The traversal description stays exactly the same as before, including NODE_PATH uniqueness ❶. The only change is that you're returning paths instead of nodes from the traversal ❷.

The console output of this code would look like this:

```
(Jane)--[KNOWS,0]-->(John)
(Jane)--[KNOWS,1]-->(Kate)<--[KNOWS,4]--(John)
```

This time it's clear why there were two john nodes as results previously—they're parts of different paths, and these results illustrate that. Based on these results, Jane has two options:

- She can contact John, who knows Ben, directly.
- She can contact Kate, who can contact John. This could be a valid alternative if Jane knows John only slightly, whereas Kate is her best friend and works with John!

NODE_GLOBAL and NODE_PATH are the most typical uniqueness types used, but Neo4j offers other uniqueness types that can be useful in some situations. We'll briefly introduce other uniqueness types in the next section.

8.3.3   *Other uniqueness types*

NODE_GLOBAL and NODE_PATH are probably the two most common uniqueness types for traversals. But for completeness, the Neo4j Traversal API includes six other types.

RELATIONSHIP_GLOBAL uniqueness states that each relationship in the graph can be visited only once. If there are multiple relationships between nodes in a graph, each node can be visited as many times as there are relationships that connect them.

RELATIONSHIP_PATH uniqueness is similar to NODE_PATH uniqueness in that relationships can be visited multiple times as long as the combination of relationships between the starting node and the current node is unique. Nodes can be visited multiple times with this uniqueness setting as well.

When either NODE_GLOBAL or RELATIONSHIP_GLOBAL is set, the traversal can be memory-hungry, especially in very connected, large graphs. Each node (in the case of NODE_GLOBAL) or relationship (in the case of RELATIONSHIP_GLOBAL) must be remembered for uniqueness constraint reasons. This is where the NODE_RECENT and RELATIONSHIP_RECENT settings come into play. When using these settings, the uniqueness constraint is loosened slightly.

With NODE_RECENT, there's a cap to the number of visited nodes that are remembered. The rule is the same as for NODE_GLOBAL—a node can be visited only once—but only the collection of recently visited nodes are remembered for comparison. The number of recent nodes to be remembered can be passed as the second argument to the uniqueness method, as in the following snippet:

```
TraversalDescription description = Traversal.description()
        .uniqueness(Uniqueness.NODE_RECENT, 1000)
```

With RELATIONSHIP_RECENT, the same rule as RELATIONSHIP_GLOBAL applies, so relationships can be visited only once. But during the traversal, only a specified number of relationships are remembered for comparison. The number of recent relationships that are remembered can be configured using the second argument to the uniqueness method, as in the following snippet:

```
TraversalDescription description = Traversal.description()
        .uniqueness(Uniqueness.RELATIONSHIP_RECENT, 1000)
```

Since Neo4j version 1.8, the Traversal API has included two more settings:

- *NODE_LEVEL*—Guarantees that nodes on the same level (nodes that have the same distance from the starting node) are only visited once during traversal
- *RELATIONSHIP_LEVEL*—Guarantees that relationships on the same level (from nodes that have the same distance from the starting node) are visited only once during traversal

In the next section we're going to look at bidirectional traversals, which allow you to significantly increase the performance of one type of traversal.

8.4 *Bidirectional traversals*

In all the traversals you've tried so far, you walked the graph from the single selected starting node until you found the solution, or until you walked the entire graph. You haven't had multiple starting points from which to start traversing the graph. This was a limitation of the Neo4j Traversal API until Neo4j version 1.8, which introduced the concept of bidirectional traversals.

Let's consider a typical social network graph with thousands of users, similar to the graph in figure 8.5. Users who know each other are connected via a KNOWS relationship. One of the typical traversal queries in such a graph would be "Are the selected two users (user 1 and user 2) in the same network?" (In other words, are the selected users connected, and, if so, how?)

You can solve this problem by using the standard Traversal API: starting from user 1, follow the KNOWS relationships; for each node you visit, check if that node is user 2. If it is, you found the connection; if it isn't, you continue further, until you exhaust the entire graph. This is a perfectly valid solution, but if the graph is very large and densely connected, finding the solution can be quite time-consuming.

What if you could start the traversal from user 1 in the direction of user 2, and at the same time start another traversal from user 2 in the opposite direction? When the two traversals meet (called the *collision point*), you'll have found the connection, and you can determine the full path between the users. This is exactly what bidirectional traversal allows you to do. Figure 8.6 illustrates bidirectional traversal in action.

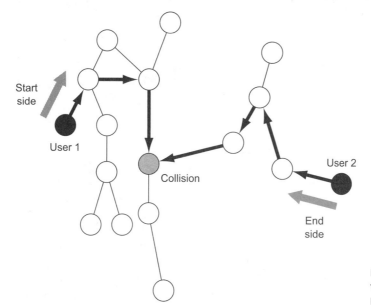

Figure 8.6 Bidirectional traversal used to find the path between two nodes

Bidirectional traversal involves additional Traversal API components, which we haven't seen before:

- *Start-side traversal*—A traversal definition for the start (outgoing or normal) side of the bidirectional traversal. The traversal description is created using the standard one-direction Traversal API used throughout this book.
- *End-side traversal*—A traversal definition for the end (incoming) side of the bidirectional traversal.
- *Collision evaluator*—Each time the start-side and end-side traversals collide, you have a potential solution of the traversal. The collision evaluator allows you to determine if the solution should be included in the traversal end result.
- *Side selector*—This component determines how quickly you should move the traverser on each side. The alternating side selector is the most commonly used; it alternates between moving the start-side and end-side traversals one step at a time.

The following listing shows the implementation of a bidirectional traverser using the Neo4j Traversal API.

Listing 8.9 Bidirectional traversal that finds paths between two users in a social network

```
BidirectionalTraversalDescription description =           ❶ Initializes Bidirectional-
    Traversal.bidirectionalTraversal()                       TraversalDescription
            .startSide(
            Traversal.description().relationships(KNOWS)     Sets traversal
                    .uniqueness(Uniqueness.NODE_PATH)         description for
            )                                                 outgoing direction
            .endSide(                                         of traversal,
            Traversal.description().relationships(KNOWS)    ❷ start side
                    .uniqueness(Uniqueness.NODE_PATH)
            )
            .collisionEvaluator(new Evaluator() {           Sets collision
                @Override                                    evaluator that
                public Evaluation evaluate(Path path) {      includes all
                    return Evaluation.INCLUDE_AND_CONTINUE; ❹ collisions found
                }
            })                                               Starts
            .sideSelector(SideSelectorPolicies.ALTERNATING, 100); bidirectional
Traverser traverser = description.traverse(user1, user2);    traversal by
Iterator<Path> iterator = traverser.iterator();            Iterates  specifying
while (iterator.hasNext()) {                                through   starting and
    System.out.println(iterator.next());                   results in the ending
}                                                           usual way ❻ nodes
```

Sets traversal description for incoming direction of traversal, end side ❸

Sets side selector that alternates between traversal directions ❺

Iterates through results in the usual way ❼

To initiate the bidirectional traversal description, you use the static helper method `Traversal.bidirectionalTraversal()`, which is similar to the regular traversal initialization ❶. Next, you set the traversal description for the outgoing direction ❷. Use the standard one-directional Traversal API to create the `BidirectionalTraversal-Description` and follow the KNOWS relationships with NODE_PATH uniqueness.

Next you repeat the same process for the incoming direction of the bidirectional traversal, using the same traversal description ❸, but note that there's nothing stopping you from using a different traversal in the incoming direction (for example, by following different relationships).

The next step is to configure the collision evaluator ❹. The collision evaluator is the regular `Evaluator` implementation, which is used to determine what should happen when incoming and outgoing traversals collide. You want to return all such collisions, so your evaluator simply returns `Evaluation.INCLUDE_AND_CONTINUE`.

The last step in building the `BidirectionalTraversalDecription` is setting the side selector ❺, responsible for determining how traversals from both sides progress. You provide the built-in `ALTERNATING` side selector, which, as its name states, alternates between traversal directions (one step in one direction, and one step in the opposite direction).

With that, your bidirectional traversal is ready, so you can kick it off by calling the `traverse` method and specifying the starting and ending nodes ❻. As usual, you iterate through the results until you exhaust the traversal ❼.

What benefit do you get from using bidirectional traversal? As we mentioned before, doing a standard, one-direction traversal on a large graph can have less-than-optimal performance. By using a bidirectional traversal in such scenarios, you effectively employ two traversals to walk the graph, splitting the size of the problem in half. With typical one-directional traversal, the number of relationships traversed increases exponentially with the depth of the traversal. When using bidirectional traversal, each side of the traversal will have to visit half of the graph depth, resulting in fewer node–relationship–node hops to perform, in turn resulting in much better performance.

> **NOTE** Built-in graph algorithms available in Neo4j, such as `shortestPath` or `a*` graph searches (from the `GraphAlgoFactory` class), use bidirectional traversal starting with Neo4j version 1.8.

You're not limited to one starting point in each direction. Bidirectional traversal allows for multiple starting points for both directions. To use that feature, all you have to do is use the overloaded `BidirectionalTraversalDescription.traverse` method:

```
BidirectionalTraversalDescription.traverse( Iterable<Node> start,
    Iterable<Node> end )
```

All this makes bidirectional traversal a very powerful tool. In a few lines of code, you can write fast traversals to find patterns based on a number of fixed nodes, such as finding all users who know each of the users from a given set. Although bidirectional traversals are a bit more difficult to set up, they offer better performance and use less memory than standard traversal, especially for longer paths.

8.5 Summary

Traversal is a very powerful way to query graph data, and in this chapter you learned advanced concepts and techniques that can help you write fast and efficient traversals.

Using correct traversal ordering can make a huge difference in the speed and memory footprint of a traversal, especially on large graph data sets. In section 8.1 you saw how different traversals benefit from common depth-first and breadth-first branch ordering strategies.

You also learned about the key concept of relationship expansion. You've seen a standard expander in action, which is good for all typical traversal use cases. But for more specific scenarios, we demonstrated how you can order relationships with an ordered expander and also how you can implement custom relationship expanders, taking full advantage of the power of Neo4j's flexible Traversal API.

The uniqueness of visited nodes and relationships was the next advanced traversal topic we covered. You learned how to make sure you visited each node or relationship only once during the traversal. We also illustrated how to use different uniqueness constraints to solve some queries.

Finally, you've seen one of the lesser known but powerful features of Neo4j: bidirectional traversals. We implemented a bidirectional traversal that started from multiple points and converged to a single point, significantly shortening the time it takes to find a solution.

You've learned a lot of new complex concepts and features of Neo4j in this chapter. But how does Neo4j work with existing popular Java frameworks? And is there an easy way you can apply graph mappings to the object-oriented programming model? This is exactly what you're going to learn about in the next chapter, which covers one of the most popular general-purpose Java frameworks—Spring Framework—and how it integrates with Neo4j.

Spring Data Neo4j

This chapter covers

- Creating a domain model using Spring Data Neo4j (SDN)
- Loading and saving your SDN domain entities
- Object-graph mapping modes work within SDN
- Performing queries with SDN

Until now we've been working directly with the core Neo4j graph primitives—nodes and relationships—to represent and interact with (that is, read and persist) various domain model concepts.

Though that approach is extremely powerful and flexible, operating with the low-level Neo4j APIs can sometimes be quite verbose and result in a lot of boilerplate code, especially when it comes to working with domain model entities. In this chapter we'll introduce you to Spring Data Neo4j (SDN), a subproject within the broader Spring Data project that aims to bring the convenience of working with the simpler, more familiar Spring-based development model to the NoSQL world, and in this case, specifically to Neo4j.

To demonstrate SDN, we'll be returning to the social network example first described in chapter 1 and used in other chapters throughout the book. This is the social network example that allows users to rate movies. We'll use this social network to demonstrate how SDN allows for the domain to be modeled using plain old Java objects (POJOs), and we'll explain how the mapping to the underlying graph structure occurs. We'll also demonstrate how to read, persist, and query these managed entities.

9.1   *Where does SDN fit in?*

In a nutshell, SDN is an object-graph mapping (OGM) framework that was created to make life easier for (currently only Java) developers who need, or would prefer, to work with a POJO-based domain model, where some or all of the data is stored in Neo4j. It aims to increase productivity by dealing with all the low-level plumbing and mapping logic required to read domain entities from and write them back into Neo4j. This should free you to focus on the important job of writing the code that makes you (or your company) money—namely, the business logic. Figure 9.1 shows where SDN fits within your broader application.

In computer software, the requirement to read data from disk, and transform it into application-specific data structures, then write it back out again is very common. In the very early days of Java/RDBMS (relational database management system) projects, many developers would handcraft their own persistence-mapping logic, using, for example,

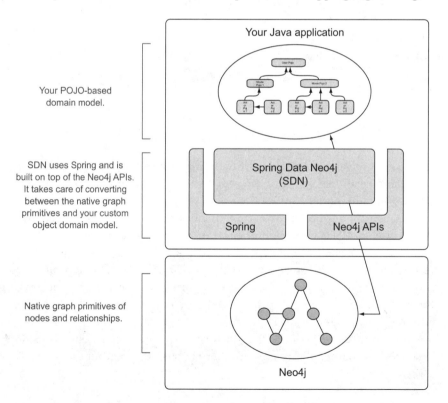

Figure 9.1   Overview of where SDN fits within your broader application

low-level frameworks such as JDBC to directly interact with databases to create and populate their domain objects. This approach proved to be quite error-prone and took up a significant amount of time in the overall development of the application, with developers doing the same thing over and over again for each new project. Various object-relational mapping (ORM) frameworks, such as Hibernate (http://hibernate.org/orm), evolved to take some of the pain out of this process and bridge the gap between translating between the physical storage structure and the model in memory.

Neo4j's native graph-based storage structure naturally provides a better fit for storing and retrieving complex object graphs than a relational database does. Relational databases often need to introduce additional structures, such as joining tables to deal with basic many-to-many relationships; Neo4j handles this natively. Nevertheless, there still exists a need to transform data from the persistence store into domain objects, and SDN seeks to play this role for scenarios where the underlying persistence technology is the NoSQL graph database Neo4j. In SDN's case, this involves mapping the native graph concepts of nodes and relationships into your chosen POJO domain model classes.

> ### What about OGMs for non-Java projects?
>
> There are other non-Java OGM frameworks out there. A current listing of some of these (interspersed among general Neo4j clients) can be found at http://neo4j.org/drivers. The following list will give you a taste of what's available, but please consult the website for the most up-to-date options:
>
> - *neo4j.rb*—A Ruby binding that includes an OGM-type implementation of the Rails Active Model and a subset of the Active Record API. See https://github.com/andreasronge/neo4j.
> - *Neo4j Grails plugin*—A plugin that integrates the Neo4j graph database into Grails, providing a GORM API for it. See http://grails.org/plugin/neo4j.
> - *neo4django*—An OGM for Django. See https://github.com/scholrly/neo4django.
> - *neomodel*—An OGM for Python. See https://github.com/robinedwards/neomodel.

9.1.1 What is Spring and how is SDN related to it?

Spring (http://projects.spring.io/spring-framework) is a very popular Java-based application development framework that provides productivity tools and utilities for Java developers.

Spring itself has many subprojects dealing with different areas, one of which is Spring Data. Within Spring Data, one of the projects is SDN. The engineers at Pivotal (formerly SpringSource) recognized that there were many data-access frameworks available for use with traditional RDBMS databases, but not so many in the brave new world of NoSQL.

The open source Spring Data project was developed as an umbrella project, with multiple subprojects being created to provide logic for specific databases (the first of which was SDN, where Emil Eifrem and Rod Johnson worked on the initial draft). Other NoSQL newcomers in this space include MongoDB and Redis.

In all cases, developers from both Pivotal and the underlying database helped get the frameworks to where they are today. All Spring Data projects leverage the existing good practices and proven functionality available within the core Spring framework to provide their flavors of data-accessing logic.

9.1.2   What is SDN good for (and not good for)?

By its very nature, SDN provides a convenient way to work with code or libraries that need or expect to operate on POJO-based domain entities. If you're already using Spring, or you're already using a rich domain model that you want to map to a graph, SDN could be for you.

Besides simply having, or wanting to work with, a rich domain model, another key consideration to take into account with SDN is the nature of, and number of, results or entities you're typically going to be dealing with. If it's in the region of a few hundred to a few thousand at a time, this scenario could lend itself well to an SDN setup. SDN isn't suited to scenarios where you'll need to perform any kind of mass data handling in a single go. Any logic where you have to load or store more than about 10,000 elements in a single swoop isn't a good candidate for SDN. Additionally, by providing a layer of indirection, SDN will be slower than simply using the core API, so if speed and performance are of the utmost importance to you, you might be better served using the native API.

> **NOTE**   The SDN framework provides a number of hooks (code providing access to the underlying `GraphDatabaseService` instance), which, if required, allow you to drop down and use the low-level core APIs to achieve maximum performance and flexibility. You can still view, query, and (with certain restrictions applied) update the graph outside of SDN using standard Neo4j tools if you so desire. Later in this chapter, the sidebar "Can SDN and Native Neo4j play nicely together?" offers more information on this subject.

9.1.3   Where to get SDN

SDN isn't part of the main Neo4j offering, but can be downloaded as a separate library and used in conjunction with an appropriate Neo4j version. At the time of writing, the latest version available for use is 3.2.1.RELEASE, which is compatible with Neo4j version 2.1.5 and can be found at http://projects.spring.io/spring-data-neo4j. This chapter (and the accompanying source code) will be using this release. Appendix C provides more detailed instructions on how to set up your project to use SDN. For more information about major changes introduced in SDN 3 in general, please also see the Neo4j blog post, "Spring Data Neo4j Progress Update: SDN 3 & Neo4j 2," at http://blog.neo4j.org/2014/03/spring-data-neo4j-progress-update-sdn-3.html.

9.1.4   *Where to get more information*

SDN is a vast project in and of itself, and we'll only be able to go so far in covering it here. In this chapter we aim to provide an introduction to some of the important aspects in the framework rather than a comprehensive reference guide. If you're looking for more in-depth coverage on any of the points covered here, as well as those we'll not be able to cover, there are good books on this subject, namely *Good Relationships* by Michael Hunger, which has also been incorporated into the official SDN reference docs, available at http://docs.spring.io/spring-data/neo4j/docs/current/reference/html/ (a free download at www.infoq.com/minibooks/good-relationships-spring-data) and *Spring Data* by Mark Pollak and others (O'Reilly, 2012). In general, the SDN documentation (http://projects.spring.io/spring-data-neo4j) is also a very useful reference resource, with more general information about the core Spring framework itself available at http://projects.spring.io/spring-framework.

9.2   *Modeling with SDN*

In this section, we'll show you how SDN can be used to transform POJOs to represent the entities within the movie-lovers' social network, where the data is stored in your Neo4j database. We'll assume that you're starting from a blank canvas and will be using SDN as the primary mechanism for driving the creation of, and setting up, your graph database. If you already have a graph database and want to know if you can apply SDN retrospectively, please refer to the sidebar "Can SDN and native Neo4j play nicely together?" later in the chapter.

In this section, you'll

1 Define a standard POJO object model to represent your domain.
2 See what's required by SDN to transform these POJOs into entities backed by Neo4j.
3 Dig a little deeper into various elements of SDN modeling, including
   – Modeling node entities
   – Modeling relationship entities
   – Modeling relationships between node entities

To recap, in this social network users can be friends with each other. Users can also mark the movies they've seen and rate them with one to five stars, based on how much they liked them. You're going to add a `userId` property so users can log in. This will also allow you to uniquely identify and refer to each user. Finally, you're going to add the ability for new users to indicate whether they were referred by anyone at joining time. This could be used to assign points to the referrer for each movie rated by new members within their first month, potentially leading to a free movie ticket or some other benefit. Figure 9.2 illustrates that John originally joined the network because he was referred by David.

9.2.1   *Initial POJO domain modeling*

If you ignore the fact for a moment that your data is actually being stored in Neo4j and take a simple stab at modeling your conceptual domain as POJOs, your first attempt

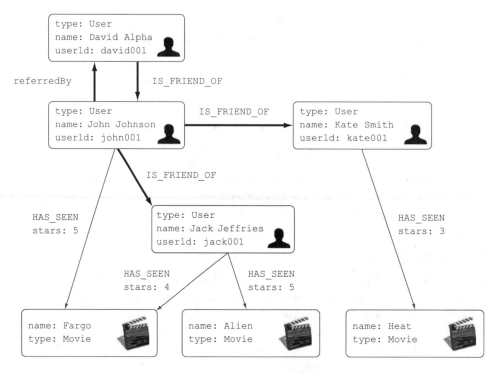

Figure 9.2   Conceptual overview of the movie-lovers' social network, with referrals

might look something like the following listing. Note that getters and setters have been omitted for brevity.

Listing 9.1   Initial POJO modeling attempt

```
public class User {                    ❶ All user's friends
    String userId;
    String name;                          All movie viewings
    Set<User> friends;                    (with associated star
    Set<Viewing> views;                   ratings assigned by users)
    User referredBy;
}                                      ❷ User who referred this
                                         user to the system
public class Movie {
    String title;
    Set<Viewing> views;
}                                         All users who have viewed this
                                          movie (with star ratings)

public class Viewing {
    User user;
    Movie movie;                          Rating (one to five stars) user
    Integer stars;                        gave for associated movie
}
```

There is nothing too complicated here—this is basic object modeling. Both the `User` and `Movie` concepts have been modeled as first-class entities—that seems reasonable enough. You've also modeled a user's viewing of a particular movie as an entity as well, namely the `Viewing` class. This is primarily because the relationship itself holds important information that you want to retain and use—namely the `stars` rating provided by the user. If you had modeled this as a simple collection type relationship between `User` and `Movie`, you'd lose this information.

At this point there is still no reference to any SDN- or Neo4j-specific concepts, just POJO stuff. Next, you'll need to map this entity into the underlying Neo4j graph model.

How close have you gotten to creating a POJO model that's easily translatable into the Neo4j world? Can you use it as is, or does it need any modifications? In this particular case you appear to have a good fit, with the `User` and `Movie` classes mapping neatly into the Neo4j nodes primitive concept with an associated `name` and `title` property, respectively.

The new `referredBy` relationship ❷ is represented as a reference to the user who did the referring, while the `IS_FRIEND_OF` relationship ❶ between users maps nicely to the set of friends. The only tricky part seems to be the modeling surrounding the `Viewing` class, which is trying to represent the scenario where a user has seen a movie and optionally rated it. Further inspection, however, reveals that this also fits perfectly into the Neo4j relationship concept. The `Viewing` class represents the `HAS_SEEN` relationship with its optional `stars` property, as well as the `User` who viewed the movie and the `Movie` reference itself.

So far so good; now it's time to do the mapping with SDN.

NOTE It won't always be possible to find a logical POJO model that's so closely tied to the physical Neo4j structure. In this case, you were quite fortunate, but in other cases you may have to adapt your model to fit. In any case, what this does highlight is how general POJO modeling concepts translate relatively well into Neo4j structures.

SDN modeling challenges
The logical model we've used for this chapter happens to translate very easily, and without much adjusting, to the physical Neo4j storage structure. It's worth highlighting two scenarios where you may have an object model that requires a bit of adjusting to fit some of the SDN mapping requirements. These are some common scenarios:

- *Using non-Set-based collections*—When modeling node entity relationships (via `@RelatedTo`, which is covered in section 9.2.5), at present only `Set`-backed collections may be used. For example, you can't have the following:

```
@RelatedTo
private Map<RelationshipType,Set<User>> users;
```

- *Entity equality*—SDN requires the database ID (the node/relationship ID) form part of an object's identity. Quoting from the reference guide, "Entity equality

(continued)

can be a grey area, and it's debatable whether natural keys or database ids best describe equality, there is the issue of versioning over time, etc. For Spring Data Neo4j we have adopted the convention that database-issued ids are the basis for equality, and that has some consequences." There are techniques for dealing with this scenario, but we won't be covering this issue in this book. Once again, we direct you to the official website for more information. See the "Entity Equality" section in http://docs.spring.io/spring-data/neo4j/docs/current/reference/html.

9.2.2   Annotating the domain model

SDN is an annotation-based object-graph mapping library. This means it's a library that relies on being able to recognize certain SDN-specific annotations attached to parts of your code. These annotations provide instructions about how to transform the associated code to the underlying structures in the graph.

Sometimes you may even find that you don't need to annotate certain pieces of code. This is because SDN tries to infer some sensible defaults, applying the principle of convention over configuration. OGM is to graphs what ORM is to an RDBMS.

The following listing shows SDN annotations added to the POJOs to identify them as entities backed by Neo4j.

Listing 9.2   SDN annotated domain model

```
@NodeEntity                                          Maps to Neo4j node
public class User {

    String name;
    @Indexed(unique=true)                            Stored as node
    String userId;                                   properties within graph

    @GraphId                                         Neo4j node ID
    Long nodeId;

    User referredBy;
    @RelatedTo(type = "IS_FRIEND_OF", direction = Direction.BOTH)
    Set<User> friends;
    @RelatedToVia
    Set<Viewing> views;
}
                                                     Stored as node        Relationships
                                                     properties            to other node
@NodeEntity                                          within graph          entities
public class Movie {                                                       involving
                                                                          this node
    String title;
    @GraphId
    Long nodeId;                                     Neo4j node ID

    @RelatedToVia(direction = Direction.INCOMING)
    Iterable<Viewing> views;
}
```

Maps to Neo4j node

Maps to Neo4j relationship

```
@RelationshipEntity(type = "HAS_SEEN")
public class Viewing {

    Integer stars;
    @GraphId
    Long relationshipId;

    @StartNode
    User user;
    @EndNode
    Movie movie;
}
```

Stored as relationship properties within graph

Neo4j relationship ID

References to node entities on either side of relationship

These annotations, along with sensible defaults assumed by SDN based on field names, directly tie elements of your Java class to physical entities in Neo4j. This means it's imperative you have a very good understanding of your Neo4j data model when modeling with SDN. Although SDN shields you from having to do the low-level mappings yourself, it expects you to be able to describe how it should be done.

The sections that follow break down listing 9.2 a bit more and explain core modeling concepts, repeated here, in more detail:

- Modeling node entities
- Modeling relationship entities
- Modeling relationships between node entities

We'll start with node entities.

9.2.3 *Modeling node entities*

Within SDN, a *node entity* refers to a Java class that's being used to represent a particular domain entity represented and backed by a Neo4j node primitive in the underlying graph database. Figure 9.3 highlights candidate nodes within the social network domain model that could be modeled as SDN node entities.

The Movie and User classes are perfect examples here. The @NodeEntity annotation is used to mark a class as a node entity, generally being placed just before the Java class definition, as shown in listing 9.2 and in the following snippet:

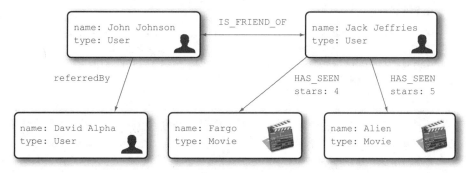

Figure 9.3 Social network model with nodes highlighted

Class backed by a Neo4j node

```
@NodeEntity
public class User {

    String name;

    @Indexed(unique=true)
    String userId;
    @GraphId
    Long nodeId;
    ...

}
```

❶ Maps to name property on underlying node

❷ Ensures userId field is indexed (using a schema-based index) and is unique

❸ Property contains Neo4j node ID

PROPERTIES

Within a class annotated with @NodeEntity, SDN will by default treat all simple fields as being representative of Neo4j properties on the backing node. In this context, *simple* means

- Any primitive or its associated wrapper class
- A string
- An object capable of being converted to a string through a Spring conversion service

Collections of any of these types are also included, where these collections are ultimately stored as an array on the Neo4j node. In the preceding domain example, this means that the name ❶ and title fields defined on the User and Movie classes, respectively, will get mapped as Neo4j properties with those same names, without you needing to lift a finger!

What about custom property types?

The core Spring framework comes with a general type-conversion system that allows you to write and register custom type-conversion logic that can transform a specific (nonprimitive) class to a string representation and back again. SDN has already registered some conversion services for you that handle enums and dates. So if, for example, you define a java.util.Date field on a node entity when the entity is due to get persisted, Spring recognizes that there is a custom converter defined for date fields and uses it to convert the Date property to a string that's then stored in the graph; the reverse occurs when reading the data out of the graph and back into the node entity field.

This means that you can take advantage of this same mechanism to handle any custom class types that you may want to use, such as a phone number object. You'll need to write a custom converter and register it with Spring. The book's sample code provides an example of how to do this by adding a phoneNumber to the User entity. For more details on this conversion mechanism, please refer to chapter 6 of the *Spring Framework Reference Documentation*, http://static.springsource.org/spring/docs/current/spring-framework-reference/html/validation.html#core-convert.

If you don't register a converter, SDN will still save a string version of your object into the database. However, it will simply be based on whatever is returned from the toString() method.

You've probably noticed that an additional field appears to have snuck into both the User and Movie node entities, namely nodeId, annotated with @GraphId. This is a mandatory SDN requirement when using simple object mapping. Without going into too much detail just yet, simple object mapping is one of the strategies employed by SDN to perform the physical mapping between your domain entity and the Neo4j-backed graph entity. Using this strategy, SDN needs to have a field where it can store the underlying ID of the node backing the entity. The @GraphId annotation ❸ serves to mark the field that you've set aside for SDN to store this value in. Read more about simple object mapping in section 9.4.1.

INDEXED PROPERTIES

As it's generally considered bad practice for an application to rely on the Neo4j node ID as an external unique identifier of an object (see the "Notes on the lookup bench-mark" sidebar in section 5.6.1 for details), it's important to have some other way of looking up a node. The addition of the @Indexed annotation ❷ on the userId field in the previous bit of code ensures that lookups and queries can be performed against this user based on this field. By default, @Indexed uses schema-based indexes, which rely on Neo4j labels. The code to look up the entity will be covered in section 9.3, but internally Neo4j uses exactly the same schema-indexing code and logic as described in section 5.5.1 to accomplish this.

> **NOTE** If you'd like to still use the legacy indexes, you can specify this using the indexType attribute; for example, @Indexed(indexType = IndexType.SIMPLE).

Under what labels and names are these annotated properties indexed?

By default, SDN employs a label-based type representation strategy that associates the underlying node for a node entity with labels whose names are the simple version of the class names in the entity hierarchy (User in this case). The schema index is then created on the property name defined against this label.

If you wanted to write some Cypher to perform a lookup on your userId property directly against the graph, you'd need to issue the following query:

```
MATCH (n:User) WHERE n.userId = {userId} return n
```

Be careful how you name and structure your domain entities. It's generally not advisable to have two domain entities with the same name, even if they're in separate packages, due to this default indexing behavior. If you had one User domain entity under a "core" package and another under "admin", they'd end up sharing the same label, which is probably not what you'd want. It's possible to override this default behavior by setting an @Alias annotation against the class, which will then create the index against the specified alias name instead. Nevertheless, it could be confusing to those who may not be aware of this behavior, and it could result in unforeseen results if you're not careful.

RELATIONSHIPS TO OTHER NODE ENTITIES

There are also relationships between node entities. You'll be pleased to learn that these are simply mapped as reference fields on the entity; this will be covered in section 9.2.5.

Before we get into the details of how this is done, you need to learn about relationship entities.

9.2.4   *Modeling relationship entities*

A *relationship entity* is the relationship version of a node entity. It refers to a Java class that's ultimately represented and backed by a Neo4j relationship in the underlying graph database. Neo4j treats relationships as first-class citizens, which, just like nodes, can have their own identifiers and sets of properties if required. Thus, SDN also allows them to be represented as entities in their own right. Figure 9.4 highlights these relationships within the domain model.

In this section we'll cover what's required to model the physical Neo4j relationship entity as a POJO itself; in section 9.2.5, we'll show what's required from the node entity's perspective to refer to other node entities through these modeled relationships, as well as through simpler mechanisms.

> **NOTE**   You will probably define many relationships within your physical Neo4j model, but this doesn't automatically mean that all of them need to be modeled as relationship entities in SDN.

SDN relationship entities are generally only required for relationships that have their own set of properties, and, together with these properties, provide context to the relationship. We'll refer to these relationships as *rich relationships* because of the additional data they contain over and above the relationship type.

The HAS_SEEN relationship is a perfect example of this, with its additional stars property providing more context to the relationship. It indicates not just that a user has seen a movie, but also how the user rated it. In the social network model, this relationship with all its associated information has been defined as the Viewing class, as

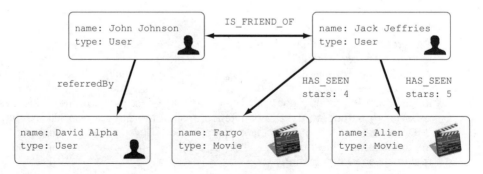

Figure 9.4   A social network model with highlighted relationships that could potentially be modeled as relationship entities

shown in listing 9.3. Contrast this to the `IS_FRIEND_OF` relationship, which alone is all that's required to understand the relationship between two users—that is, that they're friends. These *simple relationships* (relationships where the `TYPE` alone is enough to completely describe the relationship, such as the `IS_FRIEND_OF` relationship) can still be referenced, and you'll see how this is done in section 9.2.5, but there's no additional benefit in defining a whole new class to represent them.

Listing 9.3 The `Viewing` class as a relationship entity

```
@RelationshipEntity(type = "HAS_SEEN")                  ◁──┐  Class is backed by a
public class Viewing {                                     │  Neo4j relationship.
    @GraphId                          ❶ Property containing
    Long relationshipId;                 Neo4j relationship ID.

    @StartNode                        ❷ User node from which relationship
    User user;                           originates (outgoing).

    @EndNode                          ❸ Movie node at which
    Movie movie;                         relationship ends (incoming).

    Integer stars;                    ◁──┐ Maps to stars property on
}                                        │ underlying relationship.
```

The `@RelationshipEntity` annotation is applied to classes to indicate that it represents a Neo4j relationship. The annotation takes a `type` property that indicates the name of the Neo4j relationship type used within the graph itself. If the `type` property is not explicitly specified within the annotation, SDN will default the value assigned to it as the simple name of the class (which would be `Viewing` in this example). As with the node entity, the relationship entity has the same requirement for a `@GraphId` annotated field ❶, this time for storing the underlying relationship ID.

If you'd like to access the node entities on either side of this relationship, you'll need to provide a field for each of these and annotate them with `@StartNode` ❷ and `@EndNode` ❸. For the `Viewing` class example, the `User` node entity starts (has the outgoing) relationship to the ending `Movie` entity.

In terms of what's required to model a Neo4j relationship, that's it. There is, however, generally not much point in defining relationship entity classes in isolation. They're almost always referred to through one or more fields on associated node entities. In section 9.2.5 we'll go into detail about how node entities can refer to other node entities through simple references, but also through POJO-modeled relationships. To provide the full context for this example, the following listing provides a sneak preview of how the `User` node entity, as well as the `Movie` node entity, refer to the `Viewing` relationship entity class through their `views` field.

Listing 9.4 `User` and `Movie` node entity snippets

```
@NodeEntity
public class User {
```

```
     @RelatedToVia
     Set<Viewing> views;

     ...
```

❶ **Set of all HAS_SEEN relationships (from the User perspective)**

```
@NodeEntity
public class Movie {
     @RelatedToVia(direction = Direction.INCOMING)
     Iterable<Viewing> views;
```

❷ **Read-only Set of all HAS_SEEN relationships (from the Movie perspective)**

Within the `User` node entity, the `RelatedToVia` annotation ❶ on the `views` field essentially reads as "all the `HAS_SEEN` relationships (with any associated properties) between this user and any movies the user has watched." (The `HAS_SEEN` relationship type is inferred because that is what's defined in the `type` property on the annotation of the `Viewing` class itself.) The `Viewing` class represents the full context of the relationship between these two entities including the `rating` field. Note that in this case (unlike the `Movie` class detailed next) you don't explicitly specify `direction = Direction.OUTGOING` within the annotation because this is the default.

Within the `Movie` node entity, the `RelatedToVia` annotation ❷ marks the `views` field as representative of "all the `HAS_SEEN` relationships (with any associated properties) between this movie and any users who have actually watched it."

In both cases the `Viewing` class provides a way to access the extra contextual information about the relationship, over and above the fact that these two entities are merely related—in this case, the extra contextual information is the specific rating provided for each viewing. You may at this stage be wondering why in one case the relationship was modeled with a `Set` (on the `User`) and with an `Iterable` in the other (on the `Movie`). All will be revealed in the next section, so keep reading!

In the next section we'll continue to detail some of the finer points defining different types of relationships between node entities, including where the rich relationship details are required to fully understand the context.

9.2.5 *Modeling relationships between node entities*

Being able to model node and relationship entities with their simple associated properties in isolation will take you only so far. Models start getting interesting when you're able to actually connect them to explore the relationships between them, and in this section, we'll cover how to do that.

The end of the previous section provided a preview of how such a connection could be established between the `User` and `Movie` entities through the `Viewing` relationship entity. You saw how the `HAS_SEEN` relationship between `Users` and `Movies` was modeled as a physical POJO (the `Viewing` class) and was then referred to from the entities. In that particular case, a whole separate class (`Viewing`) was used to represent the relationship in context. But what about other, simpler relationships, such as "John is a friend of Jack"? Do you also need a dedicated relationship entity class for such cases? You'll be pleased to know the answer is no—they can be dealt with in a much simpler manner.

Figure 9.5 recaps the relationships between node entities that you're potentially interested in referencing from the node entities.

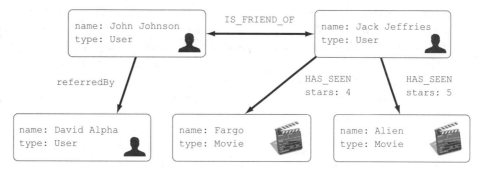

Figure 9.5   **A social network model with the relationship references between nodes highlighted**

From the node entity's perspective, relationships are also modeled as normal Java object references, and they come in a variety of flavors depending on what you're trying to convey. We've already previewed how you can use the `Viewing` class to reference the `HAS_SEEN` relationship, but let's tackle the other simpler relationships as well, such as `referredBy` and `IS_FRIEND_OF`.

The relationships involved in the `User` and `Movie` entities are shown in the next listing.

Listing 9.5   **User and Movie node entity snippets**

> **User (node entity) associated with this node through referredBy relationship**

```
public class User {
    User referredBy;
    @RelatedTo(type = "IS_FRIEND_OF", direction = Direction.BOTH)
    Set<User> friends;
    @RelatedToVia
    Set<Viewing> views;
    ...

public class Movie {
    @RelatedToVia(direction = Direction.INCOMING)
    Iterable<Viewing> views;
    ...
```

1. public class User { ... User referredBy;

2. **Users (node entities) associated with this node through IS_FRIEND_OF relationship**

3. **HAS_SEEN relationship information between this user and movies**

4. **Read-only version of HAS_SEEN between this movie and users who rated**

Basic relationships, represented by an underlying Neo4j relationship with no associated properties to exactly zero or one other node entity, can be modeled as a standard object reference within the node entity. By default, the property name will be used as the name that's mapped to the relationship type in Neo4j, in the absence of any meta-information to the contrary. The newly introduced concept of one user referring another to the social network (modeled by the `referredBy` property ❶) is an excellent example of this. Note that this property must be a reference to another node entity.

Basic relationships to zero or more other node entities are modeled with a `Set`, `List`, `Collection`, or `Iterable` class, with the referenced node entity as the collection type. The use of a `Set`, `List`, or `Collection` class signifies that the field is modifiable from the containing node's perspective; an Iterable class indicates this should be treated as read-only. Based on the contained node entity class type and its annotations, SDN will be able to work out that your intention is for this field to represent a basic relationship. If, however, you'd like to overwrite any of the defaults inferred, you can add an @RelatedTo annotation. The friends relationships ❷ between users is an example. Note how in this case we added the @RelatedTo annotation with the type property to specify the underlying Neo4j relationship type as IS_FRIEND_OF rather than the default value that SDN would have inferred if it were not there. In the absence of the annotation, SDN would have used the name of the field, friends, as the name to be used for the underlying relationship type property.

Rich relationships, those represented by an underlying Neo4j relationship with associated properties, are also modeled with the same Collection class as basic relationships. In this case, however, the type of the contained entity in the collection is a relationship entity rather than a node entity. To recap, a *relationship entity* represents the underlying Neo4j relationship along with any associated properties that were also modeled in the entity (see section 9.2.4). This provides a neat way to access the rich information on the relationship itself, while still being able to get to the entity or entities on the other end. As with basic relationships, without any annotations, SDN can work out that you're creating such references based solely on the fact that the type of class contained in the collection has been defined as a relationship entity. Again, if you wish to override any of these relationship defaults assumed by SDN, you can apply the @RelatedToVia annotation. As you've already seen, the views field reference ❸ representing the relationship between a User and a Movie is a good example; the additional stars rating serves to enhance the information about the relationship between these two entities. Notice the different Collection class used for the views property in the case of the User and Movie nodes, namely Set<Viewing> and Iterable<Viewing>. This means that the views property can be modified from the User node perspective but not from the Movie node. Conceptually, users rate movies; movies don't apply ratings to users.

Both the @RelatedTo ❷ and @RelatedToVia ❸ and ❹ annotations can take a type and optional direction element, specified to clarify whether relationships of a particular direction (valid values are INCOMING, BOTH, and the default OUTGOING) should be included in the collection of entities returned.

Note that for the friends property you need to specify the direction as BOTH, as shown in the following snippet:

```
@RelatedTo(type = "IS_FRIEND_OF", direction = Direction.BOTH)
    Set<User> friends;
```

Logically, a friends relationship is bidirectional; physically within Neo4j, however, relationships are only stored in one direction. By specifying BOTH, you're telling Neo4j to consider any IS_FRIENDS_OF relationships associated with the user, regardless of the direction in which the physical relationship is defined.

9.3 Accessing and persisting entities

You've seen how you can use annotations to provide SDN with the basic information it needs to map your POJO classes to the underlying graph-backed database without so much as a low-level node or relationship class in sight. This is a great step forward in having to only deal with business-level concepts in your domain model code. The next logical questions are how you can interact with these entities and how you can load and save your POJO entities to and from the graph database.

SDN offers a few options in this area, and we'll be focusing on two of them in this section, namely the `Neo4jTemplate` class and the more general concept of Spring data repositories. Before that, we'll look at the supporting Spring configuration, which you need to supply in order to make this all work.

9.3.1 Supporting Spring configuration

The following listing shows the minimum XML Spring configuration required to initialize SDN so it can find your domain entities and make various beans (such as the `Neo4jTemplate`) available to you.

Listing 9.6 XML-based Spring configuration

```
<beans xmlns="http://www.springframework.org/schema/beans"
       xmlns:neo4j=http://www.springframework.org/schema/data/neo4j ...>

    <neo4j:config storeDirectory="target/sample-db"
        base-package="com.manning.neo4jia.chapter09.simple.domain"/>

</beans>
```

> Core SDN configuration entry

The `neo4j:config` entry is used by SDN to perform many initialization activities; for example, you can supply the `storeDirectory` attribute as a convenient way to refer to a graph database (creating a new embedded one if it doesn't exist). From SDN 3.0 onward, it's mandatory that you use the `base-package` attribute to specify the directory or list of directories where your domain entities are defined.

> **NOTE** You can achieve the same outcome by using Spring Java configuration if you don't fancy XML.

Let's move on to look at how you can use the `Neo4jTemplate` class to interact with your entities.

9.3.2 Neo4jTemplate class

`Neo4jTemplate` is an SDN class that can be instantiated and used directly or made available to your application when Spring is initialized. Following in the spirit of the other successful Spring template classes (such as `JDBCTemplate` and `JMSTemplate`), the `Neo4jTemplate` class aims to provide a convenient and simplified API for interacting with the low-level classes and behavior requirements of the underlying Neo4j graph-based classes.

It's interesting to note that the SDN framework itself makes use of Neo4jTemplate to perform many of its own internal tasks, delegating to it as appropriate. But the template itself isn't restricted to internal use only and can also be used as one of the options for invoking basic functionality surrounding SDN entities.

> ### Neo4jTemplate: Power to the people!
> The Neo4jTemplate class also provides many other low-level utility methods for operating on, querying, and gaining access to nodes and relationships. This is one of the ways in which SDN provides a hook for you to drop down to the core low-level API if you really need to get into the "belly of the beast" and have more fine-grained control. Be sure to explore all of the other methods available to you at some point.

The following listing is an example that illustrates how to save and load the User entity using the Neo4jTemplate class in its most basic form.

Listing 9.7   A basic Neo4jTemplate example

```
GraphDatabaseService graphDB = getGraphDatabase();          Needs reference to
Neo4jTemplate template = new Neo4jTemplate(graphDB);    ◁── graph database

try (Transaction tx = template.getGraphDatabaseService().beginTx()) {
  User user      = new User("john001","John");
  User savedUser = template.save(user);
  User loadedUser = template.findOne(savedUser.getNodeId(), User.class);
  tx.success();
}
```

Only operates with domain objects (except for the template itself)

First up, the Neo4jTemplate class needs a reference to the underlying graph database it's ultimately operating on to perform its tasks. This is the same GraphDatabaseService you've used in previous chapters to work with the native Neo4j constructs.

Although you appear to be holding true to the aspiration of only having to deal with real domain objects, there's still a lot of "noise" (all that boilerplate transaction code) in listing 9.7. You could do better in this regard by making full use of the Spring framework with its dependency injection (DI) functionality and all that comes with it. Moving in this direction, your code can be transformed to what you see in the following listing.

Listing 9.8   A Neo4jTemplate example with full Spring integration

Made available via Spring DI

```
@Autowired Neo4jTemplate template;          Previous boilerplate code
                                        ◁── replaced by annotation
@Transactional
public void saveAndLoad() {
    User user      = new User("john001","John");       ❶ Saves node entity
    User savedUser = template.save(user);          ◁──    into graph

    User loadedUser = template.findOne(            ❷ Lookup via node ID
        savedUser.getNodeId(), User.class);
```

```
User loadedUserViaIndex = template
        .findByIndexedValue(User.class,
            "userId", "john001")
        .singleOrNull();
}
```

❸ **Lookup via an index**

This new code comes a lot closer to achieving your Spring nirvana of only needing to write the core business logic, deferring all low-level plumbing to Spring. The boiler-plate transaction code has now been replaced with the `@Transactional` annotation that instructs Spring to ensure that all code executed within the method is wrapped in a transaction for you.

Focusing on the core persistence logic, you can see that creating and saving a new entity is as simple as calling the `save` method ❶ on the `Neo4jTemplate` class, passing in the newly created POJO-based entity as the argument. Internally, the `Neo4jTemplate` creates a new node in the database for you, assigns a new (or reused) graph node ID, stores all associated properties (`userId` and `name`), and indexes the `userId` property.

Listing 9.7 illustrates two ways to load an entity. The first ❷ requires knowledge of and access to the graph node ID, which you have as a result of a previous call to save the entity ❶. Recall that the `@GraphId`-annotated `nodeId` property on the `User` entity was required by SDN to store the underlying node ID. You're simply making use of this information now for your own lookup purposes.

The second approach, for the cases where the node ID isn't available or known, is to look up the entity via the indexed `userId` property ❸.

Although this code isn't quite as clean as it could be, it does the job. In the next section you'll see how entities can be looked up via repositories, which does an even better job of hiding all internal plumbing required to perform index lookups as well as other functions.

9.3.3 Repositories

The second main option for loading and saving entities is via an implementation of the *repository pattern*, which you can find discussed in various books, including *Domain Driven Design* by Eric Evans (Addison-Wesley Professional, 2003) and *Patterns of Enterprise Application Architecture* by Martin Fowler (Addison-Wesley Professional, 2002).

In simple terms, a repository provides an abstraction layer between your business code, which should generally be dealing with domain-level entities, and all the logic required to convert these entities to and from their formats in any underlying data stores. Your business code should deal in the language of the domain; how these domain entities are actually loaded and saved is a job for a particular repository implementation. Using this approach, if you decided to swap out your data store, you wouldn't need to throw away all of your business code; rather, you'd replace the appropriate repository implementation with one that knows how to translate the domain entities to and from the new data store format.

SDN repositories have specifically been designed to focus on one domain class at a time, and they aim to provide a whole range of default operations specific to that domain

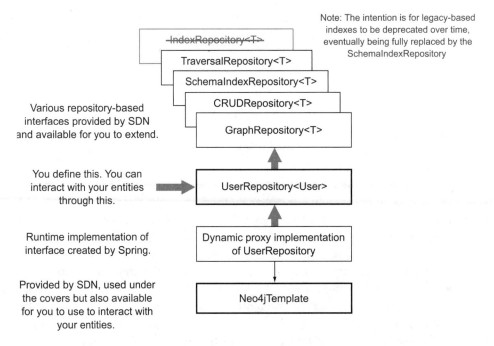

Figure 9.6   Overview of SDN repository classes involved in accessing `User` node entity

class. The really nice feature of SDN repositories is that they don't require you to write a single line of code to implement the default operations. All you need do is define an interface and specify which domain class you'd like these operations created for.

Using the User domain class as an example, let's look at how this works and what's involved. Figure 9.6 shows our starting point.

The following one-line snippet shows the definition of the UserRepository interface, specifically for the User domain (node entity) class:

```
public interface UserRepository extends GraphRepository<User> { }
```

In this case, the UserRepository interface is extending the GraphRepository interface, which defines the broadest set of default operations available for a domain class. The use of Java generics ties this repository (at compile time, anyway) to the User domain entity.

The GraphRepository interface essentially consolidates all the other interfaces and thus defines operations covering CRUD, indexing, and traversals for a user. The following list shows some of the default operations that the GraphRepository interface covers:

- `public <U extends User> U save(U entity);`
- `public <U extends T> Iterable<U> save(Iterable<U> entities);`
- `public User findOne(Long id);`
- `public boolean exists(Long id);`

- `public Result<User> findAll();`
- `public void delete(User entity);`

SDN builds on the abstraction concept defined in the Spring Data Commons module that provides shared infrastructure across Spring Data projects. SDN takes on the responsibility of implementing the base methods in the interface that your repository extends (for example, the `GraphRepository` interface in the `UserRepository` case), providing a uniform set of functionality to support common loading, saving, querying, indexing, and traversing operations specific to an entity.

The following listing depicts how the `UserRepository` can be used to save and load users.

Listing 9.9 Loading and saving data via the `UserRepository`

```
@Autowired
UserRepository userRepository;

@Transactional
public void saveAndLoad() {
User user       = new User("john001","John");
User savedUser  = userRepository.save(user);
User loadedUser = userRepository.findOne(savedUser.getNodeId());
User loadedUserViaIndex =
        userRepository.findBySchemaPropertyValue ("userId","john001");
}
```

You'll notice that this code is very similar to that used by the `Neo4jTemplate` approach in listing 9.7 (with the exception that you don't have to provide a target type). The `Repository.save` method persists the entity into the graph, with the loading being accomplished with `findOne` (based on a node ID) or `findBySchemaPropertyValue` (based on an index lookup, against the `userId` property in this case). For Spring to know about any repository interfaces you define, it needs to be told. Adding the following code into your Spring XML configuration file will do the trick:

```
<neo4j:repositories base-
    package="com.manning.neo4jia.chapter09simple.repository"/>
```

Who implemented my interface?

The astute among you may have realized that we never actually defined any concrete implementation for the `UserRepository` interface. We simply injected it through Spring's `@Autowired` annotation and then used it, somehow managing to read and save the `User` domain entities along the way. So, if we never provided any implementation, who did, and how does this work?

There's no magic involved here. What's happening is that SDN used the initial packages you provided in your XML configuration to search for your repository definitions, and then dynamically created a proxy for you that implements your interface and makes it available as a Spring bean. This proxy does all the hard work of implementing the functionality defined in the core interfaces. You get a whole bunch of functionality simply by extending one interface!

Repositories are a step up from the `Neo4jTemplate` class in that they also provide implementations for a lot of boilerplate code, but in a far more domain-targeted manner.

### 9.3.4	*Other options*

Besides using the `Neo4jTemplate` class or repositories, there's a third approach available when saving entities. This involves calling a persistence method on the entity itself. We'll cover this in section 9.4.2 as it's only available when making use of the advanced mapping mode, but it's listed here for completeness.

There may also be cases when your domain object needs to load data from multiple data stores, the so-called *cross-store persistence* scenario. Perhaps some of your data is stored in Neo4j and the rest in MySQL. You'll be happy to know that SDN also caters to cross-store persistence, although we won't be covering how to do this in this book. More information about cross-store persistence can be found in the core Neo4j SDN documentation.

Can SDN and native Neo4j play nicely together?

From a reading, querying, and traversing perspective, any data written into the underlying graph from SDN can safely be accessed in a read-only manner using any of the native Neo4j tools you've come across thus far, such as Cypher via the Web Admin Console, the Neo4j Shell, and so on.

SDN tries to be as unobtrusive as possible when it comes to storing data in the graph, but it needs to store some meta information in order to do some of the things it does. For example, there are a few different ways in which a domain model's Java hierarchy can be represented in the graph, and these options are handled by something called *type representation strategies*. These strategies rely on storing some information in the graph. The `LabelBasedNodeTypeRepresentationStrategy` (which is the default strategy from SDN 3.0 onward) creates labels against the underlying nodes based on the simple class names of the node entities. The `IndexingNodeTypeRepresentation-Strategy` creates legacy indexes as well as adding a property called `__type__` on each entity, whereas the `SubReferenceNodeTypeRepresentationStrategy` may create `INSTANCE_OF` and `SUBCLASS_OF` relationships between entities.

You'll need to understand and take this additional meta information into account if you want to update the underlying entities outside of SDN. Creating a new `Person` entity, for example, may involve more than simply adding one node in the graph with its basic attributes.

We can't cover all the scenarios where meta information is used and stored by SDN, but we can highlight this point here to make you aware of it and the possible limitations it may impose on you should you consider using SDN.

For more information about the different type representation strategies available, see the "Entity type representation"detailed in http://docs.spring.io/spring-data/neo4j/docs/current/reference/html.

Before we move on to the final functional section regarding how to perform queries and traversals using entities, let's detour to cover OGM. We've occasionally referred to *simple object mapping* throughout this chapter, and now's the time to define exactly what we mean by this.

9.4 *Object-graph mapping options*

SDN offers two modes to perform the mapping between your domain POJOs and the underlying graph entities: simple mapping and advanced mapping. Understanding the differences in how these modes operates will help you assess the trade-offs in each approach and decide which one is most appropriate for your project, should you choose to use SDN. Choosing is a little bit like deciding between DOM and SAX XML parsers—both do the same thing, parse XML, but in very different ways with implications for the choice taken.

Regardless of whether you choose the simple or advanced mapping mode, the process for determining what gets mapped to what is the same for both and was conceptually described in section 9.2.2 for annotating the domain model. Very briefly, this mapping process involves SDN parsing and analyzing all known node and relationship entities. With a little help from the Java reflection API, SDN builds up an in-memory metamodel of the mapping rules. These rules are then used by each implementation to perform the grunt work, so to speak—the work of running backwards and forwards between the domain model and graph primitives, translating when each sees fit.

> ### And then there were two ...
> Prior to the release of Spring Data Neo4j version 2.0.0, only the advanced approach (AspectJ-based mapping) was supported. AspectJ is a Java implementation of the aspect-oriented programming (AOP) paradigm—see http://eclipse.org/aspectj. Within SDN, it looks to dynamically intercept method calls on your POJOs as the mechanism for seamlessly integrating the Neo4j database and Java domain model.
>
> Reacting to feedback from the community, the simple mapping mode was added to address many of the issues and concerns that were raised in relation to the AspectJ tooling, as well as some other more general implications present with this more complicated setup. It should be noted that more effort is now being focused on upgrading and making the simple model the de facto approach to using SDN.

9.4.1 *Simple mapping*

The simple mapping mode, which is the default mode and requires no special setup, involves copying data into a node entity on any load operations, with the writing back to the graph only occurring when an explicit save operation is invoked. Figure 9.7 shows a simple mapping mode.

Although the approach is simple, you need to be aware of the memory implications inherent with simple mapping. Because this approach involves copying data

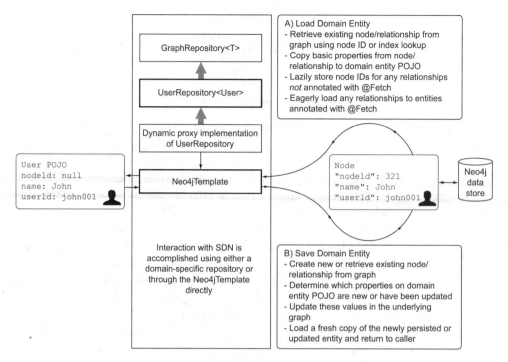

Figure 9.7 Overview of the simple mapping logic

between your domain entities and their underlying representations, you'll need to keep an eye on your memory footprint, as everything is essentially loaded twice—once via the node and then again via the domain class when everything is copied over. Additionally, this approach will also incur a performance penalty because you have to constantly keep copying the graph to perform certain operations.

That said, let's take a look at the next listing and dig a little deeper into what's happening with the loading and saving methods, as well as everything in between.

Listing 9.10 Loading and saving

```
@Transactional
public void saveAndLoad() {

    Long johnNodeId = getJohnNodeId();
    User loadedUser = userRepository.findOne(johnNodeId));    ←❶ Loads entity

    // Start: All changes between these Start/End
    //        markers are only performed in memory
    loadedUser.setName("New Name");

    User susan = new User("susan001","Susan");
    loadedUser.addFriend(susan)
    // End
                                                          ❷ Modifications saved
    User savedUser  = userRepository.save(loadedUser);   ←┘   into graph at this point
}
```

The findOne method ❶ available via the CRUDRepository interface is classified as one of the load methods. When this line of code executes, SDN will do three things:

- Create a new User object.
- Load the underlying Node class into memory.
- For each property and certain relationships (those without @Fetch annotations, which we'll come to shortly), copy the data out of the graph and into the POJO classes properties.

The next time SDN interacts with the underlying node is when an explicit save is called ❷. Nothing between these points ever results in a call to the underlying database; everything is done on the domain objects. Technically, entities that have just been created or modified but not yet saved are said to be in a *detached* state.

TRANSITIVE PERSISTENCE

The other noteworthy point to make about this code is that when John is saved ❷, Susan gets saved too. Lucky Susan! So what's special about John? Whenever a save operation is invoked, SDN will look at the object to be persisted (John, in this case) and detect what's new or changed from the perspective of the node that's being saved, including relationships. John has a new age and name *and* a new friend. Thus, SDN saves the full object graph of modified data, bringing Susan along for the ride as well. Remember relationship properties defined with read-only semantics (that is, those of the Iterable collection type) won't be persisted.

EAGER VERSUS LAZY LOADING

Susan gets saved by default when John is saved, but is she also loaded when John is loaded? The official answer is "It depends." If the SDN default configuration is in play, as in this case, the answer is initially "No." This is because, by default, SDN doesn't engage in eager relationship instantiation when loading a domain entity's relationship-based properties.

Eager loading would involve SDN actively following any relationships that may exist on an entity and then also loading these entities, including all of their properties as well as their relationships. To conserve memory and prevent potentially loading vast swathes of the graph into memory when it's not explicitly needed, SDN defaults to lazy loading.

So what happens if you ask for entities that have been lazily loaded? Take a look at the following listing.

Listing 9.11 Implications for lazy loading

```
...
User john      = new User("john001" , "John");
User sally     = new User("sally001", "Sally");

john.addFriends(sally);
template.save(john);
```

```
User loadedSally = template.findOne(sally.getNodeId(), User.class);
assertEquals(1, loadedSally.getFriends().size());
User firstFriendOfSusan = loadedSally.getFriends().iterator().next();
assertEquals( john.getNodeId(),firstFriendOfSusan.getNodeId());
assertEquals( null, firstFriendOfSusan.getName());
```

Collection of users lazily loaded where only the nodeId property is populated

For each node entity to be lazily loaded, SDN still instantiates a node entity POJO for the underlying entity, but it will only populate the property annotated with @GraphId. The unit test code in listing 9.11 shows you're able to access the nodeId, but the name is still null at this point.

When you want to load the full entity, you can make use of the Neo4JTemplate fetch method, shown in the following extension snippet, which would follow directly after the code in listing 9.11:

```
template.fetch(loadedSally.getFriends());
assertEquals( "John", firstFriendOfSusan.getName());
```

Alternatively, if you want SDN to eagerly instantiate the entities at loading time, you can annotate the appropriate property with @Fetch, as in the following snippet:

```
. . .
@Fetch
@RelatedTo(type = "IS_FRIEND_OF", direction = Direction.BOTH)
Set<User> friends;
. . .
```

You've now had a brief overview of the simple mapping mode, which can probably be summed up with the phrase "Simple, yet powerful, but potentially memory-hungry too!" Next up is advanced mapping!

Mandatory @GraphId property should be defined as a Long

Simple mapping mandates that domain modelers provide a property annotated with @GraphId to store the associated node or relationship ID, providing the library with a link to the underlying node or relationship backing it. The value will be null when the entity has yet to be persisted to Neo4j (typically when you use the new keyword to create your entity), but once it has been saved at least once, it will be populated to reflect the underlying node or relationship it's connected to in the graph.

Words of caution here. Make sure you define this property as the Long data type and not as the long primitive. The wrapper class allows for a null to be specified, indicating that the entity has yet to be persisted into the graph. If you define this field as a primitive long, this will mean that its default value will always be 0. Zero, however could represent a real node ID (prior to Neo4j 2.0, the reference node present in all graph databases was always node 'zero'). This could result in all kinds of erroneous data being stored and retrieved. What you really want is a null node ID if the entity has never been persisted.

9.4.2 Advanced mapping based on AspectJ

The advanced mapping mode relies on the AspectJ library as its mechanism for implementing the mapping and conversion logic between your POJO-annotated domain class and the underlying entity in the graph (see figure 9.8).

AspectJ (see http://eclipse.org/aspectj) is a Java implementation of the AOP paradigm (http://en.wikipedia.org/wiki/Aspect-oriented_programming). AOP, as a paradigm, aims to increase modularity within a code base, specifically for the purpose of allowing common cross-cutting concerns to be untangled and extracted out of the main code and ultimately stored separately (as aspects). A cross-cutting concern is some common logic that needs to be applied at multiple points within the code base but that isn't necessarily related to the core domain itself (typical examples cited are logging and transaction handling). This concern or aspect can then somehow (implementations differ) be configured to be applied to your code base at appropriate points.

So how does SDN make use of AOP (specifically AspectJ) to perform its common logic of converting and translating between the POJO class and underlying graph entity?

First, unlike the simple mapping that all happens at runtime, the advanced mode relies on some compile-time settings and configurations. This involves including a

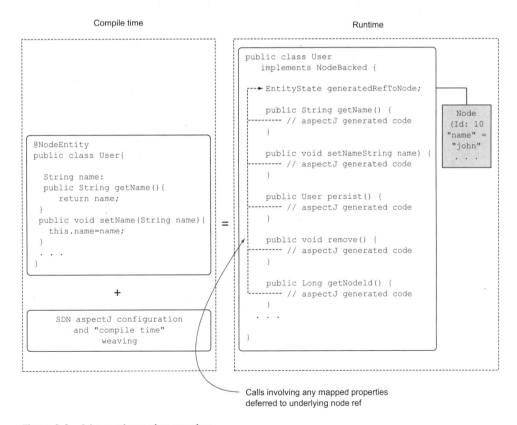

Figure 9.8 Advanced mapping overview

specific AspectJ-aware version of SDN in your project, as well as using the AspectJ (ajc) compiler. The configuration details are discussed in appendix C.

SDN will scan your code for all `@NodeEntity` and `@RelationshipEntity` classes. It will then take these POJO domain classes and, by using the special AspectJ compiler, will replace them with its own custom-generated versions.

Second, this custom-crafted class has two features worth noting. First, a direct reference to the actual node or relationship is attached to the class as an internal hidden field. The additional code generated by the AspectJ compiler, in conjunction with this hidden field, ensures that any code that's reading or writing to properties backed by Neo4j entities is modified so that it ends up delegating all calls directly to the underlying entity.

The second noteworthy feature is that additional persistence-related methods are added or mixed into the generated class, consistent with an active record type of approach—that is, a technique whereby persistence code lives side by side with the domain code. This is done by ensuring that the generated class implements either a `NodeBacked` or `RelationshipBacked` interface, providing appropriate implementations for the raft of persistence and lookup functionality. The following listing shows how you can use some of these persistence-related methods to operate on the entity directly.

Listing 9.12 Active record persistence with implicit transaction

```
public void advancedUsageWithImplicitTransactions() {        No transaction
                                                              annotation or wrapping
    User user = new User("john001","John the 1st");           code defined
    user.setName("John the 2nd");

    ((NodeBacked)user).persist();              ❶  Implicit transaction
    user.setName("John the 3rd");                 created
    ((NodeBacked)user).persist();
}
```

If you cast your eyes over the code in listing 9.12, it more than likely will conjure up a few questions, such as "Does this code even work?" The absence of any transaction code does look a bit suspect, given that all operations need to occur within a transaction.

Remember, node entities can exist in two states: *attached* or *detached*. Creating a new node entity occurs in a detached state, which simply means that the entity has not yet had its state written into the underlying graph database.

Calling `persist()` ❶ on the entity (or indeed `Neo4jTemplate`'s `save()` method) attaches the entity to the graph. Attachment ensures that the state in the entity is synchronized with that in the graph database. For new entities, new nodes and properties are created, and for entities that were at some point previously attached, they're reattached, ensuring any changes since the last attachment are written to the graph.

SDN can detect whether or not your code is operating within the context of an existing transaction. If not (as is the case in the sample code), SDN will ensure that calls to the attach-related methods (NodeBacked's persist in this case, as well as Neo4jTemplate's save) will create an implicit transaction for you. An implicit transaction is simply a new transaction created for you internally ❶ that SDN then uses to perform the mutating calls that save the state into the graph.

Although we've provided details here about how implicit transaction works, you're generally advised to provide explicit transactions yourself. Otherwise the library has to reattach detached entities all the time. Having tiny implicit transactions can also slow down your application tremendously.

It's worth being aware that use of the advanced mapping mode will generally involve a read-through down to the database whenever a property or relationship is accessed on the domain entity. To avoid multiple DB reads it may sometimes make sense to store data, or interim results, or both, in local variables rather than repeatedly querying for the data via the domain entity itself. Depending on how you're interacting with the entity, this local variable could be scoped to within a method, within the entity class itself, or even within another class. This will aid performance, but additional variables will also add to your overall memory footprint, so you need to keep this in mind.

What if I'm operating within an existing transaction?

If you have previously created or started an explicit transaction before your code executes (as opposed to relying on implicit transactions), SDN will not try to create its own new transaction. SDN will simply operate within the existing transaction boundary established, providing you with the ability to make use of all the standard transaction controls (such as rollback) that you're typically accustomed to.

This concludes our brief overview of the advanced mapping mode. In exchange for some configuration headaches as you set up AspectJ for your development environment (this was one of the primary complaints that led to the introduction of the simple mapping mode), you can better utilize your available memory compared to the simple approach, though there may be performance penalties for property read-throughs if you don't deal with them appropriately.

9.4.3 Object mapping summary

Table 9.1 compares the simple and advanced mapping modes.

Table 9.1 Comparison of simple and advanced mapping modes

	Advantages	Disadvantages
Simple mapping mode	Simple and intuitive to understand, works out of the box.	Can be memory-hungry, with data copied backward and forward between the entity and node representation.
	No special IDE requirements.	Slower.

Table 9.1 Comparison of simple and advanced mapping modes (*continued*)

	Advantages	Disadvantages
Advanced AspectJ mapping mode	Read-through approach may be more memory-efficient.	Read-through approach may have performance implications if too many fine-grained calls are occurring.
	Provides ability to use active record persistence pattern if required.	Bugs involving implicit transactions can be harder to track down and debug.
	Faster.	Tooling, specifically around support for AspectJ in IDEs such as Eclipse and IntelliJ, has been known to cause developers many headaches and sleepless nights and was one of the major gripes by the Neo4j community.

9.5 *Performing queries and traversals*

To wrap up this chapter, let's discuss how SDN extends its easy programming model to be able to specify and make use of queries and traversals in a very simple manner. Suppose you want to find information about a user's friends of friends. We'll use a submodel of the main domain to explore this scenario further, as shown in figure 9.9. Focusing on the user John, the friends of friends are ultimately identified as those users who fall into the last segment on the right.

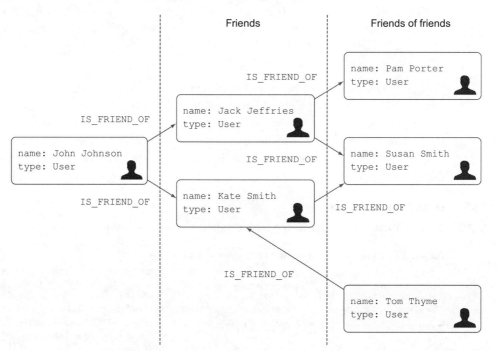

Figure 9.9 Friends-of-friends submodel

9.5.1 *Annotated queries*

It shouldn't surprise you that SDN provides an annotation (@Query in this case) for the purposes of identifying a query to be executed. This can be very helpful in cases where you want to return a filtered list of entities, or perhaps a subset of information determined at runtime. The annotation can be applied to a field on a node entity, or to methods in a repository interface. When the field is accessed on a node entity, or a method is invoked on a repository interface, the query is executed and results are returned.

ANNOTATION ON NODE ENTITIES

Let's start with how the @Query annotation can be applied to the User node entity to define some queries involving the friends-of-friends scenario:

```
@NodeEntity
public class User {

    ...
    @Query( value =
        "match (n)-[r:IS_FRIEND_OF]-(friend)-[r2:IS_FRIEND_OF]-(fof) " +
        "where id(n) = {self} " +
        "return distinct fof")
    Iterable<User> friendsOfFriends;
```

Whenever a User entity is loaded (either through Neo4jTemplate or UserRepository methods), the Cypher query specified in the annotation will be executed and the result stored in the variable (friendsOfFriends, in this case).

This is a standard Cypher query with the only new syntax being the reference to {self}, which refers to the current ID of the node backing this entity. This makes sense, as queries defined on an entity should generally be related to that entity. If your query isn't specifically related to the node entity in question, this is an indication that it probably needs to be defined in a repository as a more generic method.

You can dynamically specify parameters to your query by supplying a set of key-value pairs via the params attribute on the annotation. Following is another snippet illustrating how this can be done to answer the query, "for a given a user, for each of his or her direct friends, count the number of friends and return these counts."

```
@Query(value =
        "match (n)-[r]-(friend)-[r2:IS_FRIEND_OF]-(fof) " +
        "where id(n) = {self} " +
        "and type(r)  = {friendRelName}" +
        "return  friend.name as friendName , count(fof) as numFriends",
    params = {"friendRelName","IS_FRIEND_OF"})
Iterable<Map<String,Object>> friendsOfFriendsCount;
```

As you're not returning the whole entity, but rather a subset of the data, the result of this query will be a read-only collection (Iterable) of entries, with the keys being the names of the variables defined in the return section of the query and their values being the result. Using the example graph in figure 9.9, running this query against John would result in the following answer:

```
{friendName=Kate, numFriends=2}
{friendName=Jack, numFriends=2}
```

The next snippet shows how you can return basic aggregation-type values in Cypher, such as counts. In this case, you're looking for a count of the total number of friends of friends, which according to the submodel depicted in figure 9.9, should be four:

```
@Query(value =
        "match (n)-[r:IS_FRIEND_OF]-(friend)-[r2:IS_FRIEND_OF]-(fof) " +
        "where id(n) = {self} " +
        "return count(distinct fof)")
Long totalNumFriendsOfFriends;
```

ANNOTATION ON REPOSITORY INTERFACES

The @Query annotation can also be applied to methods that you may want to define in your entity-specific repository interfaces. Recall the UserRepository from section 9.3.3. The next listing shows what the same friends-of-friend query looks like when defined against a repository method.

> **Listing 9.13   @Query annotation on repository**

```
public interface UserRepository extends GraphRepository<User> {

    @Query( value =
"match (n)-[r:IS_FRIEND_OF]-(friend)-[r2:IS_FRIEND_OF]-(fof) " +
        "where id(n) = {0} " +
        "return distinct fof")           ◁──────  {0} maps to first argument in
Iterable<User> getFriendsOfFriends(Long nodeId);        method definition (nodeId)
...
```

Note that you're no longer using the {self} reference. Now, even more powerfully, you have access to the parameters passed into the method. The parameters are available as incrementing values starting at zero {0}, which corresponds to the first argument in the method signature, {1} to the second, and so on.

Once again there's no need for you to implement any of the logic to execute the query or do the mapping to convert the result into POJOs, primitives, and the like. SDN does this all for you.

9.5.2   *Dynamically derived queries*

Another really neat way of being able to define a query without needing to write even a line of Cypher code is to take advantage of dynamically named finder or get methods. Whenever SDN comes across a method defined in a repository interface that doesn't have an explicit @Query annotation, it will try to dynamically construct a Cypher query for you, based on the name of your method. SDN will break down the method name into parts that are matched against the metamodel. All of these parts map to properties defined on the associated domain entity class.

There are quite a few options and permutations available, including specifying sort order, specifying range queries, requesting distinct results, and much more. We can't cover them all, but the core set of rules used to recognize dynamic methods can be summarized as follows:

- Any method starting with zero or one of `find`, `read`, `get`
- Optionally followed by any alphanumeric combination of characters
- Subsequently followed by the term `By` (uppercase B)
- Subsequently followed by one or more names of any properties on the associated domain entity, with the first character of the property as uppercase, and multiple properties separated by the term `And` or other comparison separators like `GreaterThan` or `Like`

To demonstrate some of these rules in action, we've defined a few methods that all aim to find any users with a particular name (for example, find all "Susan"s). Have a look at listing 9.14 and notice how all of the method definitions on the `UserRepository` interface will ultimately result in exactly the same underlying Cypher query being generated. Note also that as with annotated queries, the parameter arguments relate to aspects of the method, in this case, the parts representing the property names.

Listing 9.14 Dynamically generated query methods

```
public interface UserRepository extends GraphRepository<User> {

    Iterable<User> name(String name);
    Iterable<User> getByName(String name);
    Iterable<User> getUserByName(String name);
    Iterable<User> readByName(String name);
    Iterable<User> readUserByName(String name);
    Iterable<User> findByName(String name);
    Iterable<User> findUserByName(String name);

}
```

All of these methods resolve to the same generated Cypher query:
match n:User
where n.name = {0} return n

HANDY HINT If you'd like to see what query SDN generates for your method, change the logging level in your application to DEBUG. SDN uses SLF4J, so any framework that supports SLF4J is acceptable; the tests in the sample code make use of Log4j.

As before, return types of `Iterable` indicate to SDN that you're expecting multiple possible entities, whereas a single domain entity indicates you're expecting just one. If you do ever specify that you only expect one entity and the underlying query results in more than one, SDN will throw an exception of the following sort:

```
NoSuchElementException: More than one element in IteratorWrapper(non-empty
    iterator)
```

MULTIPLE AND NESTED PROPERTIES
SDN is capable of understanding related property definitions. If you'd like to find all users who were referred by any other user of a particular name (say Susan), you could define a method as follows:

```
Iterable<User> findByReferredByName(String name);
```

Here the first part of the method references the `referredBy` property on the user. Then, as this property is itself of the `User` type, you proceed to search based on the name of that user.

You could string a whole lot of properties together and separate them with an `And` or `Or` term. (Currently, only `And` is supported at runtime for Cypher.) Let's pretend that your user also had an `age` attribute. In this case, if you wanted to find all users with a particular name and age, you could define a method such as this:

```
Iterable<User> findByNameAndAge(String name, int age);
```

AND MUCH, MUCH MORE

This brief section is nowhere near long enough to introduce the wealth of querying options available, including sorting, range queries, and making use of the generic query methods available through the `Neo4jTemplate` class. We hope we have provided a taste of the kind of queries that you can access and shown you the right direction should you choose to continue down this path.

9.5.3 *Traversals*

Once again we find ourselves unable to cover everything, and unfortunately, graph traversals within SDN is one area we can't cover in depth here. Not to be left out completely, however, we will point out that the traversal framework you encountered in chapter 4 is also accessible from within SDN. If you hadn't already guessed it, there's an annotation for it—namely, `@GraphTraversal`—as well a whole repository interface (`TraversalRepository`) dedicated to helping with traversals involving domain entities.

9.6 *Summary*

In this chapter we introduced the Spring Data Neo4j (SDN) framework that provides a variety of tools that allow you to use a standard POJO-based domain model backed by the powerful Neo4j database. You saw how easy it was to annotate your POJOs in a manner that allowed SDN to seamlessly take care of all the mapping logic between your domain model and the underlying graph primitives.

You learned how to make use of both the Neo4j template- and repository-backed implementations to perform CRUD and indexing operations on your entities, as well as how to define and execute queries involving node entities.

You also learned a little bit more about the two main object-graph mapping modes available to you: simple and advanced. You discovered that although they both ultimately do the same thing, they take quite different approaches to accomplishing this, which can have memory and performance implications that need to be considered.

As we stated in the section 9.1.4, we've only been able to scratch the surface of what SDN can do. We hope that this chapter has served to whet your appetite and that you'll continue to look further into what SDN has to offer. Next up, you'll delve into understanding the differences between using Neo4j in embedded versus server mode.

Part 3

Neo4j in Production

In the first two parts of the book, we covered the basics of Neo4j as well as how to use Neo4j from an application development perspective.

This final part shifts focus and looks at more operational-type areas and aspects, which need equally careful consideration and thinking. There are only two chapters in this part but they cover quite a bit of ground, so strap yourself in!

Chapter 10 explores the two main usage modes in Neo4j—embedded and server—looking at the pros and cons of using each. With much of the book having focused on the use of the embedded option, this chapter provides guidance on and examples of how to take advantage of specific server features such as plugins and extensions to get the most out of Neo4j when running in this mode. Chapter 11 finishes off by taking you on a tour of the high-level Neo4j architecture and showing how to scale and configure Neo4j to be highly available, as well as how to back up and restore your Neo4j database.

Neo4j: embedded
versus server mode

10

This chapter covers

- The two main usage modes: embedded
  and server
- How to weigh the pros and cons of each mode
- Getting the most out of your server with Cypher,
  plugins, extensions, and streaming

Now that you have a good understanding of the approaches and practical techniques required to design and model your world in the Neo4j graph database, it's time to look at the two main ways you can run Neo4j, namely in embedded or server mode. Before embarking on any serious Neo4j project, one of the first things you'll need to do is make a decision about which mode you ultimately want to run in production. This choice will influence, among other things, what languages and architectural landscapes your application can operate within, so it's an important consideration.

You'll be pleased to know that, regardless of which mode you choose, everything you've learned so far is still applicable. The semantics around using each mode are quite different, and it's important to understand what these are and how to use them appropriately, but the core principles remain the same.

In this chapter, we'll cover why there are two modes, what the main differences are, and what the trade-offs, pros, cons, and implications are of using each mode. Let's get into learning mode and get going!

10.1   Usage modes overview

When Neo4j was first released, it was aimed squarely at the Java-based world, and back then it only supported the *embedded mode*. Within the embedded mode setup, your Java application and new shiny Neo4j database were happily bundled together as a single deployable entity, and together they went forth to conquer the brave new world of interesting graph-based problems.

The broader capabilities and functionality of Neo4j, however, did not go unnoticed by other languages, which were also interested in being able to leverage and make use of this new graph database. Neo4j, although written in Java, is inherently just a JVM-based product. This means that, theoretically, any JVM-based language (provided the appropriate libraries or bindings can be found or written) can also make use of the Neo4j database. Thus, Neo4j's reach naturally began to extend to other JVM-based languages as various libraries and bindings began to evolve and become available. But it was the need to operate in more network-friendly architectures and to support other non-JVM clients that were the primary drivers behind the introduction of the *server mode*. With server mode, the Neo4j database runs in its own process, with clients talking to it via its dedicated HTTP-based REST API.

Figure 10.1 shows an overview of the two usage modes and the main ways in which Neo4j can be used by different clients through these modes.

In embedded mode, Neo4j can be used by any client code that's capable of running within a JVM. As figure 10.1 illustrates, you can use the embedded mode directly ❶ with pure Java clients, which make direct use of the core Neo4j libraries, or indirectly, through additional language-specific bindings and frameworks ❷ provided by various communities for other JVM-based languages.

In server mode, client code interacts with the Neo4j server via the HTTP protocol, specifically via a well-defined REST API, with additional options being available to extend this REST functionality when required. The API can be used directly by any HTTP-enabled client ❸, or, to make development life a little easier, by using one of the remote REST client APIs available for a variety of different languages and frameworks ❹. With the inherent network latency introduced in the server mode, performance is naturally not going to be as good as accessing the database using native code directly. To add more flexibility to the server offering, server plugins and unmanaged extensions ❺ can also be used to bolster performance and functionality. We'll be covering server plugins and extensions later in this chapter.

> **NOTE**   All of the coding examples you've seen in the book so far have used an embedded mode setup. Embedded mode is a great way to experiment with Neo4j, and it's often used to explore what Neo4j is capable of. Even if you decide to use the server mode, there will still be opportunities to make use of

native APIs on the server itself, and sometimes it may even be necessary. Additionally, with the REST API often just providing a façade over the raw embedded API, knowing and understanding exactly how the embedded APIs work can be very useful. Understanding embedded semantics and options will go a long way toward helping you get the most out of your setup, even if you opt for a server-based setup.

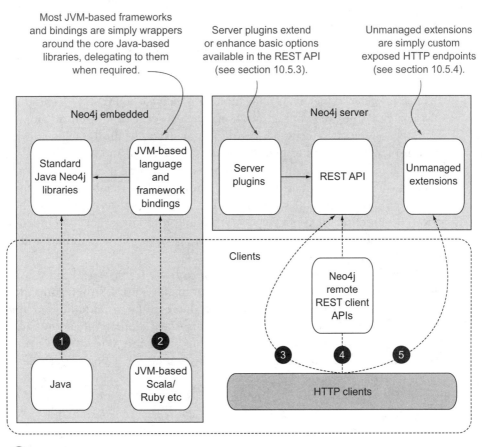

1. Direct use of native embedded Neo4j API

2. Interaction with Neo4j achieved via specific embedded Neo4j framework/binding

3. Direct use of core Neo4j HTTP REST API

4. Interaction via a supported remote REST client API.

5. Interaction via Neo4j unmanaged extensions (custom exposed HTTP endpoints; see section 10.5.4)

Figure 10.1   Overview of Neo4j usage modes and the main integration options for clients

10.2 *Embedded mode*

All the examples we've looked at so far have used the embedded mode, so it makes sense for us to explore this approach in more depth first. To clarify, embedded mode does *not* refer to the embedding of the actual physical database on disk with your application, but rather to the embedding of the Neo4j engine (the classes and associated processes) that run and manage the Neo4j database directly.

10.2.1 *Core Java integration*

The most common embedding scenario involves embedding Neo4j directly within a Java-based application, as shown in figure 10.2.

   The core Neo4j classes that are packaged and run within your application do more than simply act as a mechanism for funneling data backward and forward between the physical data store and your application. The classes themselves form an integral part of the whole database offering, handling, for example, all the logic and in-memory requirements necessary to perform traversals, queries, and so on. From an application architecture perspective, this is interesting because it means that the logic controlling your application, as well as that controlling the database, needs to be able to live in harmony within the same JVM space. The implications of this cohabitation are covered in section 10.4, but for now it's enough to know that the embedded mode means that both your application and Neo4j code will be residing and operating within the same JVM.

   Embedded mode requires that the appropriate libraries (JAR files) are bundled or made available to your application when it starts up. It's then your application's responsibility to gain access to the Neo4j database by instantiating an appropriate instance of the GraphDatabaseService interface. Your application can then use this reference to interact with Neo4j, using all of the APIs we've discussed so far. The EmbeddedGraphDatabase class typically is used for a single machine setup; the

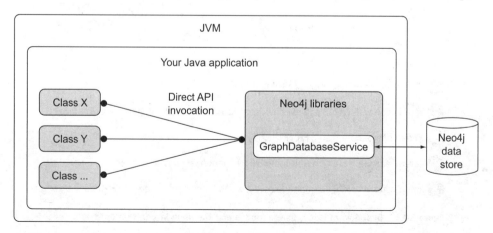

Figure 10.2 Typical Java-embedded deployment scenario, where the Neo4j libraries are embedded in the Java application

`HighlyAvailableGraphDatabase` class is used for a multimachine setup. High Availability (HA) is covered in chapter 11.

REQUIRED LIBRARIES

If you're using Maven within your project (http://maven.apache.org), the following listing shows all that's required to import the appropriate embedded Neo4j libraries into your application.

Listing 10.1 Embedded Neo4j dependencies

```
<dependency>
    <groupId>org.neo4j</groupId>
    <artifactId>neo4j-community</artifactId>
    <version>2.0.1<version>
</dependency>
<dependency>
    <groupId>org.neo4j</groupId>
    <artifactId>neo4j-kernel</artifactId>
    <version>2.0.1</version>
    <type>test-jar</type>
    <scope>test</scope>
</dependency>
```

❶ **Main dependency required for embedded development**

❷ **Test dependency useful for aiding with unit testing**

Maven will ensure that all the required dependencies ❶ will also be downloaded for you as part of its transitive dependency management system. In other words, Maven will work out what other supporting libraries also need to be downloaded in addition to the main Neo4j libraries and ensure that these are retrieved for you.

 If you don't use Maven, you'll need to download the appropriate zip/tarball from the Neo4j website and extract the necessary libraries found in the lib directory. The next listing shows the result of the Maven dependency:tree execution ❷, showing what additional libraries Maven downloads when you request the core embedded libraries.

Listing 10.2 Dependency tree of core Neo4j embedded library

```
[INFO] --- maven-dependency-plugin:2.8:tree (default-cli) @ chapter10-
    embedded ---
[INFO] neo4j-in-action:chapter10-embedded:jar:0.1.1-SNAPSHOT
[INFO] +- org.neo4j:neo4j-community:jar:2.0.1:compile
[INFO] |  +- org.neo4j:neo4j-kernel:jar:2.0.1:compile
[INFO] |  +- org.neo4j:neo4j-lucene-index:jar:2.0.1:compile
[INFO] |  |  \- org.apache.lucene:lucene-core:jar:3.6.2:compile
[INFO] |  +- org.neo4j:neo4j-graph-algo:jar:2.0.1:compile
[INFO] |  +- org.neo4j:neo4j-udc:jar:2.0.1:compile
[INFO] |  +- org.neo4j:neo4j-graph-matching:jar:2.0.1:compile
[INFO] |  +- org.neo4j:neo4j-cypher:jar:2.0.1:compile
[INFO] |  |  +- org.neo4j:neo4j-cypher-commons:jar:2.0.1:compile
[INFO] |  |  +- org.neo4j:neo4j-cypher-compiler-1.9:jar:2.0.1:compile
[INFO] |  |  +- org.neo4j:neo4j-cypher-compiler-2.0:jar:2.0.1:compile
[INFO] |  |  |  \- org.parboiled:parboiled-scala_2.10:jar:1.1.6:compile
[INFO] |  |  |     \- org.parboiled:parboiled-core:jar:1.1.6:compile
[INFO] |  |  +- com.googlecode.concurrentlinkedhashmap:
    concurrentlinkedhashmap-lru:jar:1.3.1:compile
```

Dependency tree corresponding to ❶ **in listing 10.1**

```
[INFO] |  |  \- org.scala-lang:scala-library:jar:2.10.3:compile
[INFO] |  \- org.neo4j:neo4j-jmx:jar:2.0.1:compile
[INFO] +- org.neo4j:neo4j-kernel:test-jar:tests:2.0.1:test    ◁─┐  Dependency tree
[INFO] |  \- org.apache.geronimo.specs:geronimo-                 │  corresponding to
      jta_1.1_spec:jar:1.1.1:compile                             │  ❷ in listing 10.1
[INFO] +- ...
```

GAINING ACCESS TO AN EMBEDDED NEO4J DATABASE

Assuming you have all of the appropriate dependencies available to your code, the next listing details how to obtain a reference to an embedded database, and it also, being a responsible piece of code, provides a mechanism to ensure the database is shut down properly when the JVM exits.

Listing 10.3   Starting and stopping an embedded graph database

```
private String DB_PATH = '/var/data/neo4jdb-private';
private GraphDatabaseService graphdb =
new GraphDatabaseFactory().newEmbeddedDatabase( DB_PATH );    ◁─┐  Creates an
registerShutdownHook( graphDb );                                 │  embedded
                                                                 │  database. The
...                                                              │  physical DB files are
                                                                 │  located at DB_PATH.
private static void registerShutdownHook(
final GraphDatabaseService graphDb )
{
Runtime.getRuntime().addShutdownHook( new Thread()    ◁─┐  Registers a shutdown
    {                                                     │  hook to ensure a clean
        @Override                                         │  shutdown is performed
        public void run()                                ❶ when JVM exits.
        {
            graphDb.shutdown();
        }
    } );
}
```

It's important to try to ensure Neo4j shuts down cleanly whenever your application exits. The shutdown code ❶ in listing 10.3 will be triggered even if you send a SIGINT (Ctrl-C) signal to try to terminate the process before it's finished.

Failure to shut down cleanly could result in problems the next time you start up. Neo4j is able to detect unclean shutdowns and attempt a recovery, but this will result in a slower initial startup while the recovery is in process, and sometimes may result in other issues as well. When an unclean shutdown occurs, the following warning message can generally be seen in the logs the next time the database is started up again: non clean shutdown detected.

TESTING IN EMBEDDED MODE

Testing forms an important part of any software development project. This book and most of the code detailed within are backed by unit tests proving and illustrating the scenarios and statements made in various chapters. In many cases, these tests make use of a very handy in-memory database implementation (org.neo4j.test.Impermanent-GraphDatabase) that has specifically been created with unit testing in mind.

The `ImpermanentGraphDatabase` class can be found in the test neo4j-kernel library (specified in ❷ of listing 10.1). Using Neo4j with an embedded data store (see ❶ in listing 10.3) results in the physical nodes and relationships being stored on disk. Using Neo4j with an impermanent backed data store, however, results in the data only being stored in memory rather than on the filesystem. You're strongly encouraged to unit test your Neo4j code, and this `ImpermanentGraphDatabase` implementation provides a fantastic way to test or prove certain graphing scenarios within your problem domain.

10.2.2 *Other JVM-based integration*

The Neo4j community is a diverse and active bunch, and it has already seen the creation of numerous language and framework bindings for using Neo4j in embedded mode with other languages such as Scala, JRuby, and others. This is typically accomplished through language-specific wrappers that adapt the Neo4j Core Java API into an API that can be used natively (and in some cases idiomatically) by the JVM language and framework in question. Figure 10.3 illustrates what these deployment scenarios typically involve.

What's important here is that most of these wrappers merely front the Java-based Neo4j classes and API. This means that all the properties and semantics associated with the Java-based embedded version will typically also apply to a wrapper-based implementation, with any additional peculiarities introduced by the wrapper library itself also needing to be taken into account.

A listing of the latest language wrappers available can be found at http://neo4j.org/drivers/. At the time of writing, this list included the likes of JRuby, Django, JavaScript, Scala, and Clojure.

This concludes our initial foray into how the embedded mode works and what's required to start making use of it. Next up is a similar exploration of the nature and

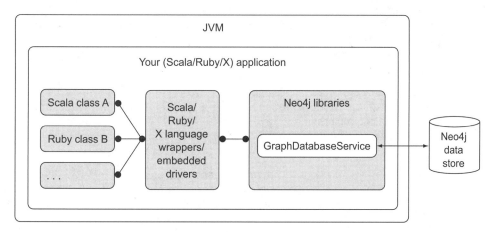

Figure 10.3   Other JVM-based embedded deployment approaches, involving language-specific wrappers and drivers for Neo4j

workings of the server mode, before we move on to looking at the trade-offs, pros, and cons of both.

10.3   Server mode

Unlike embedded mode, running Neo4j in server mode involves having all the classes and logic to access and process interactions with the Neo4j database contained within its own dedicated process, completely separate from any clients wishing to use it. As with many other server-based setups, clients need some mechanism for interacting with the server process, and in the case of Neo4j, this is achieved by using the well-defined, yet extensible, HTTP-based REST API.

What is REST?

REST is sometimes seen as a bit of an overloaded term, but officially it stands for *representational state transfer*. In a nutshell, it can be thought of as an architectural style that embraces and takes advantage of the way in which the web operates and is structured, in most cases using HTTP as the vehicle of choice to help accomplish this. For the full theoretical definition and explanation of REST, refer to Roy Fielding's doctoral dissertation, "Architectural Styles and the Design of Network-based Software Architectures" (2000), where this concept was originally proposed and first published (www.ics.uci.edu/~fielding/pubs/dissertation/top.htm).

By and large, web pages and the ways in which people interact with them follow a consistent pattern, both from the point of view of the user navigating them as well as the servers and supporting infrastructure behind them. As a user, you request pages (resources) by providing URLs. These pages are then returned with the data you requested, as well as additional links to other data or functionality associated with the resource. The server understands HTTP `GET` requests for retrieving data, and `POST` and `PUT` requests for modifying or creating new resources. Simply put, Fielding proposed that these same principles could be used for interacting with more general resources, such as those provided by application services (here, read *web services*). These resources could thus also be offered, navigated, and interacted with in a consistent and predictable manner by humans or systems if they were designed to take advantage of some of these principles that helped the web grow into what it is today.

RESTful-like web services (as opposed to SOAP, for example) are probably the de facto web service implementation nowadays, and Neo4j can be counted among them. Neo4j's REST implementation makes use of JSON as the default data format and offers a service-orientated way of interacting with and manipulating the Neo4j resources (nodes and relationships).

For more information and a pragmatic treatment of the subject, see the excellent book *REST in Practice* by Jim Webber, Savas Parastatidis, and Ian Robinson (O'Reilly, 2010). Jim Webber played a very large part in the design and development of the Neo4j REST API as well.

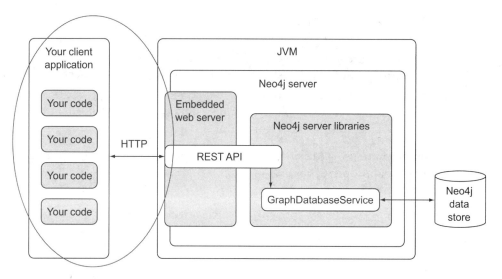

Figure 10.4   A typical Neo4j server setup with client access via the standard REST API

10.3.1 *Neo4j server overview*

Figure 10.4 depicts the core components involved in a running Neo4j in server mode, along with a client accessing the server using the standard, out-of-the-box REST API.

The Neo4j server is itself simply a JVM-based application. Under the covers, it provides its functionality by wrapping an appropriate instance of the GraphDatabase-Service interface (EmbeddedGraphDatabase or HighlyAvailableGraphDatabase), exposing the functionality to the outside world through a well-defined REST interface.

To be able to listen to and react to REST requests made to the server by clients, all Neo4j server instances will start up an embedded web server (currently a Jetty server listening, by default, on port 7474).

INSTALLING AND USING NEO4J SERVER

To install the Neo4j server, you'll need to download the appropriate tar or zip file for your particular OS, uncompress it, and then make use of the OS–specific scripts to start and stop the server. Appendix A details the exact steps required to do this.

From the client perspective, you don't necessarily need any specific Neo4j libraries. As long as you can make HTTP requests, you're good to go. If you're in a Unix environment, the curl client will do this for you. However, the raw REST API is very verbose, and more often than not you'll want some client libraries that can make your life a little easier by taking care of some of the more mundane low-level REST mappings. Using one of the appropriate remote API libraries (listed in section 10.3.4) could help immensely in this regard.

CURL AND JAVA CLIENT EXAMPLES

This chapter provides examples using two different clients:

- The `curl` command available in most Unix distributions. This client will demonstrate how to make calls directly to the low-level REST API.
- A Java client using the official Neo4j Java REST binding (`neo4j-rest-graphdb`) for the server REST API. This option shows how a remote client library can be used to simplify coding against the Neo4j REST API.

Again, if you're using Maven, the following snippet can be added to your pom.xml file to pull the appropriate libraries in:

```
<dependency>
    <groupId>org.neo4j</groupId>
    <artifactId>neo4j-rest-graphdb</artifactId>
    <version>2.0.1</version>
</dependency>
```

10.3.2 *Using the fine-grained Neo4j server REST API*

The original fine-grained Neo4j REST API was designed from the ground up to be hypermedia driven and to be able to be "discovered" as you make use of its various aspects. Each request results in only the minimal amount of information being returned, with embedded links providing the mechanism for obtaining more information. The starting URL from which all parts of the REST API can be explored or derived is http://<domain-name>:<port>/db/data. This is sometimes referred to as the *service root*. Thus a Neo4j server running on the local host, on the default port 7474, would have a service root entry point of http://localhost:7474/db/data.

The following listing shows an example of the data used in a request and the associated response for the service root, highlighting some aspects to give you a feel for the discoverable nature of the API.

Listing 10.4   HTTP service root request and response

```
HTTP Request                                          Service root URL      For all REST requests,
    GET http://localhost:7474/db/data/    ◁─┘                               explicitly set Accept
    Accept: application/json              ◁──────────────                   to be JSON if you
    Content-Type: application/json        ◁──┐                              expect the response
                                             For all REST requests,         to contain data
HTTP Response                                explicitly set Content-
    200: OK                                  Type to be JSON if you
    Content-Type: application/json           need to send data
                                                                            Base REST URL for getting
    {                                                                       information about nodes
      "extensions" : { },                                                   in the system
      "node" : "http://localhost:7474/db/data/node",    ◁──────────────┘
      "node_index" : "http://localhost:7474/db/data/index/node",
      "relationship_index" : "http://localhost:7474/db/data/index/relationship",
      "extensions_info" : "http://localhost:7474/db/data/ext",
      "relationship_types" : "http://localhost:7474/db/data/relationship/types",
```

Base REST URL for getting information about legacy indexed nodes in the system ❶

<table>
<tr><td>

Full URL for performing REST-based batch functionality

</td><td>

```
  "batch" : "http://localhost:7474/db/data/batch",
  "cypher" : "http://localhost:7474/db/data/cypher",
  "indexes" : "http://localhost:7474/db/data/schema/index",
  "constraints" : "http://localhost:7474/db/data/schema/constraint",
  "transaction" : "http://localhost:7474/db/data/transaction",
  "node_labels" : "http://localhost:7474/db/data/labels",
  "neo4j_version" : "2.0.1"
}
```

</td><td>

Full URL for performing REST-based Cypher queries

</td></tr>
</table>

Base REST URL for getting information about labels and schema-indexed nodes in the system ❷

Because REST is accessible via the standard HTTP protocol, a whole raft of clients can now be catered for, and not only those able to operate on the JVM. The following snippet illustrates how the standard Unix curl client generated the HTTP request, the response to which was detailed in listing 10.4. This code snippet includes the setting of all the required headers:

```
curl -X GET -H "Accept: application/json" -H "Content-Type: application/json"
     http://localhost:7474/db/data/
```

Suppose you wanted to explore chapter 9's social networking graph from a particular starting point, such as to get more information about Adam (an example user in the system with the user ID of adam001). You'd first need to identify your starting REST URL. You know that users in the system are indexed by their user IDs. Using listing 10.4 as our starting point, if you were using legacy indexes, you could use the base URL detailed against the node_index ❶ key as the starting point for constructing the final URL needed to look up Adam. Using schema-based indexing, you'd need to construct a URL using the node_labels ❷ key. The fine-grained requests and associated response are shown in the following listing.

Listing 10.5　HTTP request and response for getting info about Adam via his `userId`

```
Legacy Index HTTP request
 GET http://localhost:7474/db/data/index/node/userids/userId/adam001
 Accept: application/json
Label based index HTTP Request
 GET http://localhost:7474/db/data/label/Person/nodes?userId=%22adam001%22
 Accept: application/json

HTTP Response (partial response shown)
    200: OK
    Content-Type: application/json
```

URL that represents and can be used to get base-level info about this node (node ID 0) ❶

URL to get more information on all relationships connected to this node ❷

```
{
  ...
  "extensions" : { . . .},
  "traverse" :
  "property" : "http://localhost:7474/db/data/node/0/properties/{key}",
  "self" :
     "http://localhost:7474/db/data/node/0",
  "all_relationships" :
     "http://localhost:7474/db/data/node/0/relationships/all",
```

```
    "data" : {
      "userId" : "adam001",
      "name" : "Adam"
    }
    ...
}
```

❸ Data for node, detailing all properties (as key-value pairs) stored against this node

This response shows that the returned node, Adam, happens to be associated with node ID 0 ❶. It also includes all of the properties associated with this node ❸. If you wanted to explore the relationships to or from this node, another call would be required. The URL associated with all_relationships ❷ could be used to retrieve this set of information, resulting in the response shown in the following listing.

Listing 10.6   HTTP request and response for all of Adam's relationships

```
Logical HTTP Request
    GET http://localhost:7474/db/data/node/0/relationships/all
    Accept: application/json

HTTP Response
    200: OK
    Content-Type: application/json
```

For each relationship returned, a mixture of data and links is provided for clients so they can discover more info about the particular relationship in question.

```
[ { ... } ,
  { ... } ,
  {
  "start" : "http://localhost:7474/db/data/node/0",
  "data" : { },
  "property" : "http://localhost:7474/db/data/relationship/599/properties/
     {key}",
  "self" : "http://localhost:7474/db/data/relationship/599",
  "properties" : "http://localhost:7474/db/data/relationship/599/properties",
  "type" : "IS_FRIEND_OF",
  "extensions" : { },
  "end" : http://localhost:7474/db/data/node/600
  },
  { ... }
  { ... }
]
```

From these responses, you could continue exploring or discovering the graph as required with additional calls. Although this discoverable approach holds fast to the core principles behind REST, it makes the basic fine-grained REST API quite a chatty protocol, often requiring multiple over-the-wire requests to satisfy basic graph queries. This does not bode well for performance. In the following sections, you'll see what kinds of approaches can be used to reduce the chattiness, but you should now have a good basic understanding of how the core REST API is designed and functions.

10.3.3 *Using the Cypher Neo4j server REST API endpoint*

You can, more often than not, use the Cypher REST endpoint to achieve the same result as you'd get from following the various fine-grained REST API calls from a client, but with fewer network hops and more control. As you'll see moving forward, the use of Cypher is very much encouraged as a way to reduce some of the chattiness of your calls.

The following listing shows how you can execute a Cypher query over the REST API to get both the basic node info for Adam, plus a listing of all Adam's relationships, in one single call—compared to the two separate calls demonstrated in the previous section with the raw fine-grained API.

Listing 10.7   Using Cypher via REST API to get Adam's info, including all relationships

```
Logical HTTP Request
    POST http://localhost:7474/db/data/cypher          ◁─┐  REST API that executes
    Accept: application/json; charset=UTF-8               │  Cypher query
    Content-Type: application/json

{ "query" :                                            ◁─┐  Cypher query to
    "MATCH                                                │  be executed
      ( x:Person { userId: { uId } } )-[r]-()
    RETURN
     x as adam_node ,
     collect(r) as adam_rels",
  "params" :                                           ◁─┐  Values for any
    { "uId" : "adam001" }                                │  parameters
}

HTTP Partial Response
      200: OK
      Content-Type: application/json

{
  "columns" : [ "adam_node", "adam_rels" ],
  "data" : [
[ { // SAME AS CONTENT FROM LISTING 10.5 } ,
      [ // SAME AS CONTENT FROM LISTING 10.6 ]
    ]
  ]
}
```

The benefit of using the Cypher endpoint is that you're able to aggregate and consolidate the required data in a single execution, rather than requiring multiple individual network calls. Although listing 10.7 returned the raw node and relationships data, you could easily modify it to return only a subset of that data, reducing the size of the payload coming back over the wire. You could choose to only return Adam's name, and the names of friends at the end of his IS_FRIEND_OF relationships, with the following query:

```
MATCH ( x:Person { userId: { uId } } )-[r:IS_FRIEND_OF]-(y)
RETURN
   x.name as name ,
   collect(y.name) as friend_names
```

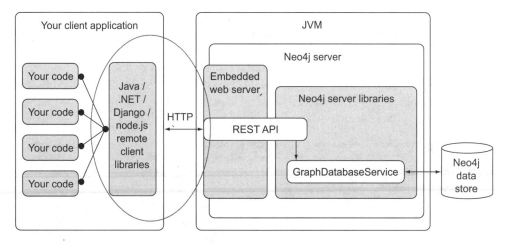

Figure 10.5   Server-based deployment approach using remote REST client libraries

10.3.4 *Using a remote client library to help access the Neo4j server*

In section 10.3.2, you saw how the curl client can be used to operate with the fine-grained low-level REST API. You also probably appreciate that this could prove to be quite tedious if you have to parse the JSON, construct appropriate URLs, and then follow them around yourself. You additionally learned how to make use of the Cypher endpoint as another means of accessing the Neo4j server. As with the fine-grained API, however, this required you to fully understand the low-level queries being executed, including parsing and constructing JSON results.

You could choose to make use of one of the community-contributed Neo4j remote client libraries to provide a more developer-friendly interface that does a lot of this plumbing for you. Figure 10.5 depicts what such a setup would look like. Many languages and framework combinations are available—a listing of remote REST wrappers (as well as general purpose wrappers) can be found at http://www.neo4j.org/develop/drivers. At the time of writing, this list includes Java, .NET, Python, Django, PHP, JRuby, JavaScript, and Clojure.

These libraries and frameworks make integrating with the various aspects of the REST API a far more pleasant experience than trying to deal with the raw API directly. Listing 10.8 shows how a Java client could make use of the java-rest-binding library (https://github.com/neo4j/java-rest-binding) to begin navigating through all of Adam's relationships. This particular binding conveniently wraps the REST calls behind the well-known `GraphDatabaseService` API, which you've already encountered in the Neo4j embedded mode.

Listing 10.8   Java REST client using the java-rest-binding library

```
...
GraphDatabaseService database
   = new RestGraphDatabase("http://localhost:7474/db/data");
```

RestGraphDatabase is a GraphDatabaseService implementation that converts all method calls to REST calls behind the scenes.

```
Node adam = database.findNodesByLabelAndProperty(
            PERSON, "userId", "adam001")
            .iterator().next();
Iterable<Relationship> adamRelationships = adam.getRelationships();
for (Relationship rel: adamRelationships) {
    logger.info("Navigating Adams Relationship, found type " +
    rel.getType().name());
}
```

Translates into an HTTP GET call on http://localhost:7474/db/data/node/0/relationships/all.

Translates into an HTTP GET call on http://localhost:7474/db/data/label/Person/nodes?userId=%22adam001%22.

NOTE The neo4j-rest-graphdb binding provides two ways to interact with the server. The first is the `RestAPIFacade` interface that provides simple wrappers around the basic Neo4j REST API. The other approach (used in listing 10.8) is to use a `GraphDatabaseService` implementation that delegates to the appropriate REST API calls behind the scenes. Although this second approach can be very convenient in that it uses the `GraphDatabaseService` interface you've come to know and love, it must be stressed that you shouldn't expect the same performance that you'll get from the embedded mode. The additional network calls involved will make the Neo4j server calls perform less optimally than simple embedded calls. You'll need to employ different tactics when using a `GraphDatabaseService` that's talking to a Neo4j server over the network to get acceptable performance. We'll be looking into these options later in the chapter.

10.3.5 Server plugins and unmanaged extensions

Neo4j provides two main mechanisms for avoiding the verbose and chatty nature of the basic REST API (aside from the Cypher REST endpoint): server plugins and unmanaged extensions, as highlighted in figure 10.6.

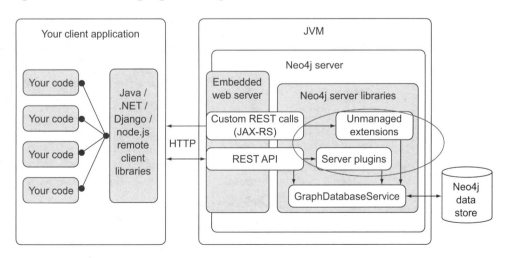

Figure 10.6 Accessing Neo4j via server plugins and unmanaged extensions

These two options allow you to write custom server-side code to supplement or enhance the existing REST API provided out of the box, and they're sometimes compared to the *stored procedures* of the relational database world. They attempt to get around some of the performance limitations inherent in the backward-and-forward nature of the server mode by providing a way to offload some of the heavy-lifting logic to the server side, with only the final result needing to be sent back to the client. Unmanaged extensions, in particular, provide the opportunity to define a more domain-friendly REST API. You'll be seeing examples of how to write server plugins and unmanaged extensions in sections 10.5.3 and 10.5.4 when we show you how to get the most out of the server setup. Before that, we're going to look at comparisons between embedded and server modes.

10.4   Weighing the options

Now that you have a solid understanding of how the embedded and server modes work and differ from each other, we'll move on to looking at pros and cons of each approach. You'll see when it might make sense to choose one over the other, and the possible implications for these choices. Table 10.1 summarizes the main points we'll be covering. Most of the points listed here can be broadly classified under architectural or performance considerations, with a few falling into the "other" category. We'll begin to attack this comparison from those perspectives.

Table 10.1   Advantages and disadvantages of Neo4j embedded and server modes

Server type	Advantages	Disadvantages
Embedded	Speed.	Language restrictions (only Java and JVM languages supported).
	Ability to take full advantage of all low-level APIs directly.	Possible common library clashes with your application.
	Ability to operate in HA setup.	Tight coupling of application process and Neo4j.
		Application may potentially impact the database's performance and vice versa.
		Inability to scale Neo4j independently of the application.
Server	Decoupled architecture: you can scale and manage Neo4j independently of the application.	Awkward and cumbersome fine-grained REST API.
	Larger set of client platforms supported (not only JVM-based).	Slower speed, though using REST streaming, Cypher, batching, server plugins, and extensions may help.
	Multiple clients can use the database.	Restricted to only being able to deal with JSON or HTML responses for raw REST API at this point in time.
	Ability to operate in HA setup.	

Neo4j has successfully been used in both embedded and server modes for startups and large corporations, including companies such as Adobe, Ebay, and GameSys, so you can rest assured that both approaches have been proven on both large and small scales. Neo Technology, the commercial backer of Neo4j, provides a list of customers (including case studies on some of them) who have successfully used Neo4j in various setups. For more information, see the Neo Technology site: http://www.neotechnology.com/customers.

10.4.1 *Architectural considerations*

One of the first things you should consider when embarking on any project is what the overall architectural requirements are, including what kind of clients will need to be supported.

For now we'll ignore considerations such as whether or not you need HA. That's not to say that HA isn't important, but for the purposes of this section, it's not part of the equation. HA is covered in chapter 11. Suffice it to say that both embedded and server modes do cater to HA.

LANGUAGE CONSIDERATIONS

When it comes to your project, if you have any specific language restrictions up front, this will naturally form one of the major factors driving your decision. The server mode can cater to a much larger set of client platforms compared to the embedded mode. With the embedded mode, you're restricted to Java or one of the other supported JVM-based languages only; the server mode can deal with any client that can "talk" HTTP.

SEPARATION OF CONCERNS: APP CONCERNS VERSUS DB CONCERNS

Choice of clients aside, one of the more fundamental items to consider is to what extent you need to be able to scale and manage your application separately from the Neo4j database.

To make this discussion more concrete, consider figure 10.7, which shows two possible ways in which you could choose to deploy the movie-based social network application from previous chapters: embedded and server modes. Let's pretend that there was a requirement for a web application to be available for general users to interact with, as well as an administration section, or separate application, where authorized administrators could perform maintenance and housekeeping tasks, such as loading new movies, deleting old users, and so on.

With the embedded mode, the lifecycle, memory, and processing capabilities of the application (social-movie.war) are tightly bound to those of the embedded Neo4j database; with the server mode, there are separate JVMs handling the application and the Neo4j database (JVM 1 and JVM 2). In the server version, the administration application is separated out into its own PHP-based web client, even further decoupling the main components and applications from one another.

In embedded mode, your application and Neo4j share the same JVM and therefore share the same Java heap; they're subject to the same garbage collection (GC) cycle

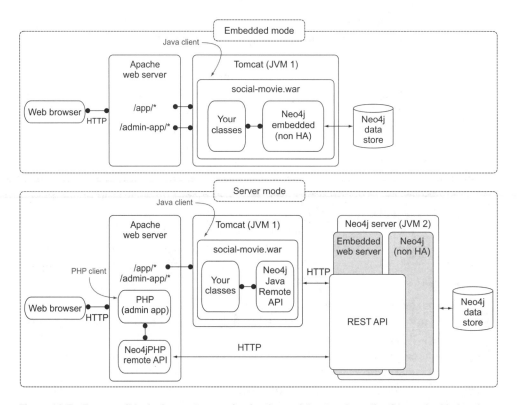

Figure 10.7   Two possible deployment scenarios for the social network application: embedded and server modes

and will essentially live and die together. If your application causes or triggers GC in embedded mode, this may impact the performance of Neo4j. What may appear to be Neo4j reacting slowly may simply be Neo4j waiting for a GC pause to complete. There may also be cases when you'll want to tune the Neo4j JVM and GC parameters separately from those of your application, as they may have fundamentally different usage patterns. Unfortunately, this isn't possible with embedded mode. You'd need to find settings that could function reasonably well for both database and application needs combined. Having said that, as stated earlier, many companies have successfully embedded Neo4j in their applications, but obviously special consideration needs to be given to this area if you do. Chapter 11 goes into more detail about how to tune and maintain the JVM for optimal Neo4j use.

Additionally, because Neo4j is a Java-based application, it will have dependencies on other common libraries. Neo4j uses Lucene as its core indexing implementation (see listing 10.2). Although care has been taken to minimize these dependencies, if your application also makes use of any of these shared common libraries, you'll need to ensure that only one appropriate version is included and used in the JVM at any given time; otherwise there may be unexpected results, either in your application or in the way the database behaves. This is generally not a big issue, but it's something to be aware of.

HARDWARE CONSIDERATIONS

Closely linked to the preceding separation of concerns issue are hardware considerations. For Neo4j to operate and function as efficiently as possible, it ideally needs a beefy machine with a lot of RAM and sufficiently fast disks (refer to chapter 11 for more details). If your setup is such that this isn't possible—for example, if you have an existing limited application server box or a set of boxes that can't be upgraded for whatever reason—then embedding Neo4j in your application may well bring your hardware to its knees.

In this case, one option may be to procure a new machine with sufficient memory where a Neo4j server instance could reside, leaving the application server boxes to deal with what would be considered a more typical application memory profile. If you can upgrade your machine to accommodate the additional Neo4j needs, the embedded approach could be a viable option.

10.4.2 *Performance considerations*

Performance is one of the key areas where the embedded and server modes differ. Neo4j in embedded mode will always outperform the server mode when doing a direct comparison of execution times for the same set of operations done via the native Java API as opposed to the REST API. This is due to the added latency and overhead associated with making calls over the network.

By way of an initial comparison, look at the results detailed in table 10.2, showing the time in milliseconds for embedded and server modes (with nodes per second in parentheses) taken to create one million new user nodes with a `name` property. Each new node was created in its own transaction (TX) using the raw Java API in embedded mode versus the raw REST API of the server mode.

Table 10.2   The initial results of embedded versus server mode performance when creating new nodes

Scenario	Description	Embedded	Server
1	1 TX per node (1,000,000 × 1)	168,815 ms (5,952 nodes/s)	2,380,140 ms (420 nodes/s)

* Run on a MacBook Pro with 16 GB of RAM and 1 TB SSD (with FileVault FS encryption turned on). The Neo4j server was run on the same local machine that the unit test was run on, and the unit test made use of the neo4j-rest-graphdb REST client library detailed earlier.

On the face of it, these numbers don't make for very good reading, even for the embedded mode. Three odd minutes to create 1 million nodes? Don't despair just yet; this example was designed to prove a point. We could argue that the question should never be a simple case of which one is faster. Rather, given a scenario, what can be done to get the best performance, and is this performance level acceptable. A few adjustments to the way in which the operations are performed can have a drastic effect on performance.

Table 10.3 shows how the performance gets a lot better when you start to make better use of transactions (native transactions in embedded mode, and batches for server mode). This simple change has a big effect on the original numbers: up to 10 times faster for the embedded mode and 16 times faster for the server mode using batches.

Table 10.3   Extended results of embedded versus server mode performance when creating new nodes

Scenario	Description	Embedded	Server
1	1 TX per node (1,000,000 × 1)	168,815 ms (5,952 nodes/s)	2,380,140 ms (420 nodes/s)
2	1 TX for all nodes (1 × 1,000,000)	25,654 ms (40,000 nodes/s)	Took too long, hung
3	Batched TXs (20 × 50,000)	16,081 ms (62,500 nodes/s)	148,357 ms (6756 nodes/s)

Whenever you're presented with performance numbers, make sure you understand how the performance test was put together and what factors are in play—or not. To lay all of our cards on the table, listings 10.9 and 10.10 show the code used to perform these comparisons.

Listing 10.9   Code used for embedded performance test comparison

```
...

@Before
public static void setup() throws IOException {          Creates new
graphDbBuilder = new GraphDatabaseFactory()              embedded database
.newEmbeddedDatabaseBuilder ("target/mytestdb");        for use in tests
graphDB = graphDbBuilder.newGraphDatabase();
}

@Test                                                    Corresponds
public void timeCreateNodesEmbeddedModeInSeparateTxs(){  to results for
    timeCreateNodes("EmbeddedModeInSeparateTxs",1000000,1);   embedded test in
}                                                        row 1 of table 10.3

@Test                                                    Corresponds
public void timeCreateNodesEmbeddedModeInOneTx() {       to results for
    timeCreateNodes("EmbeddedModeInOneTx",1,1000000);    embedded test in
}                                                        row 2 of table 10.3

@Test                                                    Corresponds
public void timeCreateNodesEmbeddedModeInMultiBatchedTx() {   to results for
    timeCreateNodes("EmbeddedModeInMultiBatchedTx",20,50000);  embedded test in
}                                                        row 3 of table 10.3

private void timeCreateNodes(
    String scenario, int numTxs, int numNodes2CreatePerTx) {
```

```
       StopWatch stopWatch = new StopWatch(scenario);
           stopWatch.start();
           for (int a = 0; a < numTxs; a++) {
               try (Transaction tx = graphDB.beginTx()) {
                   for (int i = 0; i < numNodes2CreatePerTx; i++) {
                       Node node = graphDB.createNode();          ⟵ Creates new nodes
                       node.setProperty("name","User " + i);          using native graph API
                   }
                   tx.success();
               }
           }
           stopWatch.stop();
}
```

Listing 10.10 Code used for server performance test (RAW API) comparison

```
@BeforeClass
public static void  setup() throws IOException {              Connects to
    restAPI = new RestAPIFacade("http://localhost:7474/db/data");   local Neo4j
}                                                              server to run
                                                               tests against

@Test
public void timeServerModeRawRestAPIInSeparateBatchesStreamingOff() {   Corresponds to
 timeCreateNodes("ServerModeRawRestAPIInSeparateBatchesStreamingOff",    results for server
             false, false, 1000000, 1);                                  test in row 1 of
}                                                                        table 10.3

@Test
public void timeServerModeRawRestAPIOneBatchStreamingOff () {    Corresponds to
 timeCreateNodes("timeServerModeRawRestAPIOneBatchStreamingOff",  results for server
             false, true, 1, 1000000);                           test in row 2 of
}                                                                table 10.3
@Test
public void timeServerModeRawRestAPIInMultiBatchesStreamingOff() {   Corresponds to
 timeCreateNodes("ServerModeRawRestAPIInMultiBatchesStreamingOff",   results for server
             false, true, 20, 50000);                                test in row 3 of
}                                                                    table 10.3

private void timeCreateNodes(String scenario,
   boolean stream, boolean batchMode,
   int numBatches, int numNodes2CreatePerBatch) {          Adds custom HTTP "X-Stream"
                                                            header with value of "true"
   System.setProperty(Config.CONFIG_STREAM,                to request
   Boolean.toString(stream));
   System.setProperty(Config.CONFIG_BATCH_TRANSACTION,
   Boolean.toString(batchMode));                           Instructs REST API to
                                                           use REST batch API
   StopWatch stopWatch = new StopWatch(scenario);          to implement REST
   stopWatch.start();                                    ❶ transactions if enabled
   for (int a = 0; a < numBatches; a++) {
        try (Transaction tx = restAPI.beginTx()) {
            for (int i = 0; i < numNodes2CreatePerBatch; i++) {
                Map<String,Object> props = new HashMap<String,Object>();
                props.put("name", "User " + i);
```

REST
transactions
implemented
with REST
batch API ❷

```
                        Node node = restAPI.createNode(props);      ⟵──┐  Issues request to
                    }                                                   │  create new node
                    tx.success();                                       │  over REST API
                }
        }
    stopWatch.stop();

}
```

When a REST transaction is started ❷, all subsequent REST calls are merely collected and held in memory until the transaction is marked as complete (until the `try` with resource `Transaction` block completes). At this point, the whole collection of requests is then sent over the network as a single batched request. It should be noted that this batching behavior is disabled by default. To turn it on, you need to set the system property `org.neo4j.rest.batch_transaction=true`, which is done via ❶.

As a general rule, the server mode, and in particular the REST API, will suffer more in the area of performance, due to the network-based calls required, but this doesn't mean that it should simply be avoided. There are quite a few alternative approaches and methods that can be used to improve the performance of Neo4j in server mode to the point where it performs at an acceptable level. Section 10.5 is dedicated to looking at this.

10.4.3 *Other considerations*

Besides the architectural and performance considerations already discussed, there are a couple of additional areas to consider that may also influence whether you choose to use embedded or server mode.

REST API: SUPPORTED DATA EXCHANGE FORMATS
The REST API currently only supports JSON and HTML as the data exchange formats. If you prefer XML or some other format, you're out of luck. The only way to make use of a different data exchange format is to use unmanaged extensions (see section 10.5.4), which requires that you define your own REST interface for accessing and interacting with the database. You do lose the ability to make use of all of the prebuilt REST API functionality when you go down this route.

TRANSACTIONS
Neo4j is a fully ACID-compliant database. When using the embedded mode, this is a fairly straightforward proposition, but with server mode, it can sometimes throw up a few interesting challenges.

In server mode, each HTTP request is treated as a single transaction, by default. This means, for example, that you wouldn't be able to create two nodes as part of a single transaction if all you had at your disposal was the raw REST API. (The raw REST API requires two separate HTTP POST requests that would be treated as two separate transactions.)

Approaches for handling transaction scenarios in a server context include

- Using the Cypher endpoint
- Using the REST transactional endpoint
- Using server plugins or unmanaged extensions
- Using batch operations

Depending on your situation, you may be able to define a single Cypher statement that's able to perform multiple operations in one go. Section 10.5.2 provides more details on using the Cypher endpoint. Additionally, there's also a Transactional REST endpoint (http://docs.neo4j.org/chunked/stable/rest-api-transactional.html), which allows you to execute a series of Cypher statements within the scope of a transaction, over multiple HTTP requests. With this option, the client explicitly issues commit or rollback commands via dedicated REST endpoints.

Server plugins and unmanaged extensions enable you to write server-side code that can take the data for creating the nodes in a single HTTP request, and then on the server side ensure they're created as a single transaction (see sections 10.5.3 and 10.5.4 for examples). Neo4j also provides functionality called *batch operations* that allow you to send groups or batches of low-level REST instructions over a single HTTP call, where all of the batched instructions get treated as a single unit when executed on the server side. More information about batch operations can be found in the "Transactional HTTP endpoint" section of the Neo4j Manual, at http://neo4j.com/docs/stable/rest-api-transactional.html..

10.5 *Getting the most out of the server mode*

This final section highlights options for extracting the best possible performance out of the server mode, under a given a set of circumstances. As we've said before, the server mode will suffer more than the embedded mode in the area of performance, but by using some of these techniques and approaches, server mode performance can be brought to an acceptable level.

To fully understand and appreciate the differences between the approaches we'll present, the remainder of this section will use our social network domain as an example to see how these different approaches result in different performance metrics. Let's assume you have a requirement to be able to find and return the names of all of a user's immediate friends, specifically friends whose names start with the letter *J*. In your system, there's already a user set up, Adam, who has 600 immediate friends, 15 of whom have names starting with a *J*. (Adam's userId is adam001; this user has been uniquely indexed and his node ID happens to be 0.)

You'll be using two different clients for your experiments: the first is simply the Unix curl client, and the other is the java-rest-binding client. (You can find the curl scripts and JUnit client test classes that we used for our timings as part of the provided source code. Appendix B provides instructions for running these.)

Table 10.4 provides a template for you to fill in your findings as you go along.

Table 10.4   Performance metrics log:template

Scenario	Description	Number of server calls made	Curl client		Java REST binding	
			Cold	Warm	Cold	Warm
1	Raw REST API					
2	Cypher call					
3	Server plugin					
4	Unmanaged extension					

- Time is stated in milliseconds.
- Timing for curl client is done using the bash time command.
- Timing for the Java REST binding done using Java (Spring) StopWatch.
- Cold = server first stopped then started before the first REST call was made.
- Warm = second call (same as previous) made directly after first without server restart.

Cold vs. warm timings

The first call (a cold call) made to the server includes the time required to perform one-off bootstrapping, caching, and initialization processing, which may not be present for subsequent (warm) calls. This means that cold calls will almost always be slower, and may also be slightly less predictable than warm calls. We will be providing you with both timings to provide a full picture.

10.5.1   *Avoid fine-grained operations*

As a general rule, when performing any kind of operations over a network, you should aim to minimize the number of network hops required to carry out that operation, and this same principle should also be applied to the manner in which the REST API is used. The raw, low-level REST API operations are very fine-grained, typically operating on a single node or relationship at any time. They can generate a lot of unnecessary network traffic if used inappropriately.

Rather than only using the discoverable low-level REST API for retrieving data, you should consider the following alternatives that may result in far fewer network calls and much better performance:

- Use the Cypher REST endpoint
- Use the Traversal REST endpoint
- Create a server plugin or unmanaged extension to return results

For creating data, consider these options:

- Use the mutating functionality in the Cypher API
- Use the REST batch API
- Create a server plugin or unmanaged extension to perform your task

If you use the raw REST API with its hypermedia-driven approach to get the information you need for the example scenario, you'll need a total of 602 network calls in order to accomplish this. Assuming the Neo4j server is running locally on port 7474, you'd need to do the following:

- 1 GET on http://localhost:7474/db/data/node/0 to get the initial information on data and options available for Adam.
- 1 GET on http://localhost:7474/db/data/node/{nId}/relationships/all/IS_ FRIEND_OF to get a listing of all the IS_FRIEND_OF relationships to and from Adam (see listing 10.6 for request/response details).
- 600 GETs on http://localhost:7474/db/data/node/{nId}/properties to get each of the relationship structures returned in this first call (there will be 600 entries). You'd then use the end URI to construct the next call, which will return all of the properties for the ending (friend) node. The JSON returned in each of these calls could then be parsed and used to only return those names starting with a *J*.

The updated performance metrics log is shown in table 10.5.

Table 10.5 Performance metrics log after scenario 1, raw REST API

Scenario	Description	Number of server calls made	Curl client		Java REST binding	
			Cold	Warm	Cold	Warm
1	Raw REST API	602	5726 ms	5303 ms	1066 ms	917 ms
2	Cypher call					
3	Server plugin					
4	Unmanaged extension					

10.5.2 *Using Cypher*

The Neo4j REST API makes a provision for you to run arbitrary Cypher statements against the server by posting the appropriate query or statement and parameters to the designated REST endpoint responsible for executing Cypher. Provided you have all the information you need to construct your query or statement upfront, this should require only one network call.

Using the response returned from requesting the service root URL, described in section 10.3.2, the URL defined against the cypher key (see listing 10.4) provides the entry point to use to send Cypher queries and statements to the server. The following snippet shows the service root response from listing 10.4:

```
...
"batch"  : "http://localhost:7474/db/data/batch",
"cypher" : "http://localhost:7474/db/data/cypher",
...
```

Listings 10.11 and 10.12 show the corresponding request and response to execute a Cypher query to satisfy our example scenario.

Listing 10.11   Cypher REST request

```
HTTP Request
    POST http://localhost:7474/db/data/cypher          ◁─┐ REST endpoint that executes
    Accept: application/json                              │ Cypher statements
     Content-type: application/json

{ "query" :
     "MATCH ( x:Person { userId: { lookupId } } )        ❶ "query" holds
          -[r:IS_FRIEND_OF]-(friend)                         a standard
       WHERE friend.name =~ {name2find}                      Cypher query
       RETURN friend.name ",
  "params" : {
     "lookupId" : "adam001",            ❷ "params" used
     "name2find"  : "J.*"                  in query
  }
}
```

The actual Cypher query is specified in the query key ❶ in the JSON request, with any associated parameters provided in the params key ❷ as key-value pairs.

Listing 10.12   Cypher REST response

```
HTTP Response
    200: OK                                     ❶ Ordered array of column
    Content-Type: application/json                 names indicating what data will
                                                   be returned in the data key
{
  "columns" : [ "friend.name" ],          ◁─┘
  "data" : [ [ "NonJFriend 1" , "NonJFriend 2" ,  ◁─ Ordered array of data returned
          "NonJFriend 3" , "JFriend 4"     ,         corresponding to that
          ... ] ]                          ❷         identified by the columns array
}
```

The results are returned in a structure that defines the column headers ❶ and corresponding data values ❷. You can see that the column name matches the RETURN statement specified in the Cypher request from listing 10.11, and that all the matches for this column heading are provided as an array of names under the data section in listing 10.12. The updated metrics log is shown in table 10.6.

Table 10.6   Performance metrics log after scenario 2, Cypher call

Scenario	Description	Number of server calls made	Curl client		Java REST binding	
			Cold	Warm	Cold	Warm
1	Raw REST API	602	5726 ms	5303 ms	1066 ms	917 ms
2	Cypher call	1	740 ms	45 ms	104 ms	32 ms

Table 10.6 Performance metrics log after scenario 2, Cypher call

Scenario	Description	Number of server calls made	Curl client		Java REST binding	
			Cold	Warm	Cold	Warm
3	Server plugin					
4	Unmanaged extension		.			

This approach has provided a dramatic improvement to the performance for the query.

10.5.3 *Server plugins*

Server plugins provide a mechanism for offloading some of the processing-intensive logic to the server rather than having to perform it all on the client, with multiple requests having to flow backward and forward to accomplish the same thing. Server plugins are sometimes compared to stored procedures in the relational database world.

Server plugins have specifically been designed to extend the existing REST API options returned for a node, relationship, or the global graph database. Recall that when you make a request for the detail of a particular node, you get a lot of options back, including an `extensions` key. See the following snippet for a recap:

```
{ ...
  "extensions" : { . . .},
  "property" : "http://localhost:7474/db/data/node/0/properties/{key}",
  "self" : "http://localhost:7474/db/data/node/0",
  "data" : { "name" : "Adam"  }
  ... }
```

This represents the list of extension points (server plugins available) for the node. Similar extension points will be available for relationships and the graph as a whole.

To write a server plugin, you need to first decide what it is you want to target or extend—the node, relationship, or graph database options—and then follow these steps:

1 Write a class that extends the `ServerPlugin` class.
2 Ensure that the fully qualified name of the server plugin class is listed in a file called org.neo4j.server.plugins.ServerPlugin.
3 Ensure that the plugin class and file are JAR files, and that they're placed on the class path of the Neo4j server.
4 Access the functionality by discovering and then calling the appropriate REST URL.

The following listing shows a `ServerPlugin` class we created to extend the capabilities of a node by finding all friends with names starting with a *J*.

Listing 10.13   `ServerPlugin` class

The **❷** discovery point type

Name that will get exposed in the REST API for clients to use **❸**

```
public class JFriendNamesServerPlugin extends ServerPlugin        ◁─┐   Must extend
{                                                                     │   ServerPlugin class
    @PluginTarget(Node.class)                                       ❶   to be picked up
    @Name( "get_friendnames_starting_with_j" )
    @Description( "Returns names of all friends start with the letter J" )
    public List<String> getFriendNamesStartingWithJ(
                @Source Node node )                                              ◁─────┐
    {                                                                                  │
        GraphDatabaseService database = node.getGraphDatabase();                       │
        try (Transaction tx = database.beginTx()) {                                    │
            return JFriendGraphHelper.extractJFriendNamesFromRawAPI(node);             │
        }                                                                              │
    }
}
```

Corresponding reference to discovery
point type specified in **❷**, which can then
be used within the method to perform
whatever logic or functionality is required **❹**

```
public class JFriendGraphHelper {
    private RelationshipType IS_FRIEND_OF =
        DynamicRelationshipType.withName("IS_FRIEND_OF");

    public static List<String> extractJFriendNamesFromRawAPI(Node node) {   ◁─────┐
        List<String> names = new ArrayList<String>();                             │
        for (Relationship rel: node.getRelationships(IS_FRIEND_OF)) {             │
            Node friendNode = rel.getOtherNode(node);                            │
            String friendName =                                                 │
                (String)friendNode.getProperty("name","unknown");               │
            if (friendName.startsWith("J")) {                                   │
                names.add(friendName);                  Helper method using     │
            }                                           the core native API to  │
        }                                               perform actual logic     │
        return names;
    }
}
```

ALL NODES ARE EQUAL   When a plugin targets a node, it targets all nodes. Even if logically you have different types of nodes defined within your database, such as `user` nodes and `movie` nodes, Neo4j will make this server plugin available on *all* nodes. Care should be taken to define server plugins that can be used across all nodes, or for some mechanism to be in place to ensure it gets executed on only the appropriate types of nodes.

Extending the `ServerPlugin` class **❶** will ensure that this class is picked up as a server option when the server starts. For each extension point required, a method should be created that specifies (via the `@PluginTarget` annotation **❷**) what the discovery point type is. This will be one of `Node`, `Relationship`, or `GraphDatabaseService`. Combined with the `@Name` annotation **❸**, this will determine where and under what name the additional REST endpoints are exposed in the overall REST API. A corresponding reference to the `Node`, `Relationship`, or `GraphDatabaseService` argument in the method itself **❹** will also be required so that this reference can be used to perform any functionality or logic that may be required.

The following listing shows how you could make an HTTP request to get the details for node 0 (Adam), as well as a portion of the resulting response, including a listing of what extensions are available.

Listing 10.14 Extension snippet of HTTP response for getting info on Adam node

```
Logical HTTP Request
    GET http://localhost:7474/db/data/node/0
    Accept: application/json

HTTP Response
    200: OK
    Content-Type: application/json
{
    ...
    "self" : "http://localhost:7474/db/data/node/0",
    "extensions" : {
       "JFriendNamesServerPlugin" : {
        "get_friendnames_starting_with_j" :
           "http://localhost:7474/db/data/ext/JFriendNamesServerPlugin/
node/0/get_friendnames_starting_with_j"
      }
    },
    ...
}
```

JSON key under which server plugin extensions are listed

Name (corresponds to ❸ in listing 10.13) that clients can use to look up URL to execute this plugin against this particular node

As the numbered list of steps in the beginning of this section stated, a JAR file needs to be created that contains both the plugin class and the org.neo4j.server.plugins .ServerPlugin file, as shown in the following snippet (available in the META-INF/ services directory):

```
com.manning.neo4jia.chapter10.serverplugin.JFriendNamesServerPlugin
```

This JAR file should then be placed on the server class path. This is usually done by placing the JAR file in the plugin directory of wherever the server is installed.

The results of this server plugin execution, which under the covers is using the native embedded API, are detailed in table 10.7. Again, there's quite a drastic improvement over the plain REST API.

Table 10.7 Performance metrics log after scenario 3, server plugin

Scenario	Description	Number of server calls made	Curl client		Java REST binding	
			Cold	Warm	Cold	Warm
1	Raw REST API	602	5726 ms	5303 ms	1066 ms	917 ms
2	Cypher call	1	740 ms	45 ms	104 ms	32 ms
3	Server plugin	1	147 ms	20 ms	76 ms	16 ms
4	Unmanaged extension					

10.5.4 *Unmanaged extensions*

If you require complete control over your server-side code, then *unmanaged extensions* may be what you're looking for. Unlike server plugins, which merely allow you to augment the existing REST API at specific points, unmanaged extensions essentially allow you to define your own domain-specific REST API. Instead of nodes and relationships, you can now deal in users and movies if you so choose.

Neo4j makes this possible by allowing you to deploy arbitrary JAX-RS (Java API for RESTful web services) classes to the server. JAX-RS provides a set of APIs that are supposed to make developing REST services a piece of cake for developers. Broadly speaking, you define a Java class, which, through a set of annotations, binds the class to a particular URL pattern and mount point within the Neo4j server. When this mount point is invoked, control is transferred to this class, which can have full access to the Neo4j graph database, allowing the class to perform whatever actions or functionality is required, returning the data in whatever format is desired. Though the protocol still needs to be over HTTP, the data format isn't restricted to only JSON and HTML, as with the REST API and server plugins.

> **WARNING!**   Unmanaged extensions essentially give you unrestricted access to use and influence the resources of the Neo4j server. This is extremely powerful, but you need to be careful you don't accidentally shoot yourself in the foot, so to speak. This could be done by consuming all of the JVM heap space while performing an expensive traversal of some sort. Provided you understand what you're doing, this can be a powerful tool in your toolbox, but as the saying goes: With great power comes great responsibility!

The next listing shows an implementation of an unmanaged extension that looks up a user based on their name and then returns all of the user's immediate friends whose name starts with a *J*.

Listing 10.15   An unmanaged extension

```
@Path( "/example" )                                        Beginning part of URL under
public class JFriendNamesUnmanagedExt {                    which this functionality will
                                                           be exposed
    private final GraphDatabaseService database;
    private static final Label PERSON = DynamicLabel.label("Person");

    public JFriendNamesUnmanagedExt(                       @Context annotation injects
    @Context GraphDatabaseService database )               GraphDatabaseService into class,
    {                                                      providing full access to database
        this.database = database;
    }                                                      Remaining path of URL pattern under
                                                           which the functionality defined in the
    @Path( "/user/{userid}/jfriends" )                     method will be exposed
    @GET
    @Produces( MediaType.APPLICATION_JSON )                Will result in content being
                                                           produced with Content-Type
                                                           response header of JSON
```

Will only respond to an HTTP GET method

Binds
whatever
value was
specified in
the userid
variable
defined in
#C to the
Java userId
property for
use within
the method

```
public Response getJFriends( @PathParam( "userid" ) String userId )
{
    List<String> names = null;
    try (Transaction tx = database.beginTx()) {
        Node theUser = database.findNodesByLabelAndProperty(
                        PERSON, "userId", userId)
                        .iterator().next();
        names=JFriendGraphHelper.extractJFriendNamesFromRawAPI(theUser);
    }

    ObjectMapper mapper = new ObjectMapper();
    String jsonString = mapper.writeValueAsString(names);
    return Response.status( Status.OK ).entity(jsonString ).build();
}
}
```

Serializes a list of
names to JSON

As with server plugins, this class needs to be a JAR file and made available to the Neo4j server. By convention, this is done by placing the JAR file in the plugins directory of your Neo4j server.

Additionally, you'll need to add and map any unmanaged extensions in the neo4j-server.properties file against the org.neo4j.server.thirdparty_jaxrs_classes key. (This can usually be found in the conf directory of the Neo4j server installation.) The mapping consists of defining the Java package that contains the extension classes. You map this to the base mount point as shown in the following snippet:

```
org.neo4j.server.thirdparty_jaxrs_classes=com.manning.neo4jia.chapter10.unman
    agedext=/n4jia/unmanaged
```

This means that to execute the unmanaged extension and get all of Adam's friends' names starting with the letter *J*, you'd need to issue an HTTP GET against http://local-host:7474/n4jia/unmanaged/example/user/adam001/jfriends.

Table 10.8 shows how the unmanaged extension in listing 10.15 fares against the other approaches you've seen so far.

Table 10.8 Performance metrics log after scenario 4, unmanaged extension

Scenario	Description	Number of server calls made	Curl client		Java REST binding	
			Cold	Warm	Cold	Warm
1	Raw REST API	602	5726 ms	5303 ms	1066 ms	917 ms
2	Cypher call	1	740 ms	45 ms	104 ms	32 ms
3	Server plugin	1	147 ms	20 ms	76 ms	16 ms
4	Unmanaged extension	1	158 ms	20 ms	119 ms	18 ms

Besides providing yet another mechanism for improving the performance of the server, unmanaged extensions provide benefits in allowing you to define a domain-specific REST API, as well as the ability to use whatever data interchange format—JSON, binary, text, or otherwise—you choose. We reiterate our warning, however, that this powerful tool needs to be managed carefully lest you inadvertently open Pandora's box.

10.5.5 *Streaming REST API*

As of Neo4j version 1.8, the option to "stream" the JSON responses to REST requests has been introduced as another means for improving the performance of the Neo4j REST API. By default streaming is turned off.

At present, from the client's perspective, all that's required to have the results streamed back is to provide an extended header (X-stream=true), as shown in figure 10.8.

Note that this is still new functionality and it may be subject to change as clearer usage patterns emerge and the API evolves. We won't go into too much detail at this time.

To demonstrate the additional improvement in performance gained by using the streaming API, we executed a Cypher query that returned all the nodes in the example

```
           tmp — bash — ttys008 — 98×43
04:52:08(/tmp)$
04:52:09(/tmp)$
04:52:09(/tmp)$
04:52:09(/tmp)$ # --------------- Current number of nodes in DB ---------------
04:52:09(/tmp)$
04:52:09(/tmp)$ curl -X POST -d '{ "query" : "start n=node(*) return count(n)" } '
               -H "Accept: application/json" -H "Content-type: application/json"
               http://localhost:7474/db/data/cypher
{
  "columns" : [ "count(n)" ],
  "data" : [ [ 120602 ] ]
}04:52:09(/tmp)$
04:52:09(/tmp)$
04:52:11(/tmp)$
04:52:11(/tmp)$
04:52:11(/tmp)$
04:52:12(/tmp)$ # ------------ Returning ALL nodes (Streaming OFF) ------------
04:52:19(/tmp)$
04:52:19(/tmp)$ curl -X POST -d '{ "query" : "start n=node(*) return n " } '
               -H "Accept: application/json" -H "Content-type: application/json"
               --limit-rate 12m -H "X-Stream: false"
               http://localhost:7474/db/data/cypher > /dev/null
  % Total    % Received % Xferd  Average Speed   Time    Time     Time  Current
                                 Dload  Upload   Total   Spent    Left  Speed
100  168M  100  168M  100    42  9740k      2  0:00:21  0:00:17  0:00:04 11.5M
04:52:37(/tmp)$
04:52:37(/tmp)$
04:52:39(/tmp)$
04:52:44(/tmp)$
04:52:45(/tmp)$ # ------------ Returning ALL nodes (Streaming ON) ------------
04:52:46(/tmp)$
04:52:46(/tmp)$ curl -X POST -d '{ "query" : "start n=node(*) return n " } '
               -H "Accept: application/json" -H "Content-type: application/json"
               --limit-rate 12m -H "X-Stream: true"
               http://localhost:7474/db/data/cypher > /dev/null
  % Total    % Received % Xferd  Average Speed   Time    Time     Time  Current
                                 Dload  Upload   Total   Spent    Left  Speed
100  149M    0  149M  100    42  11.9M      3  0:00:14  0:00:12  0:00:02 12.0M
04:52:59(/tmp)$
04:52:59(/tmp)$
04:55:06(/tmp)$
04:55:07(/tmp)$
04:55:08(/tmp)$
```

Figure 10.8 Result of turning streaming on/off

database. We added an extra 120,000 nodes to generate data resulting in a total of 120,602 nodes, including Adam and his friends existing within the database. The streamed results came back in about 14 seconds for 149 MB compared to 21 seconds for 168 MB.

> **NOTE** The payload is smaller because the streamed results are compressed (whitespace removed) when being sent back. Streaming can also reduce the memory required by the server to perform this task. This is possible because the data requested is streamed directly back to the client as it's read from the database, without having to temporarily store it in any nodes or relationship objects along the way.

10.6 *Summary*

You've seen how both the embedded and server modes provide the ability to access and interact with the Neo4j database, but the manner in which this is done is fundamentally different.

With the embedded mode, you have quite a cozy relationship with Neo4j, which is only available to Java and a select number of other JVM-based languages. Though you get direct access to all of Neo4j's low-level APIs and can leverage the performance gains associated with this, you're also required to share your resources (memory and the like) with Neo4j as well. This could potentially introduce additional overhead and complications to the management of your application, and that needs to be taken into account.

In the server mode, the Neo4j process is isolated and can be managed completely separately from that of the application, which is a big win in large distributed architectures. All the interactions, however, need to be done through the REST abstraction layer, which although it casts a wider net in terms of the clients it supports, has some performance implications that need to be understood and dealt with appropriately.

These performance issues are not insurmountable, with options like server plugins, extensions, streaming, and appropriate use of Cypher statements all helping to allow the server mode to operate at a better performance level.

The next logical query is how to run your Neo4j database in a production environment. You now have all the basics under your belt, but what will you need to take into account when you actually want to go live? The next, and final, chapter will cover this topic. You'll learn about some of the operational considerations involved in using Neo4j in the real world.

Neo4j in production

This final chapter covers some of the more operational aspects involved in running Neo4j in a real production environment.

This includes looking at features such as running Neo4j in "High Availability" mode, paying particular attention to ensuring that Neo4j can operate in a fault-tolerant and scalable manner. It additionally covers how to back up and restore your database, for the scenarios where things have gone a little bit pear-shaped, as well as providing insight and instructions for how to configure important memory and cache settings, which play a large part in determining how well Neo4j performs.

To help you get the most out of this chapter, and indeed out of this book as a whole, this final chapter begins with a high-level tour through the Neo4j architecture, peeking under the hood in certain places. The primary purpose of this tour is to provide context, and a structured path for introducing and discussing operational and configurational aspects key to this chapter. It additionally provides us with a great opportunity to recap and reinforce some important and significant concepts covered in previous chapters along the way.

So, let's begin!

11.1 *High-level Neo4j architecture*

As with any database, Neo4j has some configurations—knobs and levers that can be applied, pushed, or tweaked in order to direct or influence how the database operates and performs. We could provide a simple listing of what settings and options are available where, but we want you to get more out of this chapter than just knowing *what* you can change. Ideally, we want you to gain a little bit of mechanical sympathy for Neo4j—a basic feel for how Neo4j works under the covers. This will allow you to understand *why* certain setups, and the tweaking of certain settings, cause Neo4j to operate in the way it does, rather than just knowing that particular options exist.

> ### Mechanical sympathy?
>
> *Mechanical sympathy* is a metaphor that's gaining in popularity in the computing world. It's basically used to convey the idea that in order to get the most out of a tool or system properly (Neo4j in this case), it helps if you understand how it works under the covers (the mechanics). You can then use this knowledge in the most appropriate way.
>
> The original metaphor itself is attributed to the Formula 1 racing car driver Jackie Stewart, who is believed to have said that in order to be a great driver, you must have mechanical sympathy for your racing car. Stewart believed that the best performances came as a result of the driver and car working together in perfect harmony.
>
> Martin Thompson of LMAX fame was the first to popularize the use of this metaphor (as far as I'm aware) in the computing sense, when describing how the LMAX team came up with the low-latency, high-throughput disruptor pattern. His use of the metaphor can be seen in the presentation "LMAX—How to Do 100K TPS at Less than 1ms Latency" at www.infoq.com/presentations/LMAX.

The high-level Neo4j architecture is shown in figure 11.1. Your tour through the architecture will begin at the bottom of this figure and wind its way up to the top.

Because this is an introductory book, we won't be able to delve too deeply into all the aspects of Neo4j's internals. Rather we aim to go just deep enough to help you appreciate and work in harmony with Neo4j, without getting too bogged down in low-level details. For a more in-depth treatment of the subject of how Neo4j works internally, see chapter 6, "Graph Database Internals" in *Graph Databases* by Jim Webber, Ian Robinson, and Emil Eifrem (O'Reilly, 2013). Although it's a general-purpose graph database book, chapter 6 uses Neo4j's architecture as an example to explain how a good, performant native graph database is laid out and implemented. Additionally,

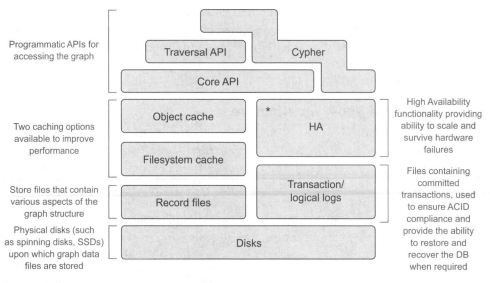

* *Only available in Neo4j Enterprise Edition*

Figure 11.1   High-level overview of the Neo4j architecture

Tobias Lindaaker has done presentations on Neo4j internals, one of which, "An overview of Neo4j internals," can be found here: www.slideshare.net/thobe/an-overview-of-neo4j-internals.

11.1.1 Setting the scene …

The time has come for you to plan to put your application into production. From an operational perspective, there will typically be three main questions, or categories of questions, that will be asked of you regarding your new graph database:

- *Physical storage*—What kind and how much of it will be needed?
- *Memory*—How much memory (RAM) and CPUs are required to support efficient and performant running of the application and database?
- *Scalability and redundancy*—What's required to ensure Neo4j can scale to accommodate a growing load, to ensure that it's highly available (or available enough), and to ensure it can be properly backed up and restored in the event of failure?

Working backward, recovery and backups are covered in section 11.3, HA is covered in section 11.2, and the memory- and CPU-related questions in section 11.1.4. First up, we'll tackle the question of storage and disks, which leads us neatly to our starting point at the bottom of Neo4j's architectural stack.

11.1.2 Disks

At the bottom of the architectural stack are the physical disks where Neo4j actually stores the graph data.

WHAT KIND OF DISKS SHOULD BE USED?

Neo4j doesn't dictate what kind of disks should be used, but it goes without saying that faster disks will lead to faster performance whenever physical disk IO is required. Making use of disks that provide lower seek times (such as solid state drives, a.k.a. SSDs) will generally provide a read-performance boost of 10 to 20 times that of traditional spinning disks.

As you'll learn in section 11.1.4, you should aim to keep as much of the graph in memory as possible, as this reduces disk IO, which helps enable Neo4j to perform at its best. At some point, however, your application or database will need to go to disk to read data. At the very least, this will occur when you initially start up your database and begin to access cold parts of the graph. It may also occur if your graph is simply too big to fit into memory (see section 11.2.4 on cache sharding).

Avoiding disk IO is one of the key factors in maximizing Neo4j performance, and having speedy disks for the times when this IO can't be avoided can make quite a difference.

HOW MUCH SPACE DO I NEED FOR MY GRAPH DATABASE?

The amount of space required obviously depends on how much data you plan on storing in Neo4j, and on any additional space required to support the runtime operation of Neo4j.

All Neo4j data lives under a single, top-level Neo4j directory (by default, data/ graph.db in a server-based setup). This includes the core graph data, which lives in a set of store files (covered in section 11.1.3), transaction logs (covered in section 11.1.5), and the rest (including things like indexes and other minor files) in other files.

All of the main store files that contain the core graph structure are consistent in the amount of space they occupy—they have fixed record sizes, which can help you estimate the ultimate file sizes. This helps greatly in calculating what the core database sizing requirements are, although this alone isn't always enough to work it out exactly. This is partly due to the fact that Neo4j itself will sometimes create additional files as part of its internal runtime optimizations, which can't necessarily be anticipated upfront. Indexes and labels will also take up more space.

You can do rough math based on your estimates of the number of nodes, relationships, and properties required. The general formula for calculating the space required for the core graph data is

```
Core Graph Size (in bytes) =
    (num nodes          X node store record size in bytes) +
    (num relationships X relationship store record size in bytes) +
    (num properties     X average bytes per property)
```

The fixed record sizes are discussed in more detail in the next section, but at the time of writing, the node store uses 14 bytes and the relationship store uses 33 bytes. Remember that there will be additional disk storage requirements for indexes, transaction logs, and the like, and these should also be taken into account when calculating the total amount of disk space required. Having said that, calculating the core graph data size, which is usually what takes up much of the disk space used by Neo4j, is relatively straightforward.

Neo4j hardware sizing calculator

Neo Technology provides an online hardware sizing calculator to provide rough estimates for the minimum hardware configuration required, given a certain set of inputs, such as the expected number of nodes, relationships, properties, number of users, and so on. This calculator deals not only with disk storage capacity, but also RAM and clustering setup recommendations.

It should be stressed that this calculator is only meant to provide a rough estimate. If you're embarking on a mission-critical project, you're advised to seek a more accurate assessment from qualified engineers, which can take many other factors into consideration. But for a rough and ready starting calculation, this calculator will generally serve just fine.

You can find the hardware sizing calculator on the Neo Technology site, www.neotechnology.com/hardware-sizing.

11.1.3 *Store files*

Neo4j stores various parts of the graph structure in a set of files known as *store files*. These store files are generally broken down by record type—there are separate files for nodes, relationships, properties, labels, and so on. The structure and layout of the data in these files has specifically been designed and optimized to provide an efficient storage format that the Neo4j runtime engine can exploit to provide very performant lookups and traversals through the graph. One of the core enablers is the fact that Neo4j stores data according to the index-free adjacency principle.

The index-free adjacency what?

The index-free adjacency principle (or property) is a fancy term that refers to graph databases that are able to store their data in a very particular way. Specifically, each node stored within the database must have a direct link or reference to its adjacent nodes (those nodes directly connected to it) and must *not* need to make use of any additional helper structures (such as an index) to find them.

By storing its data in this manner, Neo4j is able to follow pointers directly to connected nodes and relationships when performing traversals, making this type of access extremely fast compared to non-index-free adjacency stores, such as the traditional relational database. In Neo4j there's no overhead incurred when trying to locate immediately connected nodes; non-index-free adjacency stores would first need to use a supporting (index) structure to look up which nodes were connected in the first place. Only then would they be able to go off and access the nodes. Index-free adjacency allows for query times that are proportional to how much of the graph you search through, rather than to the overall size of the graph.

(continued)

Recall the football stadium analogy from the sidebar in chapter 1—"What is the secret of Neo4j's speed?"

> Imagine yourself cheering on your team at a small local football stadium. If someone asks you how many people are sitting 15 feet around you, you'll get up and count them—you'll count people around you as fast as you can count. Now imagine you're attending the game at the national stadium, with a lot more spectators, and you want to answer the same question—how many people are there within 15 feet of you. Given that the density of people in both stadiums is the same, you'll have approximately the same number of people to count, taking a very similar time. We can say that regardless of how many people can fit into the stadium, you'll be able to count the people around you at a predictable speed; you're only interested in the people sitting 15 feet around you, so you won't be worried about packed seats on the other end of the stadium, for example.

This analogy provides a practical demonstration of how a human would naturally employ the index-free adjacency principle to perform the counting task.

Store files are located under the main graph database directory (by default, data/graph.db in a server setup) and are prefixed with neostore. Table 11.1 shows the main store files used by Neo4j, as well as some of their key properties.

Table 11.1 Primary store files in use and their associated properties

Store filename	Record size	Contents
neostore.nodestore.db	14 bytes	Nodes
neostore.relationshipstore.db	33 bytes	Relationships
neostore.propertystore.db	41 bytes	Simple (primitive and inlined strings) properties for nodes and relationships
neostore.propertystore.db.arrays	120 + 8 bytes	Values of array properties (in blocks *)
neostore.propertystore.db.strings	120 + 8 bytes	Values of string properties (in blocks *)

* Block size can be configured with the `string_block_size` and `array_block_size` parameters. Default block size is 120 bytes with 8 bytes for overhead.

The main store files have a fixed or uniform record size (14 bytes for nodes, 33 bytes for relationships, and so on). Besides playing an important part in enabling fast lookups and traversals, the fixed length makes calculations about how much space and memory to allocate for your graph a little easier to reason about and plan for, as mentioned in section 11.1.2.

The node and relationship store files simply store pointers to other nodes, relationships, and property records, and thus fit neatly into fixed record sizes. Properties, on the other hand, are slightly harder to deal with because the actual data that they represent can be of variable length. Strings and arrays, in particular, will have variable length data in them, and for this reason they're treated specially by Neo4j, which stores this dynamic type of data in one or more string or array property blocks. For more information, refer to the Neo4j Manual (http://docs.neo4j.org/chunked/stable/configuration-caches.html). The details are scattered throughout subsections of the manual, currently sections 22.6, 22.9, and 22.10.

How do fixed-length records improve performance?

The use of fixed-length records means that lookups based on node or relationship IDs don't require any searching through the store file itself. Rather, given a node or relationship ID, the starting point for where the data is stored within the file can be computed directly. All node records within the node store are 14 bytes in length (at the time of writing). IDs for nodes and relationships are numerical and are directly correlated to their location within a store file. Node ID 1 will be the first record in the node store file, and the node with ID 1000 will be the thousandth.

If you wanted to look up the data associated with node ID 1000, you'd be able to calculate that this data would start 14000 bytes into the node store file (14 bytes for each record x node ID 1000). The complexity involved in computing the starting location for the data is much less ($O(1)$ in big O notation) than having to perform a search, which in a typical implementation could cost $O(log\ n)$. If big O notation scares you, fear not; all you really need to understand here is that it's generally much faster to compute a start point than it is to search for it. When a lot of data is involved, this can often translate into significant performance gains.

The fixed record size also plays an important part in providing a quick mechanism for calculating where in the file a contiguous block of records is stored; this is used by the filesystem cache (see section 11.1.4) to load portions of the store files into cache.

There are two key features that you should be aware of when it comes to the store file structure.

The first is that these fixed record sizes can be used to help estimate the amount of space that the core graph files will take up on disk, and thus how big your disks may need to be (see section 11.1.2).

The second is that these store records have a direct 1:1 mapping when it comes to the filesystem cache and how it works. Caching is covered in the next section, but basically, the filesystem cache is responsible for loading portions of the store files into available RAM for fast access. Paying close attention to the size of these store file records is an important factor in being able to calculate what your memory and caching requirements may be.

11.1.4 *Neo4j caches*

Even with super-fast disks and Neo4j's efficient storage structure, a latency penalty will always be incurred whenever processing requires a trip from the CPU to disk. This latency penalty can be dramatically reduced if the data to be accessed can be held in

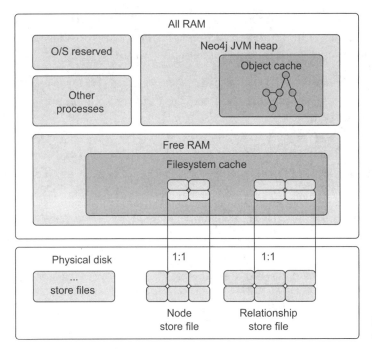

Figure 11.2   Neo4j's use
of RAM for caching

memory (RAM of some sort) where disk IO is reduced or even eliminated. Neo4j operates optimally when data is cached in memory.

So what does *in memory* mean, as far as Neo4j is concerned? Neo4j makes use of a two-tiered caching strategy: the filesystem cache and object cache. These caches, as well as where they live within the overall memory of a single server, are illustrated in figure 11.2.

FILESYSTEM CACHE

The filesystem cache is an area of free RAM (RAM that hasn't yet been allocated to any process) that the OS sets aside to help speed up reading from and writing to files. The filesystem cache makes use of something called *memory-mapped IO*. Whenever a process requests a file, the filesystem cache is checked to see if it has already been loaded there. If not, the physical file (or part of the file requested) is read from disk into this memory area. Subsequent requests for the same file (or a portion of the file) can then be served from memory, dramatically increasing performance by eliminating the need for physical disk IO. Changes to the data are also written to the filesystem cache, rather than immediately to the physical disk. The performance lift gained from accessing a file through the filesystem cache, rather than going to a spinning disk, is around 500 times faster.

The OS is in charge of managing this memory, including making decisions about when to flush changes written to this memory area down to the physical disk. Although the OS has the final say as to when data is read into and written from this area, processes can request certain files, or portions of files, to be loaded into this memory area for processing.

Neo4j takes advantage of this OS feature (through the Java NIO packages) to efficiently load, read, and write to and from the store files. This provides the first level (sometimes called the *low-level*) caching functionality within Neo4j.

What happens if the system crashes and the data has only been written to memory and not to disk?

If the OS is in control of when data is flushed to disk for the filesystem cache, what happens to that data in the event of a system failure?

In short, data held in this memory area is lost. Fear not, however, as Neo4j makes use of a separate, durable, transaction log to ensure that all transactions are physically written to a file that is flushed to disk upon every commit. Whenever a commit happens, although the store files themselves may not yet have physically been updated, the transaction log will always have the data on disk. The transaction log (covered in section 11.1.5) can then be used to recover and restore the system when starting up after a failure. In other words, this transaction log can be used to reconstruct the store files so that they fully reflect what the system looked like at the point of the last commit, and thus what the store files would have looked like had the data been flushed to disk before the crash.

CONFIGURING THE FILESYSTEM CACHE

Ideally, you should aim to load as much of your persistent graph data (as stored within the physical store files on disk) into memory as possible. You can control what parts, and how much, of the persistent graph you want loaded into memory. In practice, as all graph data lives in the store files, this generally involves looking at how much space these files occupy on disk (or how large you expect them to become), and trying to reserve an appropriate amount of RAM for each one.

Suppose you have a top-level Neo4j database directory that occupies approximately 2.2 GB of data, made up of the following store files and sizes:

```
 20M neostore.nodestore.db
 60M neostore.propertystore.db
1.2G neostore.propertystore.db.strings
900M neostore.relationshipstore.db
```

The following snippet shows a configuration that will ensure that the whole of the graph can fit into the memory allocated to the filesystem cache. The settings shown in this configuration file reserve approximately 2.5 GB of RAM, which allows for about 10% data growth:

```
neostore.nodestore.db.mapped_memory=22M
neostore.propertystore.db.mapped_memory=66M
neostore.propertystore.db.strings.mapped_memory=1.4G
neostore.relationshipstore.db.mapped_memory=1.0G
neostore.propertystore.db.arrays.mapped_memory=0M
```

When running Neo4j in server mode, these settings are specified in the neo4j.properties file found under the conf directory.

For an embedded setup, the configuration settings can be passed in when the graph database is constructed, either via a reference to a neo4j.properties file, accessible from somewhere on the classpath, or directly within Java via a Map.

You'll have noticed that there's a 1:1 mapping between the configuration settings and the physical store files on disk. Within the broader filesystem cache memory area, Neo4j ensures that separate, individual file buffer caches are maintained for each store file, and thus allows cache configuration on a per store basis as well. This makes it is possible to configure how much of each store file should be loaded into RAM independently of one another.

Different applications will have different usage patterns, and being able to independently tune these cache areas enables you to ensure that the app can perform as well as possible, especially if there isn't enough free RAM available to load the whole graph into memory.

> **NOTE** When we cover HA, we'll also look at the concept of *cache sharding*, which can be used to help load appropriate portions of the graph into memory across multiple machines.

Specific scenarios and configuration examples for the memory-mapped IO caches are provided in the "Memory mapped IO settings" section of the official Neo4j Manual at http://docs.neo4j.org/chunked/stable/configuration-io-examples.html.

> **DEFAULT CONFIGURATION** In the absence of any configuration from the user, Neo4j will try to work out what it thinks is best, given its knowledge of the system and the amount of RAM available to it.

OBJECT CACHE

The filesystem cache goes a long way to improving performance by reducing disk IO, but Neo4j is a JVM-based application that deals with the concepts of nodes and relationships (stored as Java objects) rather than only interacting with raw files.

Neo4j's object cache is an area within the JVM heap where Neo4j stores the Java object versions of nodes and relationships in a form that's optimized for use in traversals and quick retrievals by the core Neo4j APIs.

The previous section showed you how utilizing the filesystem cache could provide a performance boost of up to 500 times compared to accessing the same data on a spinning disk. The object cache allows for yet another performance boost over and above the filesystem cache. Accessing data from within the object cache (as opposed to going to the filesystem cache) is about 5,000 times faster!

CONFIGURING THE OBJECT CACHE

There are two aspects to configuring the object cache. The first involves configuring the JVM, and specifically the JVM heap, which is done by providing an appropriate -Xmx???m parameter to the JVM upon startup. The second is choosing an appropriate cache type, which is controlled by setting the cache_type parameter in the neo4j.properties file.

We'll tackle the JVM configuration first, as this can have a massive impact on the performance of your application and database. The general rule of thumb is that the larger the heap size the better, because this means a larger cache for holding and processing more objects, and thus better performance from the application. This statement holds true for the most part, but it's not always that simple.

One of the attractive features of JVM-based development is that, as a developer, you don't need to worry about allocating and deallocating memory for your objects (as you'd need to in other languages like C++). This is instead handled dynamically by the JVM, which takes responsibility for allocating storage for your objects as appropriate, as well as cleaning up unreferenced objects via the use of a garbage collector. Garbage collectors can be tuned and configured, but in general, heap sizes larger than 8 GB seem to cause problems for quite a few JVMs.

Large heap sizes can result in long GC pauses and thrashing—these are exactly the types of wasteful scenarios you want to avoid. Long GC pauses and thrashing are horrendously detrimental to performance, because the JVM ends up spending more time trying to perform the maintenance activities of cleaning up and freeing objects than it does enabling the application to perform any useful work.

So how much memory should be allocated to the JVM for Neo4j to operate optimally? This is one of those areas where you may need to play around a bit until you can find a sweet spot that makes use of as much of the JVM heap space as possible without causing too many GC-related problems. Configuring the JVM with the following startup parameters and values provides a good starting point:

- Allocate as much memory as possible to the JVM heap (taking into account your machine and JVM-specific limits—6 GB or less for most people). Pass this in via the `-Xmx???m` parameter.
- Start the JVM with the `-server` flag.
- Configure the JVM to use the Concurrent Mark and Sweep Compactor garbage collector instead of the default one, using the `-XX:+UseConcMarkSweepGC` argument.

For a more detailed discussion about JVM- and GC-based performance optimizations within Neo4j, consult the official documentation at http://docs.neo4j.org/chunked/stable/configuration-jvm.html.

Construct a sample graph early on to help determine memory (and disk) requirements

There's generally no foolproof and completely accurate way to calculate exactly how much heap space the JVM will require to hold and process your graph in memory. What many people choose to do is construct a small, but relatively accurate (if possible) representation of their graph as early on in the development process as possible. Even though this sample graph may change as time goes on, it can be used to help work out how much space and memory might be required for a larger dataset with a similar structure and access patterns.

This is useful for working out appropriate settings for the filesystem cache, object cache, and general storage requirements.

The second configuration is the cache_type parameter in the neo4j.properties file. This controls how node and relationship objects are cached. For the purposes of brevity, we'll list the options available with the brief descriptions specified in the official documentation; this can be seen in table 11.2. For more information see the "Caches in Neo4j" section of the Neo4j Manual at http://docs.neo4j.org/chunked/stable/configuration-caches.html.

Table 11.2   Object cache-type options as per the official documentation

cache_type	Description
none	Doesn't use a high-level cache. No objects will be cached.
soft *	Provides optimal utilization of the available memory. Suitable for high-performance traversal. May run into GC issues under high load if the frequently accessed parts of the graph don't fit in the cache.
weak	Provides short life span for cached objects. Suitable for high-throughput applications where a larger portion of the graph than can fit into memory is frequently accessed.
strong	Holds on to all data that gets loaded and never releases it again. Provides good performance if your graph is small enough to fit in memory.
hpc **	Provides a means of dedicating a specific amount of memory to caching loaded nodes and relationships. Small footprint and fast insert/lookup. Should be the best option for most scenarios. A high-performance cache.

* Default cache_type
** Only available in Neo4j Enterprise edition. (Note: this cache has successfully been used by some customers with heap sizes of up to 200 GB.)

As increasing the JVM heap size eats into the overall RAM available on the box, the setting of the heap size and the settings for the filesystem cache should really be considered together. Remember to include other factors as well, such as the OS's requirements for RAM and any other processes that may be running on the box. If you're running in embedded mode, the Neo4j database will be sharing the JVM heap with your host application, so ensure that this is catered to as well!

CACHING SUMMARY
Your caching approach can be summarized as follows:

- At a minimum, aim for a setup that allows for all, or as much as possible, of the graph to fit into the filesystem cache.
- Thereafter, make as much use of the object cache as feasible.

11.1.5 *Transaction logs and recoverability*

Shifting to the right side of our high-level architecture diagram (see figure 11.3), we'll focus on providing a brief overview of how the transaction log files (sometimes also referred to as the *logical files*), are used to ensure Neo4j is ACID-compliant. But more importantly for this chapter, we'll look at how the transaction logs are used to promote self-healing and recoverability.

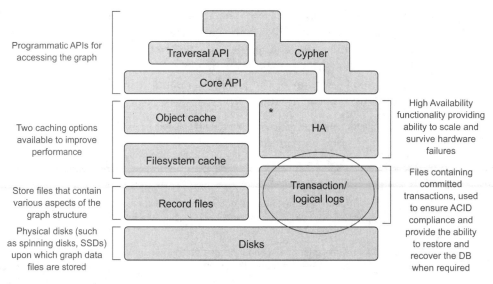

Programmatic APIs for
accessing the graph

Two caching options
available to improve
performance

High Availability
functionality providing
ability to scale and
survive hardware
failures

Store files that contain
various aspects of the
graph structure

Files containing
committed
transactions, used
to ensure ACID
compliance and

Physical disks (such
as spinning disks, SSDs)
upon which graph data
files are stored

provide the ability
to restore and
recover the DB
when required

*Only available in Neo4j Enterprise Edition

Figure 11.3   Recap of where transaction logs fit into the overall Neo4j architecture

In chapter 7 you learned that Neo4j is a fully ACID-compliant (atomic, consistent, iso-lated, durable) database. Many ACID-based systems (Neo4j included) use what's known as a write-ahead log (WAL) as the mechanism for providing the atomicity and durability aspects of ACID. The use of a WAL means that whenever a transaction is committed, all changes are written (and physically flushed) to the active transaction log file on disk before they're applied to the store files themselves. Recall that the use of the filesystem cache means that writes to the store files may still only be in mem-ory—the OS is in charge of deciding when to flush these areas to disk. But even if the system crashes and committed changes haven't been applied to the physical store files, the store files can be restored using these transaction logs.

All transaction log files can be found in the top level of the Neo4j database direc-tory and they follow the naming format nioneo_logical.log.*.

Behind the scenes—recovering from an unclean shutdown

Unclean shutdown usually refers to the scenario where a Neo4j instance has crashed unexpectedly. It can also refer to situations where Neo4j was intentionally shut down, but the key point is that Neo4j was not allowed to perform its usual cleanup activities for whatever reason. When an unclean shutdown occurs, the following warning mes-sage can generally be seen in the logs the next time the database is started up—non clean shutdown detected.

When Neo4j starts up, the first thing it will do is consult the most recent transaction log and replay all of the transactions found against the actual store files. There's a

(continued)

possibility that these transactions will already have been applied to the store (remember that the OS controls when the filesystem cache is flushed to disk—this may or may not have happened). Replaying these transaction again isn't a problem, however, as these actions are deemed to be *idempotent*—the changes can be applied multiple times without resulting in a different result in the graph.

Once the Neo4j instance has started up, its store files will have been fully recovered and contain all the transactions up to and including the last commit—and you're ready to continue!

Besides aiding with transactions and recoverability, the transaction log also serves as the basis upon which the HA functionality is built—the ability to run Neo4j in a clustered setup.

11.1.6 *Programmatic APIs*

At the very top of the Neo4j architectural stack are the three primary APIs (Cypher, Traversal, and Core), which are used to access and manipulate data within Neo4j (see figure 11.1). Previous chapters have covered these APIs in-depth so we won't be covering that ground again.

Technically, there isn't any operational aspect to these APIs; there are no specific settings to tune these APIs in the same way as, for example, the caches. They do form part of the overall Neo4j architecture that you're touring, so they get a special mention here.

The only thing we want to highlight in this section is that, although each of these APIs can be used individually to interact with the graph, they build on each other to a certain extent (in a bit of a stack-like manner). More importantly, they each have their own sweet spots. Depending on what you're trying to do, it's up to you to choose the right tool for the job. Figure 11.4 provides an overview of the primary goals and approaches used by each API.

If performance is of the utmost importance, you'll probably want to drop down and use the Core API, as this provides you with the most flexibility and control over your interaction with the graph. This comes at a price, as it requires explicit knowledge of exactly how the graph data is laid out in order to interact with it, and this interaction can be quite verbose.

The Traversal API provides a slightly more friendly API, where users provide goals such as "do a depth-first search to depth 3," allowing Neo4j to take care of interacting with the core API to realize the results. Although this API is easier for the developer to use, the slightly higher level of abstraction means that it may not perform quite as optimally as the Core API.

Then there's Cypher—the declarative, humane, graph query language, and arguably the most intuitive and friendly of all the APIs to use. Many would say Cypher represents the future of Neo4j, as so much development effort is being directed in this

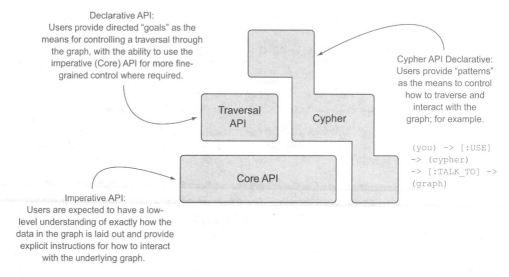

Declarative API:
Users provide directed "goals" as the means for controlling a traversal through the graph, with the ability to use the imperative (Core) API for more fine-grained control where required.

Cypher API Declarative: Users provide "patterns" as the means to control how to traverse and interact with the graph; for example.

```
(you) -> [:USE]
-> (cypher)
-> [:TALK_TO] ->
(graph)
```

Traversal API

Cypher

Core API

Imperative API:
Users are expected to have a low-level understanding of exactly how the data in the graph is laid out and provide explicit instructions for how to interact with the underlying graph.

Figure 11.4 Programmatic API stack

area. Its general appeal and ease of use and understanding (aimed at developers and operational staff alike) has made it a very compelling part of Neo4j's product surface. At present, Cypher can't match the performance of the core API in most cases. In Neo4j 1.x, Cypher binds to the Core and Traversal APIs (so it can never do any better than those APIs), but in the future (especially from Neo4j 2.0 onward) Cypher will bind lower in the stack to a sympathetic API that will support query optimization and other runtime efficiencies. Although Cypher can't match the Core API today for performance, there's no reason to think it won't be on par, or even outperform the Core API in the future—time will tell.

11.2 *Neo4j High Availability (HA)*

The Enterprise edition of Neo4j comes with a Neo4j HA component that provides the ability for Neo4j to run in a clustered setup, allowing you to distribute your database across multiple machines. Neo4j makes use of a master-slave replication architecture and, broadly speaking, provides support for two key features: resilience and fault tolerance in the event of hardware failure, and the ability to scale Neo4j for read-intensive scenarios.

> **HA VERSUS CLUSTERING** You'll often hear the terms HA and cluster used interchangeably when referring to a multimachine setup within Neo4j. In essence, these are referring to the same concepts but with different names.

Resilience and fault tolerance refer to the ability of Neo4j to continue functioning and serving clients even in the presence of network disruptions or hardware failures. If one of the machines in your cluster blows up, or a link to your network dies, Neo4j should be able to continue without a total loss of service.

Besides being able to handle hardware failure scenarios reliably, the master-slave architecture has the added benefit of providing a way to scale Neo4j horizontally for read-mostly scenarios. In this context, read-mostly scenarios can refer to applications with high throughput requirements where there's a need, or desire, to scale reads horizontally across multiple slave instances. It's additionally used to support caching sharding (discussed in section 11.2.4), which enables Neo4j to handle a larger read load than could otherwise be handled by a single Neo4j instance.

11.2.1 Neo4j clustering overview

A Neo4j HA cluster involves a set of Neo4j Enterprise instances that have all been configured to belong to a single logical unit (cluster). At any given time, it's expected that there will always be a single master present, with zero or more slaves configured as required.

Neo4j's HA architecture has recently undergone a bit of an overhaul in an effort to simplify the setup and operational running requirements. Prior to Neo4 1.9, Neo4j used Apache ZooKeeper (http://zookeeper.apache.org) to provide the cluster coordination functionality. Although ZooKeeper is a fine product, its use within the Neo4j architecture posed a number of problems, including having to deal with the additional operational overhead, setup, and integration of a separate coordinator component. It also had restrictions in terms of being able to dynamically reconfigure itself; for some cloud-based setups, this proved somewhat restrictive.

For these, as well as some other reasons, Neo Technology decided to roll its own cluster-coordination mechanism, and from Neo4j version 1.9 onward, including Neo4j 2.0, ZooKeeper is no longer used. The Neo4j implementation is based on the Paxos protocol, which primarily handles master election, but Neo4j also takes responsibility for the handling of all general cluster-based management tasks. It's not necessary to understand the finer details of the Paxos protocol (that's well beyond the scope of this book), but if you're interested, Leslie Lamport's article, "Paxos Made Simple" (2001), provides a simple introduction to the subject: www.cs.utexas.edu/users/lorenzo/corsi/cs380d/past/03F/notes/paxos-simple.pdf.

Figure 11.5 shows the key workings of the new Neo4j cluster coordination mechanism based on the Paxos protocol.

Within a Neo4j HA cluster, each database instance is self-sufficient when it comes to the logic required to coordinate and communicate with other members of the cluster. When an HA database instance starts up, the first thing it will try to do is establish a connection to its configured cluster. The neo4j.properties file contains the various properties controlling the HA configuration (all prefixed with ha*), including the property listing the initial set of other members belonging to the cluster—ha.initial_hosts).

If the cluster doesn't exist upon startup, meaning this is the first machine to attempt a connection to the cluster, then this process will take care of establishing the initial cluster, installing this instance as the master.

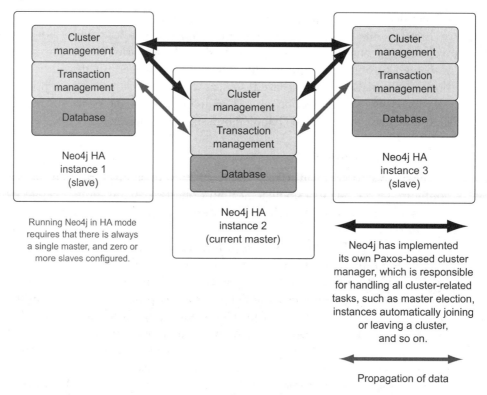

Figure 11.5   Sample Neo4j HA cluster setup with 1 master and 2 slaves

All write requests are ultimately performed through the master, although it's possible to send the request to a slave. Doing so, however, is significantly slower than going directly to the master. In this scenario, the slave has logic built into it to synchronously ensure the write is first performed on the master, and then applied to itself as well.

Changes are propagated back out of slaves through a configurable push- and/or pull-based mechanism.

WHAT ABOUT CAP AND ACID?

Running in a clustered setup has some implications for the ACID guarantee provided by Neo4j. Neo4j's single-machine consistency guarantee loosens to become *eventually consistent* in a cluster. What does that mean?

A NoSQL book isn't complete without some mention of, or reference to, the CAP theorem. Neo4j claims to be an ACID-compliant database, and when running on a single machine, this guarantee is absolute. As soon as you introduce the ability for your database to be partitioned across a network, however (through the master-slave setup), the perfect ACID guarantee (at least the availability and consistency aspects) needs to be loosened or somewhat redefined.

An example always helps to clarify things, so let's pretend that your database has now been spread (replicated) across three instances, and you update a node on one (the master) of them. What happens to the slaves? When one of them tries to read this data, will it see this update straight away (will all the slaves be able to see a consistent view of the data at all times), or will there be any periods where it's slightly out of date? If there's a network failure, can you still read and write through any machine, including the slaves?

For the purposes of this discussion, the CAP theorem, originally proposed by Eric Brewer in 2000, with his own subsequent retrospective update posted 12 years later,[1] implies that you can't have both consistency and availability 100% of the time when partitions are involved—there needs to be a trade-off of some sort.

Neo4j is an AP database, which means it's eventually unavailable in the presence of partitions (it becomes read-only for safety reasons if the network is extremely fragmented). Slaves will become eventually consistent by having updates either pushed to, or pulled by, them over some period of time. These values are configurable, so the inconsistency window can be controlled as each application or setup dictates. We'll discuss this more in section 11.2.3.

Before we dive into more specifics around how certain HA features work within Neo4j, we'll go through an exercise of setting up a three-machine cluster. This allows you to get your hands dirty, so that you can then play and experiment with some of the setup options as we discuss them in this chapter.

Switching from a single machine setup to a clustered setup

For clients currently making use of an existing single-machine (embedded or server) setup, switching to a clustered environment should be a relatively straightforward and pain-free affair. This is possible because Neo4j HA was designed from the outset to make such a transition as easy as possible. There will obviously be additional configuration involved in order to ensure the server can establish itself as a member of a cluster (we'll be covering this shortly), but from the client's perspective, the operations available and the general way in which the interaction with the server is undertaken should remain largely unchanged.

Embedded mode

For embedded clients, the Neo4j JAR dependencies will need to be changed from the Community to the Enterprise edition, if this hasn't already been done. The only change required thereafter is in the way the `GraphDatabaseService` instance is created. Instead of using the `GraphDatabaseFactory` to create the `GraphDatabaseService`, a `HighlyAvailableGraphDatabaseFactory` should be used. As both of these factories generate implementations that make use of the same (`GraphDatabaseService`) interface, there are no additional changes required for any clients using it.

---

[1] Eric Brewer, "CAP Twelve Years Later: How the 'Rules' Have Changed" (2012), www.infoq.com/articles/cap-twelve-years-later-how-the-rules-have-changed.

(continued)

The following code snippet shows this code in action, with the HA-specific changes highlighted:

```
graphDatabaseService = new HighlyAvailableGraphDatabaseFactory()
            .newHighlyAvailableDatabaseBuilder("/machineA")
            .loadPropertiesFromFile(machineAFilename)
                .newGraphDatabase();
```

Server mode

Single server instances that are not currently running against the Enterprise edition will first need to be upgraded to the Enterprise edition. Then it's simply a case of configuring the server to be part of an appropriate cluster.

11.2.2 Setting up a Neo4j cluster

Let's go through the process of setting up a three-machine, server-based cluster. Neo4j HA works just as well for embedded instances. As this is primarily going to be used for demo purposes, we'll run all three instances on the same machine; but in production you'd more than likely run different instances on different machines.

NOTE   These instructions are for *nix environments (the actual examples were done on OS X 10.9.2), but an equivalent process can be followed for a Windows setup. We ran this HA setup against Neo4j version 2.0.2.

INITIAL SETUP

Follow these steps to perform the initial setup:

1 Create a base parent directory, such as ~/n4jia/clusterexample.

2 Download the Enterprise version of Neo4j and unpack the zip file (for Windows) or tar file (for Unix) into this folder. On the Mac, this would look like the following:

```
~/n4jia/clusterexample/neo4j-enterprise-2.0.2
```

3 Rename this folder machine01, and duplicate the directory, along with all of its content, into directories machine02 and machine03. Your resulting file structure should look like this:

```
~/n4jia/clusterexample/machine01
~/n4jia/clusterexample/machine02
~/n4jia/clusterexample/machine03
```

4 Within each machine's base directory, locate the conf/neo4j-server.properties file and ensure the following properties are set:

Property name	machine01	machine02	machine03
org.neo4j.server.webserver.port	7471	7472	7473
org.neo4j.server.webserver.https.port	7481	7482	7483
org.neo4j.server.database.mode	HA	HA	HA

5 Within each machine's base directory, locate the conf/neo4j.properties file and ensure that the following properties are set:

Property name	machine01	machine02	machine03
ha.server_id	1	2	3
ha.server	127.0.0.1:6001	127.0.0.1:6002	127.0.0.1:6003
online_backup_server	127.0.0.1:6321	127.0.0.1:6322	127.0.0.1:6323
ha.cluster_server	127.0.0.1:5001	127.0.0.1:5002	127.0.0.1:5003
ha.initial_hosts	127.0.0.1:5001	127.0.0.1:5002	127.0.0.1:5003

STARTUP AND VERIFY

Follow these steps to start up and verify your servers:

1 Startup the servers in each directory by issuing the start command as shown below:

```
~/n4jia/clusterexample/machine01)$ bin/neo4j start
~/n4jia/clusterexample/machine02)$ bin/neo4j start
~/n4jia/clusterexample/machine03)$ bin/neo4j start
```

2 Visit the Web Admin Console (see appendix A) on a browser for each server once you have given it a bit of time to start up to verify that it started correctly and explore the details provided:

```
http://127.0.0.1:7471/webadmin/#/info/org.neo4j/High%20Availability/
http://127.0.0.1:7472/webadmin/#/info/org.neo4j/High%20Availability/
http://127.0.0.1:7473/webadmin/#/info/org.neo4j/High%20Availability/
```

Figures 11.6 and 11.7 show the Web Admin pages for machine01 and machine02.

In this particular startup scenario, machine01 **1.1** was started first, and, as there were no other machines started in the cluster yet, machine01 assumed the role of the master, as you can see in figure 11.6 **1.2**. If machine03 had started first, it would have assumed the role of the master.

The Web Admin Console provides a rich set of details about the HA cluster, including which other machines are involved in the cluster. This information can be found under the InstancesInCluster section **1.3**. The first machine shown here is actually machine01, but further down the page (not shown in figure 11.6), machine02 and machine03 would also be listed as slaves, provided they had been started and successfully joined the cluster.

In figure 11.7, you can see that machine02 **2.1**, having joined the cluster after machine01 was started, has taken the role of a slave **2.2**.

Great! You should now have your cluster set up and running. We can now continue on to discuss some of the HA features in more detail. Feel free to experiment as we go along and try things out—this is often the best way to learn!

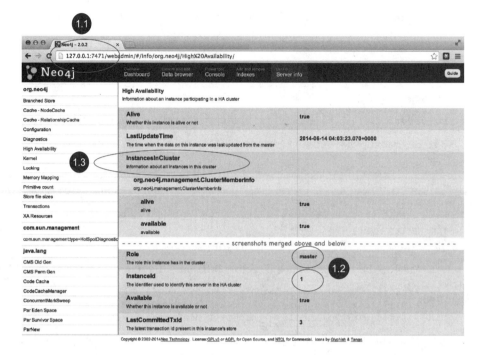

Figure 11.6   Web Admin Console view of HA setup from machine01's perspective

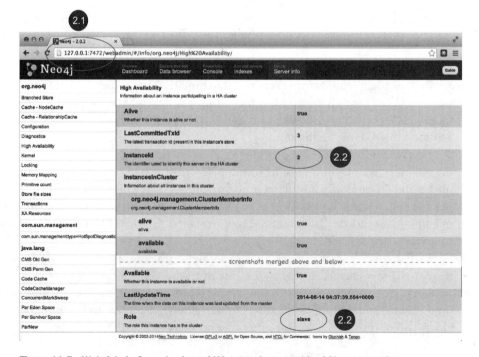

Figure 11.7   Web Admin Console view of HA setup from machine02's perspective

11.2.3 Replication—reading and writing strategies

Unlike typical master-slave replication setups that require all write requests to go through the master and read requests through slaves, Neo4j is able to handle write requests from any instance in the cluster. Likewise, Neo4j can process read requests from any instance, master or slave.

Write requests are processed quite differently depending on whether they're received directly by the master or via a slave. Figure 11.8 shows the sequence of events that occur when a write request is sent directly to the master.

Any write requests received directly by the master will operate in much the same manner as a standard non-HA transaction does; the database acquires a lock and

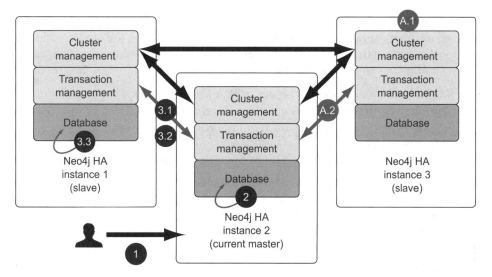

Client sends write request to a master ...

1 Client issues a commit.

2 Master acquires lock and applies the transaction as per normal non-transaction rules to the master DB instance.

3.1 Master consults `ha.tx_push_factor` setting and attempts to optimistically push change to n (default 1) configured slaves—but if this fails, (2) still succeeds.

3.2 Slave ensures it is up to date first, and if not, pulls any outstanding transactions from master.

3.3 Slave applies transaction locally.

In the background ...

A.1 Slave consult `ha.pull_interval` setting to determine if/when to pull updates from the master (default is not to pull updates regularly, only during write transactions).

A.2 When interval is in range, any new transactions are pulled from the master and applied locally to the slave.

Figure 11.8 Sequence of events when a write request is sent to the master instance

performs a local transaction. The only difference is that after the commit on the master has occurred, there are some configurable properties (`ha.tx_push_factor` and `ha.tx_push_strategy`) that additionally push the transaction out to *n* (default 1) slaves in an *optimistic* fashion. By optimistic, we mean that the master makes its best effort to ensure the transaction is propagated to the configured slaves, but if this propagation is unsuccessful for whatever reason, the original transaction on the master will still not fail.

Other slaves can also catch up by periodically polling for the latest updates from the master. This is done by setting the `ha.pull_interval` property to an appropriate value for your setup, such as `2s` (every 2 seconds). This pulling and pushing mechanism is what is used to control the speed with which Neo4j becomes eventually consistent across the cluster.

> **NOTE** The use of the term *optimistic* here isn't meant to be equated with the traditional database *optimistic locking* concept, where the whole transaction (including the one on the master) would be expected to be rolled back if a conflicted DB state is detected.

Moving on to the second scenario, if a slave receives a write request, a different sequence of events takes place, as illustrated in figure 11.9.

Slave-directed writes rely on the master being available in order for the update to work. This is because the slaves will synchronously need to take out a lock on both the master and slave before it can move forward. Neo4j has reliable, built-in logic to automatically detect when instances, including masters, potentially die or can't be reached for whatever reason. In such cases, a new master is elected, and if need be, brought up to date as much as possible. If a new master is unable to be elected for whatever reason, this essentially stops all updates to the database.

Updates are always applied on the master first, and only if this is successful are they then applied to the slave. To ensure overall consistency, Neo4j requires that a slave be up to date before any writes are performed, so as part of its internal communication protocol, Neo4j will ensure that the slave has all the latest updates applied to it before performing any local writes.

Watching an update propagate through the cluster

In order to see the pulling and pushing of updates occurring within a cluster, you can play with the various Neo4j HA settings, and then, in combination with the Neo4j Web Admin Console, create nodes and relationships and watch them replicate around the cluster.

Follow these steps to try this:

1 Ensure all of your servers are up and running as described in section 11.2.2.
2 Verify on each server that there are no nodes to begin with. This can be done by going to the console tab and issuing the following Cypher query (it should return zero rows):

```
start n=node(*) return n;
```

(continued)

3 On the master server, machine01 in this instance, use the Web Admin Console to create two nodes and a relationship using the following Cypher statement:

```
CREATE (n1)-[:LOVES]->(n2);
```

4 Wait until the pull interval has passed (the default value is 10 seconds—see the `ha.pull_interval` setting in the neo4j.properties file), and then verify that these values are now also present on the slave instances by running the query in step 2 again on each server. You should now see two nodes listed on each server.

That's it; you've just seen Neo4j's data propagation mechanism in action!

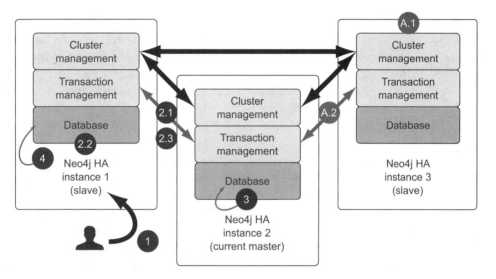

Client sends write request to a slave ...

1 Client issues a commit.

2.1 Lock is acquired on master database.

2.2 Lock is acquired on slave database.

2.3 As part of its internal protocol, slave ensures it is up to date first, and if not, pulls any outstanding transactions from master.

3 Update is committed to master.

4 Provided master commit was successful, local slave transaction is also commited.

In the background ...

A.1 Slave consults `ha.pull_interval` setting to determine if/when to pull updates from the master (default is not to pull updates regularly, only during write transactions).

A.2 When interval is in range, any new transactions are pulled from the master and applied locally to the slave.

Figure 11.9 Sequence of events when a write request is sent to a slave instance

TO WRITE THROUGH THE SLAVES—OR NOT TO WRITE THROUGH THE SLAVES—THAT IS THE QUESTION!

Being able to send write requests to either the master or one or more slaves provides greater flexibility in deployment options, but choosing one over the other has implications that you need to consider.

- *Writing through a slave will be significantly slower than writing through a dedicated master.* There will naturally be higher latency involved when writing through a slave, due to the added network traffic required to sync and coordinate the data and activities of the master and slave.

- *Writing through a slave can increase durability, but this can also be achieved by configuring the master to replicate changes upon commit.* By writing through a slave, you're guaranteed that there will always be at least two Neo4j instances that will always be up to date with the latest data (the slave itself, as well as the master). Alternatively, or in addition to this, durability can be increased by configuring writes on the master to be replicated out to a specified number of slaves upon commit. Although this occurs on a best-effort basis (via the `ha.tx_push_factor` property), the end result is that your data ends up on as many machines as you have configured. Distributed durability is important, as it provides a greater degree of confidence that you have the full set of data stored in multiple places, but it comes at a price.

- *A load balancer of some sort will be required to ensure that writes are only, or predominantly, handled by the master.* Neo4j doesn't provide any built-in load-balancing functionality. Rather, it relies on an external mechanism of some sort to provide this capability. For clients requiring such functionality, HAProxy (www.haproxy.org) is a popular choice. The logic around when to route to the master versus a slave then needs to be built into the load-balancing mechanism, which can be a tricky proposition. How do you know if something is a read or write request? There's generally no 100% accurate way to determine this based purely on traffic. This often results in a scenario where the application itself needs to possess some knowledge of whether its action is classified as a read or write, and then help route the request appropriately.

Whether you write through the master or a slave doesn't have to be an all or nothing decision. It's possible to use a hybrid approach (mostly write to the master, mostly read from the slaves) if this makes more sense for your system. Be pragmatic about making such decisions. The general recommendation provided to most clients nowadays is to try to ensure writes are predominantly sent to a master, where feasible, with data subsequently being pushed out to the slaves using the `ha.tx_push_*` settings. This tends to offer the best trade-off in terms of flexibility and performance.

11.2.4 Cache sharding

There will be some instances where your graph is simply too big to fit into the amount of RAM available. The advice up to now has always been to aim for this ideal situation, but what if it's simply not possible?

In these circumstances, it's recommended that you consider using a technique known as *cache sharding*. Cache sharding isn't the same as traditional sharding.

Traditional sharding (such as the sharding employed by other data stores, like MongoDB) typically involves ensuring that different parts of the data are stored on different instances, often on different physical servers. If you have a massive customer database, you may choose to shard your database on customer groups. For example, all customers with usernames A to D are stored in one instance, E to F in another, with further divisions stored in yet others. The application would need to know which instance has the data it's looking for and ensure that it goes to the correct one to get it. Of course, many shard-enabled databases provide automated ways of partitioning and accessing the appropriate instance, but the main point here is that not all of the data is stored on each instance or server; only a subset is.

With Neo4j, each HA instance expects to have access to the full set of data. Cache sharding, unlike traditional sharding, which is a physical data partitioning technique, is more of a routing-based pattern. Using this pattern, requests for data that is typically accessed as a collective unit are always directed to the same Neo4j instance. By consistently routing such requests to the same instance, you increase the likelihood that this data will be held in memory when you access it, thereby allowing this instance to exploit the memory-accessing performance that Neo4j provides for such cases.

Let's look again at the previous customer database example. With Neo4j, *all* the data (for customers A to Z) is present on each HA instance, but by using some kind of load-balancing mechanism, you can ensure that all local requests related to one group of customers (customers with "A" usernames) will always be routed to the same HA instance, "B" to another, and so on. Figure 11.10 illustrates how cache sharding might work for such a graph.

> **Why does Neo4j not do traditional sharding?**
>
> The short answer is that this is a very, very hard problem for graph databases to solve. So hard, in fact, that this problem falls into a category of "really hard mathematical problems" that have been given their own name: "NP-hard problems" (http://en.wikipedia.org/wiki/NP-hard).
>
> Traditional sharding typically involves splitting a full data set such that different portions are stored on different instances. Provided certain conditions hold true, this approach is a way to scale large databases while at the same time maintaining a predictable level of performance as the data grows.
>
> The key to the preceding statement is "provided certain conditions hold true." In most shard-enabled databases, the keys against which data is held in a shard are stable

(continued)

and predictable. Additionally, the access patterns generally used are such that you can look up the data you need from one shard (with a key), look up data in another, and then have the application take care of wiring it back together if required.

The sweet spot for graphs, however, and for Neo4j in particular, lies in local graph queries—starting at a given point and exploring the data and immediate connection patterns around it. This may involve traversing very different types of data—the types of data that would typically be spread across different shards. Say you had a query that said, "Given customer A, tell me which stores are within 1 km of where she lives where any of her immediate friends have purchased a product greater than £100 in the last month." If you decided to partition data such that users and friends were stored in one shard, and retail stores in a separate area, with purchase history in yet another, a built-in graph query would end up following data spread across physical servers, resulting in unpredictable and slow data-retrieval times as the network is crossed and navigated.

You may argue that we could try to partition the data based on the pattern described, which may or may not be possible. This would, however, potentially negate other traversals that you may also want to perform—ones that start from some other node within the broader data set, not specifically customer A, and explore from there.

Until such time as we can perform such traversals across network boundaries in an acceptable and predictable manner, the best solution for such cases involving Neo4j in the interim is to make use of cache sharding. The sharding of Neo4j is still actively being looked into as a problem in its own right, but it's not a problem that looks like it will be solved in the immediate future.

ROUTING STRATEGIES

As you learned in section 11.2.3, there's no routing or load-balancing functionality built into an HA setup as far as the client is concerned; Neo4j expects clients to provide or implement their own, with tools such as HAProxy (www.haproxy.org) proving a popular choice. Regardless of the physical mechanism used, each application will need to decide on the most appropriate strategy for the routing of the data.

Some options include

- *Routing requests based on some data characteristic*—This is the approach used in our customer example.
- *Using sticky sessions*—This involves ensuring that requests from one client always go to the same server, no matter what was asked for. This may or may not be appropriate depending on the circumstances.
- *Employing geography-based routing*—This involves ensuring that all requests related to, or originating from, a common geographic location are always routed to the same instance.

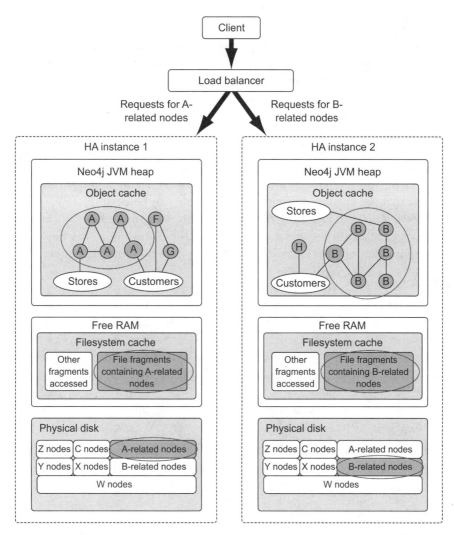

Figure 11.10   Cache sharding

11.2.5 *HA summary*

As with many of the subjects discussed in this book, we're only able to cover a small fraction of what's actually available, and HA is no exception. For more information on HA in general, see the "High Availability" chapter in the Neo4j Manual (chapter 23): http://docs.neo4j.org/chunked/stable/ha.html.

You've now learned how you can scale and ensure Neo4j can continue to operate and serve its clients, even in the event of a hardware failure. We'll now move on to the final section in this chapter, which covers backing up and restoring the database when such disasters do actually strike.

11.3 *Backups*

Your social network site is whirring along nicely, generating great revenue and kudos for you, then suddenly...bam! Your administrator informs you that there was a hardware failure, and the current data is corrupted.

At this point, your heart will either sink, and you'll say, "I really should have thought about backing the data up," or you'll sit back and think, "No worries, we have backups."

Assuming you choose to be in the latter camp, this section aims to provide all the information needed to ensure that if and when such disasters do strike, you're prepared, and it doesn't mean the end of the world.

We'll begin by looking at what's involved in performing a simple offline backup, a process that *does* involve downtime, but one that can be performed on any edition of the Neo4j database, including the free Community edition. For the cases where you really can't afford for the database to be offline, the online backup functionality comes into play, but this is available only in the Neo4j Enterprise edition.

11.3.1 *Offline backups*

At the end of the day, the physical files that comprise the Neo4j database all reside under a single directory on a filesystem, and this is what ultimately needs to be backed up. As stated in the introduction to this section, this process will work on any edition of the Neo4j database, but it will most probably only be used on the Community edition. (If you have access to the Enterprise edition, you may as well make use of the online backup functionality.)

The process itself is relatively straightforward and involves the following steps:

1 Shut down the Neo4j instance.
2 Copy the physical Neo4j database files to a backup location.
3 Restart the Neo4j instance.

Let's look at these steps in turn.

SHUT DOWN THE NEO4J INSTANCE

If you're running in a single server mode, you simply need to execute the `neo4j` script with a `stop` argument. Assuming Neo4j was installed in /opt/neo4j/bin, you could stop the server by issuing this command:

```
/opt/neo4j/bin/neo4j stop
```

If you have embedded Neo4j in your application, then unless you've explicitly provided a mechanism to only shut down the Neo4j database, you should stop your application with whatever mechanism you have chosen to use. This could be as simple as sending a SIGINT signal (for example, issuing Ctrl-C in a terminal window if your application has been launched in this manner), or it may be more elaborate, involving a special script or custom application functionality.

Whatever the mechanism, you should ensure that Neo4j is also shut down when this process occurs. You saw in listing 10.3 in the previous chapter what was required to ensure this occurred when running in embedded mode. To refresh your memory, here's the snippet of code that registers a shutdown hook:

```
private String DB_PATH = '/var/data/neo4jdb-private';
private GraphDatabaseService graphdb =
    new GraphDatabaseFactory().newEmbeddedDatabase( DB_PATH );
registerShutdownHook( graphDb );
...
private static void registerShutdownHook(
            final GraphDatabaseService graphDb )
{
    Runtime.getRuntime().addShutdownHook( new Thread()
    {
        @Override
        public void run()
        {
            graphDb.shutdown();
        }
    } );
}
```

It's important to ensure that Neo4j shuts down cleanly whenever your application exits; failure to do so could result in problems the next time you start up. You don't need to worry about a clean shutdown when using Neo4j server—this will be done for you.

COPY THE PHYSICAL DATABASE FILES

Locate the directory that contains the physical Neo4j database files. For applications that run in embedded mode, this will be the path you supply in the startup code. To refresh your memory, the following snippet shows the code required to start up an embedded database where the physical files reside in the directory /var/data/neo4jdb:

```
private GraphDatabaseService graphdb =
    new GraphDatabaseFactory().newEmbeddedDatabase("/var/data/neo4jdb" )
```

If you're working with the server mode, the database files will be located at the location specified by the `org.neo4j.server.database.location` key in the neo4j-server.properties file. That setting will look something like the following:

```
org.neo4j.server.database.location=/var/data/neo4jdb
```

Copy the directory and all subfolders and files to a separate backup location.

RESTART THE DATABASE

For Neo4j server, use the appropriate Neo4j start command, and for embedded applications, restart the application as appropriate.

> **NOTE** Neo4j is able to detect unclean shutdowns and attempt a recovery, but this will result in a slower initial startup while the recovery is in process, and it sometimes may result in other issues as well. When an unclean shutdown occurs, the following warning message can generally be seen in the logs the next time the database is started up again—non clean shutdown detected. You should verify that your shut down processes, both graceful and forced, do their best to ensure Neo4j is shutdown cleanly.

11.3.2 *Online backups*

The online backup functionality is available only in the Enterprise edition of Neo4j, but it's a robust and reliable way to back up your single, or clustered, Neo4j environment without requiring any downtime.

You have two options available for online backups: a full or incremental backup. In both cases, no locks are acquired on the source Neo4j instances being backed up, allowing them to continue functioning while the backup is in progress.

FULL BACKUP

A full backup essentially involves copying all of the core database files to a separate backup directory. As the database being backed up isn't locked, there's a very real possibility that a transaction may be running when the backup is initiated. In order to ensure that the final backup remains consistent and up to date, Neo4j will ensure that this transaction, and any others that occurred during the copy process, make it into the final backed-up files. Neo4j achieves this by making a note of any transaction IDs that were in progress when the backup began. When the copying of the core files is complete, the backup tool will then use the transaction logs (covered in section 11.1.5) to replay all transactions starting from the one just noted and including any that occurred during the copy. At the end of this process, you'll have a fully backed up and consistent Neo4j instance.

INCREMENTAL BACKUP

Unlike the full backup, the incremental backup doesn't copy *all* of the core store files as part of its backup process. Instead, it assumes that at least one full backup has already been performed, and this backup serves as the initial starting point for identifying any changes that have subsequently occurred. The first incremental backup process will only copy over the transaction logs that have occurred since that initial full backup, thus bringing the backed-up data store to a new last-known backup point. This point is noted, and the next incremental backup will then use this as the new backup starting point, only copying over transaction logs that have occurred since that last incremental backup point up to the current point. These logs are replayed over the backup store, bringing it to the next last-known backup point. The process continues for each incremental backup requested thereafter. The incremental backup is a far more efficient process of performing a backup, as it minimizes the amount of data to be passed over the wire, as well as the time taken to actually do the backup.

THE PROCESS OF DOING A BACKUP

Whether or not a full or incremental backup is performed, the process for enabling and performing the backup is the same. Figure 11.11 illustrates an example backup scenario for a single server setup.

Whenever any of your Neo4j instances start up (embedded or server, single or HA), they check to see whether their online_backup_enabled configuration parameter is set to true. If it is, a separate backup service (which comes as part of the Neo4j distribution) is started as well. It defaults to port 6362 for a single server setup and 5001 for

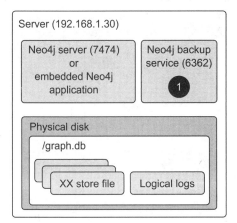

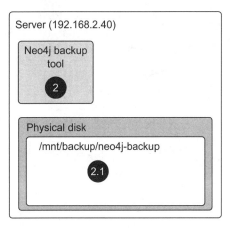

① When Neo4j starts up, if the config param `online_backup_enabled=true` (default=true from Neo4j 1.9) starts, the Neo4j backup service (default port 6362) will also be started.

② Neo4j backup tool invoked with example Unix command line for single server:
`./neo4j-backup -from single://`
`192.168.1.30 -to /mnt/backup/`
`neo4j-backup`

2.1 Neo4j backup tool inspects target backup directory to determine whether to perform a full or incremental backup (full performed if directory is empty, incremental performed if previous backup already exists in dir).

Figure 11.11   Example backup scenario for a single server setup

an HA setup. This service provides the access point for the Neo4j backup tool to connect to, in order to read the underlying store and transaction log files to backup.

The Neo4j backup tool is merely a Unix or Windows script (found in the bin folder of your distribution) fronting a Java application that understands how to connect to one or more Neo4j backup services. The backup tool can be run from any machine on the network, provided it has the ability to connect to the backup service. The backup command takes the following format for Unix:

```
./neo4j-backup -from <source-uri> -to <backup-dir>
```

For Windows it looks like this:

```
neo4j-backup -from <source-uri> -to <backup-dir>
```

The parameters are as follows:

- *backup-dir*—Directory where the backup should be stored. In order to perform a full backup, this directory needs to be empty. If the backup tool detects a previous version of a graph database in there, it will attempt an incremental backup.
- *source-uri*—This provides the backup tool with all the information it needs to connect to the appropriate backup service, and this needs to be specified

in the following format. (Details taken from man docs found here: https://
github.com/neo4j/neo4j/blob/2.0-maint/enterprise/backup/src/docs/man/
neo4j-backup.1.asciidoc)

```
<running-mode>://<host>[:port]{,<host>[:port]*}

running-mode:
     'single' or 'ha'. 'ha' is for instances in High
     Availability mode, 'single' is for standalone databases.

host:
     In single mode, the host of a source database; in ha mode,
     the cluster address of a cluster member. Note that multiple
     hosts can be given when using High Availability mode.

port:
     In single mode, the port of a source database backup service;
     in ha mode, the port of a cluster instance. If not given, the
     default value 6362 will be used for single mode, 5001 for HA
```

How do I schedule backups?
Neo4j itself doesn't provide any scheduling functionality. It's expected that you'll use
an external scheduling tool (such as cron) to do this for you. Using something like
cron, you can set up incremental backups to be performed every hour, or at whatever
frequency suits your needs.

11.3.3 Restoring from backup

To restore a Neo4j database from a backup, simply follow these steps:

1 Shut down the specific Neo4j instance to be restored.
2 Delete the folder that contains the old or corrupted version of the Neo4j database and replace it with the backed-up version.
3 Restart the Neo4j instance.

That's it! You're done! It seems a bit too easy, doesn't it? But that really is all there is to it!

11.4 Topics we couldn't cover but that you should be aware of

Security and monitoring are two topics we couldn't cover, but that may be worth looking into if you have specific requirements in these areas.

11.4.1 Security

Ensuring that you can run Neo4j securely in your production environment should
form an important part of your configuration. Depending on how you're making use
of Neo4j, there are different aspects to consider.

There are no out-of-the-box security options provided for those making use of the
embedded mode—Neo4j doesn't provide any data-level security or encryption facilities.
Most of the out-of-the-box options (as well as supplementary security configuration setups and approaches) are geared to the use of Neo4j in standalone mode (Neo4j server).

The official documentation provides relatively good coverage on the types of things to look out for, as well as basic instructions on how to begin securing these aspects of your Neo4j system. For more info, see the "Securing access to the Neo4j Server" section in the Neo4j Manual: http://docs.neo4j.org/chunked/stable/security-server.html.

11.4.2 Monitoring

Being able to monitor the health of your Neo4j system and understand when it's getting into trouble is a good way to ensure a stable and long-running system. Most of Neo4j's monitoring features are only available in the Enterprise edition of Neo4j, and they're generally exposed through the Java Management Extensions (JMX) technology (http://docs.oracle.com/javase/7/docs/technotes/guides/jmx/index.html).

More information on what is available, and how to get hold of this information, can be found in the "Monitoring" chapter (chapter 26) of the Neo4j Manual: http://docs.neo4j.org/chunked/stable/operations-monitoring.html.

11.5 Summary

Congratulations! You've reached the end of your Neo4j journey through this book. In this final chapter, you took a tour through the high-level Neo4j architecture, periodically dipping beneath the covers, gaining some valuable insight into some of the will and whys of certain Neo4j internals, especially in the context of configuring Neo4j to operate optimally for a production environment.

Specifically, you gained insight into the factors required to calculate rough disk usage and memory requirements for your Neo4j system. You also learned about Neo4j's two-tiered caching strategy involving the filesystem cache and object cache, and how these can be configured to suit your needs.

As this was the last chapter in the book, we recapped some of the basic concepts you encountered in the previous chapters in the book. With a solid understanding of the basic Neo4j architecture, your final task involved learning how to perform the key tasks of configuring Neo4j to run in a clustered High Availability setup, and also how to back up and recover the database.

Phew! We packed quite a bit into this last chapter, and you've done well to get to the end of it—congratulations!

11.6 Final thoughts

Although this chapter marks the end of this book, we hope that for you it marks the start of your onward journey with Neo4j. There's so much more to Neo4j than we could cover; we've only scratched the surface here. We do hope that we've provided enough basic grounding and references to help you on your way as you begin to discover all that Neo4j has to offer. We've enjoyed writing this book and sharing our experiences with you, and we'd love to hear how you're getting on and using Neo4j in new and interesting ways.

appendix A
Installing Neo4j server

The instructions detailed in this appendix are geared toward installing Neo4j server from the compressed tar.gz (Mac/Unix) or zip (Windows) files.

Windows users are lucky enough to be the first recipients of the binary installer package, with binary installers for Mac/Unix coming in due course. If you'd prefer to use the binary Windows installer, please follow the instructions on the Neo4j website at http://neo4j.org/download.

> **Neo4j versions and official documentation references**
>
> This book targets Neo4j 2.0; unless specified differently in a particular discussion, Neo4j 2.0.1 is the version against which all code was run and verified. As you can appreciate, writing a book while trying to keep up with the latest version of a fast-moving product can be challenging at the best of times. You should be able to substitute the latest version of Neo4j for 2.0.1, provided there are no major breaking changes.
>
> To ensure you always have links to the latest information, we have endeavored to use references that point to the latest stable release of the official documentation. At the time of writing, all Neo4j documentation URLs follow a common pattern, namely http://docs.neo4j.org/chunked/<version> where *version* is the Neo4j version of the docs you wish to view, with *stable* being an alias that always points to the latest, most stable released version.
>
> For the 2.0.1-specific information, please consult http://docs.neo4j.org/chunked/ 2.0.1. For the latest stable release, consult http://docs.neo4j.org/chunked/stable.

A.1 Installing and configuring a single Neo4j server

Follow these steps to install and configure a single Neo4j server:

1 Make sure you have the latest Oracle 7 JDK installed. If you don't, it can be downloaded at www.oracle.com/technetwork/java/javase/downloads/jdk7-downloads-1880260.html.

2 Locate and download the appropriate Neo4j install file. (As stated in the sidebar, all sample code in the book has been verified against version 2.0.1 and all instructions here are for that version; feel free to try using the latest version available, provided no major breaking changes have been introduced). Choose Windows or Linux/Mac as appropriate) from http://neo4j.com/download/other-releases/:

   – Linux/Mac: neo4j-community-2.0.1-unix.tar.gz
   – Windows: neo4j-community-2.0.1-windows.zip

3 Unpack the compressed file to a location on your disk that we'll refer to as your NEO4J_HOME; for example, a location such as this: /users/xxxx/devstuff/neo4j-community-2.0.1.

   For Linux/Mac, use this command:

   ```
   tar zxvf neo4j-community-2.0.1-unix.tar.gz
   ```

   For Windows, use an appropriate unzipping tool such as 7-zip or winzip.

4 If required, modify the configuration files that control how Neo4j starts up. Neo4j server allows you to configure many aspects of how it works via two files located in the conf directory:

   – conf/neo4j-server.properties
   – conf/neo4j.properties

   To change the location of the core database files (the default resides under the data/graph.db directory), update the `org.neo4j.server.database.location` property in the neo4j-server.properties file, as follows:

   ```
   org.neo4j.server.database.location=
   /users/xxxx/devstuff/neo4j-in-action/code-samples/chapter10/
   performance-demos-server/the-chapter10-server-db
   ```

   For more information on what all the options are, refer to the "Server Configuration" section in chapter 22 of the Neo4j Manual: http://docs.neo4j.org/chunked/stable/server-configuration.html.

5 Open up a terminal (Mac/Linux) or command prompt (Windows) in your NEO4J_HOME directory, and start the database by executing the `neo4j` script with the `start` command :

   – Linux/Mac: `bin/neo4j start`
   – Windows: `bin\neo4j.bat start`

6 Verify that the server is up by going to http://localhost:7474 and checking that the Neo4j browser window is displayed (see section A.2).

7 To shut down the server, execute the neo4j script with the stop command:
   - Linux/Mac: bin/neo4j stop
   - Windows: bin\neo4j.bat stop

The official installation procedure can also be found in the "Server Installation" section in chapter 21 of the Neo4j Manual: http://docs.neo4j.org/chunked/stable/server-installation.html.

A.2   Neo4j browser

Neo4j server comes with a neat browser available out of the box. Visit http://localhost:7474/browser on a running server instance to have a look. The first screen you encounter will be the splash page and will look something like figure A.1.

You can click the Intro button to get a guided tour of the browser. At its core, however, the browser allows you to run ad hoc queries and easily visualize the results of your queries in tabular or graphical format.

If you click the Neo4j three-dot icon on the left side of the page, you'll be presented with a sidebar presenting an initial view of the main labels and relationships in the system. You can begin navigating from here, or type in a specific Cypher query at the top of the page. Figure A.2 depicts the options available for some of the sample data from chapter 10.

Clicking the asterisk (*) under Node Labels executes the default Cypher query MATCH n RETURN n LIMIT 25 which allows you to visualize the first 25 nodes and their relationships within the graph, as shown in figure A.3.

Figure A.3 shows the first 25 nodes from some of the sample performance data from chapter 10.

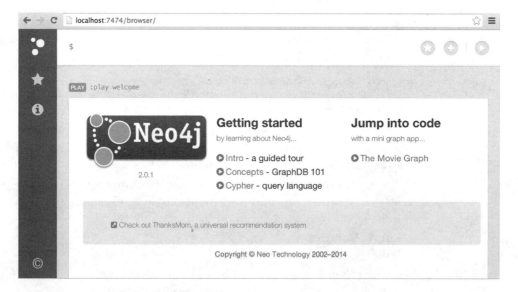

Figure A.1   The Neo4j browser splash page

Figure A.2 The Neo4j browser splash page with expanded sidebar

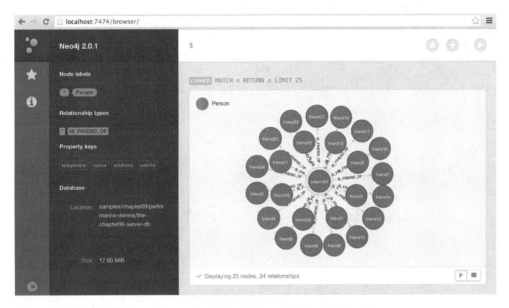

Figure A.3 The Neo4j browser's graphical visualization of nodes in the system

A.3 *Neo4j Web Admin Console*

The Neo4j browser was made available with Neo4j 2.0 onward, and it's the preferred GUI moving forward. Prior to version 2.0, users needed to make use of the Web Admin Console. The Web Admin Console is still available from http://localhost:7474/ webadmin for those wishing to access it, and figure A.4 shows what this looks like.

Figure A.4   Neo4j Web Admin Console

appendix B
Setting up and running
the sample code

All of the source code used in the book is available for download from www.manning .com/Neo4jinAction as well as at https://github.com/opencredo/neo4j-in-action.

All of the code and demos use Java so you'll need to have an appropriate version of Java installed. Additionally, we use Maven as the primary framework for providing the automatic building, compiling, and running of the code.

JUnit-based tests have primarily been used to demonstrate features in the book, but there are some standalone classes as well (which are not run as part of the test suite) that can also be executed to view their results.

This appendix provides the instructions required to set up your system to run the examples and associated source code.

B.1 Setting up your environment

This section describes how to prepare your machine for running the associated samples and demo code.

Download the sample code

Download and unpack the sample code into a directory that we'll refer to as N4JIA_SAMPLE_HOME. The source code is provided in zip format and can be downloaded from www.manning.com/Neo4jinAction. Alternatively you can simply clone the github repository available at https://github.com/opencredo/neo4j-in-action.

Install JDK (Oracle SE 7)

Neo4j requires Java 7 as the minimum JDK (Java Development Kit) to run and has officially been tested against Java 7. For those wishing to try it out with Java 8, though in theory you can give it a bash, there are no guarantees at this stage and so we recommend you stick with Java 7 for now until Java 8 is officially supported. Maven is also a Java-based tool, and it specifically requires a JDK to be installed rather than simply a JRE (Java Runtime Environment).

You should download and install the latest Oracle JDK (Java SE 7u60 at the time of writing) into a JAVA_HOME directory. OS-specific downloads can be found at www.oracle.com/technetwork/java/javase/downloads/index.html with installation instructions provided at http://docs.oracle.com/javase/7/docs/webnotes/install/index.html.

REMEMBER   Follow the JDK installation instructions, not the JRE instructions!

Install Maven (3.0.5+)

Maven (http://maven.apache.org) is a Java-based development framework that's used to help manage the setup, building, compiling, and dependency resolution aspects of your code, including the running of tests. These are all part of its well-known and standardized process called the *Maven lifecycle*, which is controlled by a project object model file, a.k.a. the pom.xml file.

With its standardized structure and process, one of the nice things about Maven is that whenever a user encounters a new Maven project, they'll generally be able to get up and running quickly. Everything will be in the places they expect, and common commands are used to build and execute the code.

Another benefit to using Maven is its dependency management system. You simply need to tell Maven what libraries you are dependent on, and it will generally go and fetch them (as well as any subdependencies)—no manual downloading is required. That means all the source code can be built and tests can be run through Maven.

A snippet of the dependency section from a pom.xml file is shown next, demonstrating how you can specify that version 3.1.1.RELEASE of the spring-data-neo4j library is required:

```
<dependencies>
    <dependency>
        <groupId>org.springframework.data</groupId>
        <artifactId>spring-data-neo4j</artifactId>
        <version>3.1.1.RELEASE<version>
    </dependency>
    ...
</dependencies>
```

You can find the appropriate binary files as well as OS-specific installation instructions at http://maven.apache.org/download.cgi. Please ensure you use Maven 3.0.5 or greater. The setup process described on the Maven site will help you to set up your Maven home (the M2_HOME directory), and it should be a relatively simple process.

If, however, you're running in a restricted environment (behind a firewall or on a machine with restricted rights), you may need to do a bit more configuration. The "Building a Project with Maven" page of the Maven site provides a more detailed set of instructions for setting up Maven to build a project, including its use in restricted situations: http://maven.apache.org/run-maven/index.html.

B.2 *Running the demos and samples*

This section provides specific instructions for running the samples and demo code that accompany this book. This assumes you have already followed the setup instructions detailed in section B.1.

General instructions

The instructions here are for running the samples from a command line, but you can just as easily run them from an IDE such as Eclipse or IntelliJ, provided the appropriate (Maven) plugins are available and basic setup has been performed:

1 If you haven't already, follow the instructions in section B.1 to install Java and Maven.
2 Open a command prompt (Windows) or terminal (Unix) window.
3 Change to the base N4JIA_SAMPLE_HOME directory.
4 Type in the following command, which will build, compile, and run various tests for all the main code samples detailed within this book:

```
mvn clean install
```

5 You should see a lot of output in the terminal window; if everything was successful, you should see something like the following output at the end:

```
[INFO] ------------------------------------------------------------
[INFO] Reactor Summary:
[INFO]
[INFO] neo4j-in-action-reactor ......................... SUCCESS [0.298s]
[INFO] chapter01 ....................................... SUCCESS [1.898s]
[INFO] chapter02 ....................................... SUCCESS [0.035s]
[INFO] chapter03 ....................................... SUCCESS [2.319s]
[INFO] chapter04 ....................................... SUCCESS [1.494s]
[INFO] chapter05 ....................................... SUCCESS [1.556s]
[INFO] chapter06 ....................................... SUCCESS [3.873s]
[INFO] chapter07-core .................................. SUCCESS [5.450s]
[INFO] chapter07-spring ................................ SUCCESS [2.420s]
[INFO] chapter08 ....................................... SUCCESS [0.290s]
[INFO] chapter09-current-simple ........................ SUCCESS [7.704s]
[INFO] chapter09-current-advanced ...................... SUCCESS [6.123s]
[INFO] chapter09-legacy-simple ......................... SUCCESS [7.815s]
[INFO] chapter09-legacy-advanced ....................... SUCCESS [5.268s]
[INFO] chapter10-embedded .............................. SUCCESS [0.053s]
[INFO] chapter10-server ................................ SUCCESS [0.201s]
[INFO] chapter10-performance-demos-server .............. SUCCESS [0.535s]
[INFO] chapter10-performance-demos-embedded ............ SUCCESS [0.122s]
[INFO] chapter11-community-embedded .................... SUCCESS [1.042s]
[INFO] chapter11-enterprise-embedded ................... SUCCESS [3.832s]
[INFO] ------------------------------------------------------------
[INFO] BUILD SUCCESS
[INFO] ------------------------------------------------------------
```

```
[INFO] Total time: 52.638s
[INFO] Finished at: Sat Jul 05 22:13:59 BST 2014
[INFO] Final Memory: 38M/305M
[INFO] -------------------------------------------------------------------
```

If you only want to run the tests for one of the chapters, you can change directories to the appropriate chapter (ensure that this is the directory with a pom.xml file in it) and run the mvn clean install command again. Alternatively, staying in the N4JIA_SAMPLE_HOME directory, you can use the following command (substituting the appropriate directory where the pom.xml file resides as required):

```
mvn clean install -f chapter04/pom.xml
```

Chapter 10 instructions

The sample code in chapter 10 includes tests and demos that involve running Neo4j in server mode. As quite a few of these tests are used for gauging performance-related metrics using different options, we decided to have the server start up independently of the tests running against them, to get as accurate a measurement as possible. This also enables you to go through the process of setting up a server for yourself.

Unlike all the other tests, which up until now have made use of Java JUnit-based tests, the performance-related tests in chapter 10 are to be initiated from the command line via a series of bash scripts.

As one of the clients chosen to execute some performance tests was the simple Unix-based curl (http://curl.haxx.se) client, the performance-testing scripts are only available as bash scripts that can be run in (*nix) environments. If you're on Windows, you could try installing Cygwin (www.cygwin.com), which provides a form of Linux emulation, and then run the scripts from within there:

1 By default, when you run the standard mvn clean install, the performance-related tests in chapter 10 are not run. If you look at the output in the console, when it gets to chapter 10, you should see something like figure B.1.

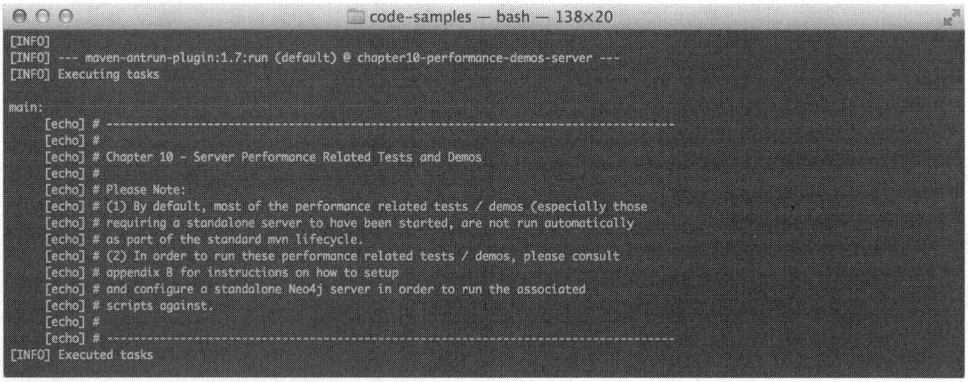

Figure B.1 Default Maven output for chapter 10

This is to be expected. It's been done this way to ensure that the basic tests can all run without you having to first install a Neo4j server or wait a long time for the performance tests to run. The instructions that follow detail the additional steps required to run the performance-related demos and tests.

2 To run some of the embedded performance related tests, run with the Maven profile `include-embedded-perfdemos`:

```
mvn clean test -f chapter10/performance-demos-embedded/pom.xml -P
include-embedded-perfdemos
```

3 Follow the instructions in appendix A that detail how to set up and install a single Neo4j server (the samples use version 2.0.1). We'll refer to the directory where the Neo4j server has been installed as <<NEO4J_HOME>>.

4 Within the <<NEO4J_HOME>>/conf/neo4j-server.properties file,

a Ensure that the location of the Neo4j server database is set to that expected by the performance tests by modifying the following property value as shown here:

```
org.neo4j.server.database.location=<<N4JIA_SAMPLE_HOME>>/chapter10/
performance-demos-server/the-chapter10-server-db
```

b Ensure the unmanaged extension (to be installed in the upcoming steps) has been registered. This can be done by uncommenting and modifying the following property value as shown here:

```
org.neo4j.server.thirdparty_jaxrs_classes=com.manning.neo4jia.chapter
10.unmanagedext=/n4jia/unmanaged
```

5 Provided you have performed at least one successful general `mvn clean install`, a jar file containing the server plugins and extensions will have been generated here:

```
<<N4JIA_SAMPLE_HOME>>/chapter10/server/target/chapter10-server-1.0-
SNAPSHOT.jar. Copy this file to the server's plugin directory located
here: <<NEO4J_HOME>>/plugins.
```

6 Create and export a `NEO4J_HOME` variable within your terminal window, as this will be expected by the scripts. Do this by executing the following command:

```
export NEO4J_HOME=<<NEO4J_HOME>>
```

7 Change to the base directory from which the bash scripts will be run: <<N4JIA _SAMPLE_HOME>>/chapter10/performance-demos-server/src/test/scripts/bash.

8 Seed the performance database by executing the following script from within the bash directory:

```
./seed_performance_db.sh
```

You should now be ready to run the bash scripts.

9 Ensure that you're still in the base directory from which the bash scripts will be run:

```
<<N4JIA_SAMPLE_HOME>>/chapter10/performance-demos-server/src/test/
scripts/bash.
```

10 Run the bash-based tests:

a To run the curl-based demo/performance test scripts, use this command:

```
./curl_adams_friends.sh
```

b To run the Java REST-binding-based demo/performance test scripts use this command:

```
./javarestbinding_adams_friends.sh
```

Note: As this is a Java REST client, these scripts essentially call certain Java-based demo/JUnit tests under the covers.

This will spew out quite a bit of information. If you're only interested in seeing the stopwatch details, the recommended way to call script is as follows:

```
./javarestbinding_adams_friends.sh | grep StopWatch
```

appendix C
Setting up your project to use SDN

This appendix will walk you through the setup instructions required to run SDN. Specifically, these instructions are for version 3.2.1.RELEASE of SDN, which is officially compatible with Neo4j 2.1.5. The SDN 3.2.1.RELEASE version is the one referred to in the dedicated SDN chapter (chapter 10), and it's the version used by the accompanying source code as well.

The easiest way to configure your project to use SDN is through a Maven build, which is also used for the accompanying source code. General instructions for setting up and installing Maven are provided in appendix B. SDN can also be built with Gradle or Ant/Ivy if you'd like; instructions for how to do this can be found at http://docs.spring.io/spring-data/data-neo4j/docs/current/reference/html/#setup.

This appendix will also provide details of the minimal Spring configuration required to make SDN function appropriately.

Depending on whether you want to make use of the simple or the advanced mapping mode, the setup will be a bit different. The source code for chapter 9 provides a configured setup for both simple and advanced mapping modes.

The most up-to-date set of instructions, as well as options not specified here, can be found in Michael Hunger's *Good Relationships*: http://docs.spring.io/spring-data/data-neo4j/docs/current/reference/html/#setup.

SDN versions and official documentation references

This book targets SDN version 3.2.1, compatible with Neo4j version 2.1.5. As you can appreciate, writing a book while trying to keep up with the latest versions of open source software can be challenging at the best of times. To ensure you always have

---

(continued)

links to the latest information, we have endeavored to use references that point to the latest stable release of the official documentation. At the time of writing, all SDN documentation URLs follow a common pattern, namely http://docs.spring.io/spring-data/data-neo4j/docs/<version>/reference/html where version is the SDN version of the docs you wish to view, with current being an alias that always points to the latest, most stable released version.

For the 3.2.1-specific information, please consult http://docs.spring.io/spring-data/data-neo4j/docs/3.2.1.RELEASE/reference/html. For the latest stable release, please consult http://docs.spring.io/spring-data/data-neo4j/docs/current/reference/html.

C.1   Maven configuration

If you're using Maven, you need to ensure that one of the following sets of Maven dependencies (either listing C.1 or C.2 as appropriate) is included in your pom.xml file. The choice depends on which mapping mode you are using.

The following listing shows the dependencies for the simple mapping mode.

Listing C.1   Maven dependencies required for the simple mapping mode

```
<dependencies>
    <dependency>
        <groupId>org.springframework.data</groupId>        Primary SDN
        <artifactId>spring-data-neo4j</artifactId>          dependency
        <version>3.2.1.RELEASE</version>
    </dependency>

    <dependency>
        <groupId>org.hibernate</groupId>                   Hibernate implementation
        <artifactId>hibernate-validator</artifactId>        of the JSR-303 Bean
        <version>4.2.0.Final</version>                      Validation Spec API
    </dependency>
</dependencies>
```

In theory, the core `spring-data-neo4j` artifact should be all that's required, but in reality there's currently one other library that also needs to be included in order for SDN to function correctly, and it is an implementation of the JSR-303 Validation Spec API. In our sample code, we've chosen the Hibernate implementation. The SDN library itself makes use of the validation API, so users need to provide an actual implementation at runtime.

Both the simple and advanced versions of the SDN library make use of Maven's transitive dependency management system to ensure that all of the supporting libraries required for development are automatically pulled down.

The following listing shows the dependencies for the advanced mapping mode.

Listing C.2 Maven dependencies required for the advanced mapping mode

```
<dependencies>
    <dependency>
        <groupId>org.springframework.data</groupId>
        <artifactId>spring-data-neo4j-aspects</artifactId>
        <version>3.2.1.RELEASE </version>
    </dependency>

    <dependency>
        <groupId>org.hibernate</groupId>
        <artifactId>hibernate-validator</artifactId>
        <version>4.2.0.Final</version>
    </dependency>
</dependencies>
```

Primary SDN dependency (for advanced mapping)

Hibernate implementation of the JSR-303 Bean Validation Spec API

As with the simple mapping mode, you'll need to explicitly include a dependency to a concrete JSR 303 implementation library. Again, we've used the Hibernate one here.

In addition to the dependencies themselves, the advanced mapping mode requires you to configure the Maven build to use AspectJ for the build-time weaving of entities. The following listing shows the snippet of configuration that will need to be added to your pom.xml file to achieve this.

Listing C.3 AspectJ build configuration for the advanced mapping mode

```
<build>
<plugins>
    <plugin>
        <groupId>org.codehaus.mojo</groupId>
        <artifactId>aspectj-maven-plugin</artifactId>
        <version>1.4</version>
        <dependencies>
            <dependency>
                <groupId>org.aspectj</groupId>
                <artifactId>aspectjrt</artifactId>
                <version>1.7.4</version>
            </dependency>
            <dependency>
                <groupId>org.aspectj</groupId>
                <artifactId>aspectjtools</artifactId>
                <version>1.7.4</version>
            </dependency>
        </dependencies>
        <executions>
            <execution>
                <goals>
                    <goal>compile</goal>
                    <goal>test-compile</goal>
                </goals>
            </execution>
        </executions>
```

```
        <configuration>
            <outxml>true</outxml>
            <aspectLibraries>
                <aspectLibrary>
                    <groupId>org.springframework</groupId>
                    <artifactId>spring-aspects</artifactId>
                </aspectLibrary>
                <aspectLibrary>
                    <groupId>org.springframework.data</groupId>
                    <artifactId>spring-data-neo4j-aspects</artifactId>
                </aspectLibrary>
            </aspectLibraries>
            <source>1.7</source>
            <target>1.7</target>
        </configuration>
    </plugin>
</plugins>
</build>
```

C.2   Spring configuration

This section looks at what's required to set up and configure Spring within your application. The setup is relatively minimal, so even if you don't know Spring, it shouldn't prove too painful.

The Spring configuration itself can be done either via an XML file or Spring's Java bean configuration (using `@Configuration` annotations). As most of the SDN documentation at the time of writing provides examples using XML, we'll do likewise here, but you can look up how to make use of the Java bean approach in chapter 21 of Michael Hunger's *Good Relationships*: http://docs.spring.io/spring-data/data-neo4j/docs/current/reference/html/#setup.

Core XML configuration

You need to tell Spring what beans need to be created and instantiated. With the XML approach, this is done by providing an XML file with initial content that looks like the following.

Listing C.1   XML configuration using a store directory

```
<?xml version="1.0" encoding="UTF-8" standalone="yes"?>
<beans xmlns="http://www.springframework.org/schema/beans"
    xmlns:context="http://www.springframework.org/schema/context"
    xmlns:xsi="http://www.w3.org/2001/XMLSchema-instance"
    xmlns:neo4j="http://www.springframework.org/schema/data/neo4j"
    xsi:schemaLocation="
        http://www.springframework.org/schema/beans
        http://www.springframework.org/schema/beans/spring-beans.xsd
        http://www.springframework.org/schema/context
        http://www.springframework.org/schema/context/spring-context.xsd
        http://www.springframework.org/schema/data/neo4j
        http://www.springframework.org/schema/data/neo4j/spring-neo4j.xsd">
```

```
    <context:annotation-config/>
                                            Activates various annotations
    <neo4j:config                           to be detected in bean classes
        storeDirectory="target/config-test"
        base-package="com.manning.neo4jia.chapter08.simple.domain"/>

</beans>
                                            Uses Neo4j namespace to concisely
                                            define basic SDN configuration
```

The Neo4j-specific XML namespace element, neo4j:config, provides a simple way of concisely configuring SDN. It creates or exposes the core graph database bean as well as other helper classes, such as the Neo4jTemplate.

The neo4j:config element itself has four attributes (storeDirectory, graph-DatabaseService, entityManagerFactory, and typeRepresentationStrategyFactory) that can be configured. For convenience, there is a storeDirectory attribute that when set points to a particular directory where a new EmbeddedGraphDatabase will be created if one doesn't exist (if one is already there, it will be used). This is the approach used in the sample code.

You can make use of the graphDatabaseService attribute to point to a particular pre-configured Neo4j instance that should be used. In that case you'd also need to define a factory bean to create an appropriate Neo4j instance, as shown in the following snippet:

```
<neo4j:config graphDatabaseService="graphDatabaseService" />
<bean id="graphDbFactory"
      class="org.neo4j.graphdb.factory.GraphDatabaseFactory"/>
<bean id="graphDatabaseService"
      scope="singleton"
      destroy-method="shutdown"
      factory-bean="graphDbFactory"
      factory-method="newEmbeddedDatabase">
    <constructor-arg value="target/config-test"/>
</bean>
```

As of SDN 3.0, the base-package XML element is mandatory, and you're expected to supply a list of all the packages that SDN should search to find your annotated domain entities. If you're engaging in cross-store persistence, you'll also need to supply the entityManagerFactory attribute value (not shown here).

If you'd like to make use of a type representation strategy other than the default one (SDN 3.x defaults to label-based; SDN 2.x defaults to legacy indexed-based), you can optionally define a bean named typeRepresentationStrategyFactory of type org .springframework.data.neo4j.support.typerepresentation.TypeRepresentation-StrategyFactory, as shown in the following snippet, choosing an appropriate value for the second constructor argument:

```
<bean id="typeRepresentationStrategyFactory"
class="org.springframework.data.neo4j.support.typerepresentation.TypeRepresen
    tationStrategyFactory">
    <constructor-arg index="0" ref="graphDatabase"/>
    <constructor-arg index="1" value="Indexed"/>
</bean>
```

More information on the available options can be found in the "Entity type representation" section in chapter 20 of Michael Hunger's *Good Relationships* at http://docs.spring.io/spring-data/data-neo4j/docs/current/reference/html/#reference_programming-model_typerepresentationstrategy.

For more configuration options see the official website.

Repository configuration

Within the XML configuration approach, SDN repositories can be configured using the `<neo4j:repositories>` element. The following snippet shows an example of how to instruct Spring to look within the `com.manning.neo4jia.chapter09.simple.repository` Java package to find repository classes that need to be made available as Spring beans for use by SDN:

```
<neo4j:repositories base-package=
    "com.manning.neo4jia.chapter09.simple.repository"/>
```

You'd replace the package name with the location where your specific repository implementations live. The package element defines the base-package (or packages) to search through to find repositories.

> **ADDITIONAL SPRING DATA COMMONS CONFIGURATION OPTIONS** SDN is built on top of the infrastructure and libraries provided by the Spring Data Commons project. The additional configuration options made available via SD Commons should also work here.

How does Spring know where to find the XML configuration file?

The short answer is that you need to tell it, but this will generally depend on what kind of application you are creating.

If you're building a web application, the Spring Web framework provides a custom `ContextLoaderListener` class that you can use within your web.xml file to create the container, as shown in the following snippet. Note that in this case, the XML configuration file (applicationContext.xml) is referred to from its location within the WEB-INF directory:

```
<context-param>
    <param-name>contextConfigLocation</param-name>
    <param-value>/WEB-INF/applicationContext.xml</param-value>
</context-param>

<listener>
    <listener-class>
        org.springframework.web.context.ContextLoaderListener
    </listener-class>
</listener>
```

Alternatively, if you're building a standalone Java application, you could make use of the `ClassPathXmlApplicationContext` class, as shown in the following snippet:

(continued)

```
ClassPathXmlApplicationContext ctx
= new ClassPathXmlApplicationContext(
"classpath:applicationContext.xml");
UserRepository userRepository =  ctx.getBean(UserRepository.class);
...
```

For more options on other ways you can provide Spring with its configuration details, see the "Introduction to the Spring IoC container and beans" section of the *Spring Framework Reference Documentation*: http://docs.spring.io/spring/docs/4.0.x/spring-framework-reference/htmlsingle/#beans-introduction.

appendix D
Getting more help

When there's something strange in your Neo4j neighborhood ... who you gonna call? The community, of course!

Because it's an open source project, there's a wide and diverse Neo4j community that is happy to help out with problems, and they'd also love it if you chose to get involved and contribute to the project as well. The following resources are the main places where you can go to find more help, and to contribute to the cause.

 Find answers, or reach out to fellow developers with your questions: http://stackoverflow.com/questions/tagged/neo4j.

 Share your experiences and expertise with fellow graphistas: http://groups.google.com/group/neo4j.

 Found an issue with Neo4j? Raise it here: https://github.com/neo4j/neo4j/issues.

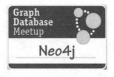 Neo4j meetups occur all over the world. Connect or start a new group yourself: http://neo4j.meetup.com.

index

RELATED MANNING TITLES

Java 8 in Action
Lambdas, streams, and functional-style programming
by Raoul-Gabriel Urma, Mario Fusco, Alan Mycroft

> ISBN: 9781617291999
> 424 pages, $49.99
> August 2014

Functional Programming in Scala
by Paul Chiusano and Rúnar Bjarnason

> ISBN: 9781617290657
> 320 pages, $44.99
> August 2014

Spring in Action, Fourth Edition
Covers Spring 4
by Craig Walls

> ISBN: 9781617291203
> 624 pages, $49.99
> November 2014

Spring Integration in Action
by Mark Fisher, Jonas Partner,
  Marius Bogoevici, Iwein Fuld

> ISBN: 9781935182436
> 368 pages, $49.99
> September 2012

For ordering information go to www.manning.com